JUST UNPLUG
AND GO

How Traveling the World Saved
One Man's Soul!

Stan Crossland II

First published by Dog Ear Publishing
4011 Vincennes Rd
Indianapolis, IN 46268
www.dogearpublishing.net

ISBN: 978-1-4575-5347-9

This book is printed on acid-free paper.

Printed in the United States of America

CHAPTER SEQUENCE:

GREETINGS, DEAR READER...

First and foremost, thank you.

Thank you for spending your hard-earned money on this book.

More importantly, thank you for sharing with me one of your most valuable possessions—your time! I sincerely hope my efforts prove worthy of such a gift.

Know that, if you should happen to think this book is drivel, I can live with such an assessment and still be so very appreciative you gave it a try. Also know I gave this endeavor my very best.

I went into this with the goal of giving you the truth regarding my experiences, thoughts, and feelings. Thus, if my truth is not yours, so be it.

At the very worst, maybe you can find consolation in the fact that some of the purchase price went to charity. On the other hand, should you find partial joy in reading this, you can be sure it will make me very happy. Happy to know you might have found something to take away from my walkabout that serves you well in the future.

I think there is a silent epidemic sweeping the world today. It is the disease of loneliness. We have all these ways and means of connecting, yet too many have forgotten real con-nection comes from face-to-face interaction with others. From reaching, not for your cell phone, but across the table!

Too many suffer in silence, feeling as if nobody out there is either like them or even listening. Too many have nothing to stand on. No foundations beneath their feet providing support when the earth starts shaking all around them.

You have to stand for something or you will fall for everything.

My greatest accomplishment would be for this book to help you find out what you stand for, or maybe simply to remind—you used to stand for something.

Something that gave you hope!

Something that sustained you when times were dark!

Something that pushed you to seek out more of what life has to offer!

Something that seems missing, lost, or hazy!

Lord knows I was close to losing that something before I went on this journey. Thankfully, I found that something again. And that something was me!

The guy who is beautiful, loving, curious, vibrant, funny, appreciative and, once again, very much alive!

The guy who came way too close to losing sight of himself, then decided the best thing he could do to get a clear view again was to get lost.

The guy who felt the same crippling loneliness many of you do and decided he needed to disconnect in order to reconnect.

So I sold everything I owned and went on a walkabout. Just said forget it, jumped in my car, and drove cross-country for six weeks visiting old friends and re-solidifying dear relation-ships. Then I dropped my beloved dog off with some friends and jumped on a plane to Thailand. From there it was off to visit eleven countries in four and a half months.

I was determined to get my mojo back if it still was out there to be found and wanted to be my friend again.

Listen, peeps, the world is fucking awesome! Flat-out mind-blowing. There are still people, places, and experiences you simply can't fathom until you get out and go exploring.

If you have lost your verve, your sense of wonder, your lust for life or yourself, well, read onward. Maybe we, you and I, can help you find the way back to you.

At the minimum, maybe this book will provide a few laughs, inspire your imagination, and rekindle your desire to live with passion again. Possibly find your passion for the first time.

It is there, ya know, the passion, just below the surface. Waiting for you to light a match... I know this because mine was, and, well, we are the same, you and I.

Two more housekeeping notes.

First, I wrote this book as if I were talking with a friend. This means I dropped a lot of formal writing techniques and rules in favor of a more "spoken word" approach. Colloquial. The bottom line for you is a relaxed writing style. Hopefully, it makes you feel as if you were right there with me.

May the format provide a more enjoyable presentation; help you sit back, take a break, and turn off the noise that is life these days.

Second, this is neither a story nor presented in sequential order of events/places/people. It is a smattering of situations, events, thoughts, epiphanies, insights, and interactions.

When a certain moment occurred is much less relevant than what the moment provided me upon reflection.

Absorb each piece for what it is, one moment or collection of moments that left an imprint.

Let the critic in you go to bed.

Let the reader in you stay up an extra hour to absorb.

Let your mind freely roam with me and without expectation.

Chillax! After all, it's a travel book.

> With heartfelt gratitude,
>
> Stan

RANDOM STATISTICS:

** Eleven countries inhabited; feet touched ground in fifteen countries

** Four continents

** Went from the Northern Hemisphere to the Southern Hemisphere to the Northern Hemisphere to the Southern Hemisphere and back again to the Northern Hemisphere

** Flew approx. 31,000 miles

** Eleven major cities sauntered around and thirty-plus smaller meandered through

** Chillaxed on six islands

** Dipped my toes in the Atlantic and Pacific oceans, the Indian Ocean, the Andaman Sea, the South China Sea, the Gulf of Tonkin, the Gulf of Thailand, the Rading Strait, the Alboran Sea, the Mediterranean Sea, the Marmara Sea, the Black Sea, the Bosphorus Strait, the North Sea, the English Channel, the Mekong River, the Rio Blanco River, the Ayung River, and the Chao Phraya River

** Uncomfortably sat on nineteen different planes

** Used, and sometimes got used by, fifteen different airline companies

** Rode on two cross-country trains

** Suffered through eight extended (six- to ten-hour) bus rides

** Floated on nine different boats

** Cruised on three hydrofoils

** Paid for 150+ taxis. Got overcharged about ten times; flat-out "bent over" maybe five times

** Number of times driver of said taxi had me reciting the Hail Mary and promising the Good Lord I would never swear, drink, or smoke again = three

** Three also happens to be the number of times I exited said taxi, uttered some unceremonious epithet at said driver, walked into a bar, ordered an alcoholic beverage, lit up a smoke, held now delivered elixir up in the air, and thanked the Lord I survived the ride

** Choked down smog during the obligatory tuk-tuk ride five times

** Rented scooters on foreign soil five times

** One = number of scooter crashes. Minor road rash and lifelong permanent "artwork" included

- ** Eight = number of times I scuba dove; which led to
- ** 258 = number of times I giggled with glee underwater
- ** Gleefully zip-lined on the world's longest run, 900 meters over a jungle valley
- ** Two ecstatic whitewater rafting adventures through jungles
- ** Three riverboat cruises through big cities, another three through jungle terrain
- ** Seventy hostels/guesthouses/homestays
- ** Two fleabag shacks stayed in and regretfully paid for
- ** Four luxury hotel/resort "treats" to myself
- ** Laid me head down on ninety-eight different beds
- ** Three = sets of floors slept on
- ** Six = number of major city subway systems navigated
- ** Fifteen Buddhist temples, six famous mosques, eight prestigious churches, fourteen renowned museums, twenty-eight beautiful beaches, and countless tranquil city/national parks visited
- ** Nine volcanoes viewed
- ** Hiked three mountains over 14,000 feet
- ** Three = number of times I swam with giant prehistoric sea turtles spanning up to eight feet in length
- ** Thirty-five massages received; all for $12 or less
- ** Three hundred+ delicious meals devoured for less than $2 each
- ** Sixty = number of Doner kebabs eaten. Cheap, tasty, nutritious enough, and ubiquitous around the world!
- ** Two hundred+ = number of delightful roadside food stands enjoyed. Trust me, despite what they tell you, it is the best representation of their culture in most countries, and often the safest too
- ** Practiced yoga overlooking numerous oceans, rice paddy fields and valleys, temples, farmlands, huge and small rivers, city rooftops, city parks, friends' living rooms, tiny hostel rooms, multiple mountain ranges, and a fair number of airports around the world
- ** Forty+ = number of different nationalities I thankfully both "broke bread" with and had meaningful conversations with
- ** One = number of times I rode a horse at a canter and an exhilarating gallop
- ** Against any said desires did the following for the first and last time = A) rode a horse sideways, yes, that's right, at

a perfect ninety-degree angle to the right, for around fifty feet and B) fell off a horse at full gallop and was dragged by a horse for about forty feet

** Zero = number of times I ever felt threatened whatsoever
** Zero = number of items stolen
** Zero = number of truly bad experiences I had
** 7,777,777 = times I thanked God for the privilege of such a journey at this time in my life

STAN'S TURKISH BATHHOUSE EXPERIENCE, OTHERWISE KNOWN AS "WHAT THE FUCK JUST HAPPENED!"

So it's my third day in Istanbul.

Between my last day in Bali, the seventeen hours flying over, deciding to forego a nap and instead having two Turkish coffees at lunch beside the Blue Mosque and the subsequent adrenaline rush said coffees provided, which boosted my energy enough to wander for about six hours, then sharing a hookah with my new friend Julian—I stayed up for forty-one hours straight.

A new record for me! Who says new plateaus can't be reached after forty?

That night I slept maybe five hours. I can never, ever get a good night's sleep when I am in a room for the first time.

The following day I get up, do some yoga, and begin to wander the streets. I walk around for six hours to explore the city, have dinner, and then drink beers with my fellow mystery hunter Julian, a sweet and soulful Canadian Indian, until about 11 p.m.

Folks, this is indeed a walking city. Except it's similar to San Francisco in that it is up steep grades and then down steep grades, mostly on cobblestone roads. It wears you out!

Day three I wake up absurdly early again, have some breakfast, write a bit, and decide I need to relax my weary bones.

***

Let me digress for a second. Throughout all the Asian lands I visited, I must have had approximately thirty massages. I mean, after all, they usually ranged from $8-12. How can you not, right?

Most of these occurred on a beach, about fifteen feet from the ocean, while a warm breeze washed over me; wonderful Asian ladies showing subtlety, tenderness, and care performed every one. Often they included either coconut oil or aloe vera oil. A few were stupendous! During one particular massage, I felt as if I was in my mother's womb. I was spoiled rotten!

***

Debating whether I have the energy and willpower to do some yoga, I notice a sign in the lobby at the hostel that advertises a trip to a Turkish bathhouse, ride included, for the price of $30.

When in Rome, I think to myself. *How can I not go see what these infamous places are all about?*

Hot saunas, steam rooms, and warm pools to enjoy. Plus, they offer a Turkish massage in the package.

Done!

I ask the front desk attendant to book me a ride. Twenty minutes later I am picked up by a driver who speaks nary a word of English and off I go.

On the way there the driver takes a left-hand turn down a one-way street and we come to a dead stop. This is not your typical traffic jam.

We are on what is known as Shoe Road. Every store on the street is a shoe store. I mean every single store. And there has to be about sixty stores. We are talking 60,000 pairs of shoes to choose from in a thousand-foot stretch of road. Carrie Bradshaw from *Sex and the City* would never, ever, ever leave here.

Thus we wait. And wait. And wait.

After twenty minutes the driver shuts his car off. As I stated, he speaks not a word of English whatsoever.

So I sit with him in silence, no music on the radio at all.

After a half hour I step out of the car to see what the deal is, and basically every shop is getting their delivery that day. There are men with makeshift forklifts unloading boxes from the trucks onto dollies and then scurrying around, crisscrossing the road to and fro, dropping off orders at all the stores.

A giant human bumper car game, with the occasional fifty-box spill here and there.

Did I mention it is a one-way street with no exit possible?

We sit some more. I say to myself, *Well, this is what patience is all about, Stan. You have to take the good with the bad when it comes to travel.*

And I have no clue where I am. None. It's not like he can tell me how to get to the place—'cause he doesn't speak English.

I am once again at the mercy of the travel gods. Silence fills the car while the sands of time slowly flow through the hourglass. Every once in a while he would look at me, make the "what can ya do" gesture with raised hands, palms up, and shrug his shoulders.

After forty-five minutes, traffic moves. Yesss!

We drive another, say, two hundred meters and stop. He points to the left and says, "Sauna!"

You mean to tell me we were literally two hundred meters from the front door, a door which resides on the same street where we have sat for three-quarters of an hour, and it never occurred to you to get out of the car and just point to the place? Son of a bitch! Oops, I mean Sweet Mother Mary and Joseph.

Of course, this is what is going through my mind; 'cause to say anything now is pointless.

As I walk toward the door, I see a sign that says the place was built in 1492, meaning the structure is over six hundred years old.

Wow!

Seeing as how I have renovated well over three hundred homes in my life, two thoughts immediately come to mind: 1) How awesome! I can't wait to see this place and, 2) Ha, America has no clue. How many times have I heard someone brag about a home being built in 1945?

I walk in and it's like going back in time seventy years as far as decorum. Dark, musky, and covered in lacquered wood!

There is a big open area that rises about thirty-five feet to a domed ceiling. The dome has small glass-plated openings that let in small rays of sun. On both sides are little wooden rooms with doors.

I pay the man at the front desk, and he points to one of the rooms, saying, "Change!"

"All righty then."

I go inside, take my clothes off, hang them on a metal hook, and wrap a Turkish towel, known as a *fouta*, around my waist. As I exit I see a pair of slippers next to the door. I put them on.

Or at least try. I wear a size eleven; these are a size nine.

I try to jam my feet into them, get about three-quarters of the way in, and my toes will go no further. My heels are hanging off the back about two inches.

As I walk across the big room, a slipper flies off my feet two or three times. Each time I jam my feet back in and make it another four steps before one of them flies off again.

I get to the door that appears to be the entrance to the sauna area. Standing there is a gruff-looking Turkish man. He grabs me by the arm, and I mean *grabs*.

No, he *clenches* me by the arm and says, "I show you!"

As we enter the sauna area, my slipper falls off again. I replace it. I look up to see a giant room covered in marble. The walls are marble, the benches are marble, and the wash-basins are marble.

In the middle is a huge marble platform, probably twenty feet in diameter, except it is in a hexagonal shape. The room is warm, moisture dripping down every wall. Again, there is a domed ceiling at the top with small glass panes allowing the sun to ever so gently illuminate the room.

As he continues to clench my arm, he leads me around the sauna area. Twice more a slipper falls off. He looks at me, gives an expression that translates, "Are you sure you know how to walk?"

I sling the slippers off and say, "For Christ's sake, too small!"

Still clenching my arm as if I am a toddler he fears will be run over by a train, he shows me the various rooms I can utilize.

There is a wood door to the dry sauna room, a wood door to the wet sauna room, two different coves that have shower areas, what seems to be a massage room and, lastly, a small alcove off the back with a pool.

All along the wall in the main area there are marble benches and next to these filled-up marble sinks with faucets above them.

Finally, mercifully, he releases his circulation-killing grip on my arm and says, "Good?"

"Good!" I reply.

"Massage man come in fifteen, twenty minutes, okay?" he states.

"Okay!" I retort.

He goes back outside.

I decide I will start in the wet sauna room first. I want to get a sweat going, open up my respiratory system, and let my skin breathe. So, I go into the room and sit on a bench area.

My skin is immediately singed. Marble retains heat as if it were a stovetop. I jump off the bench and let out a "Yikes!" I decide to take off my fouta and lay it on the marble bench. Slowly and carefully I lie down. *Okay, I can handle this; just relax, Stan.*

Three minutes later a rather plump, older Turkish man comes into the room. I close my eyes and try to chill out, let my muscles release the tension and tiredness.

Within minutes I get that feeling. You know the one—someone is staring at me. Sure enough, I open my eyes, turn my head to the left, and the Turkish man has his eyes affixed on my naked body.

Spidey-sense starts to tingle. I think, *Aw, man, not here. Not now.*

"Maresh!" he says. Means hello.

I reply in kind.

"Very hot," he states.

"Yes, but good," I return. I close my eyes and begin to chill again. *Maybe he is just being friendly*, I tell myself.

I am in the room for ten minutes max; my body is just beginning to adapt to the stifling heat, the merciless marble, and the strange surroundings. My mind has barely begun to unwind.

The door opens and I hear, "Massage, you!"

I open my eyes, look at the guy, and say, "Me?"

"Yes, you!"

"All righty then." I grab my fouta off the table, wrap it around my waist, and walk out of the room.

Once again, this guy clenches my arm as if he is a cop arresting me for having child porn and leads me over to one of the benches next to a marble sink. "Sit!" he commands. And I do.

He reaches down, grabs a big bowl, and dips it into the water. He swings it over my head and dumps the whole bowl over me.

It is scalding hot water. I mean skin-searing, eyeball-popping-out hot. A few degrees below boiling, if you ask me. It takes every ounce of energy not to shriek out loud. He does this four times. My skin is now numb from the pain.

He slings me back up against the marble wall. My back ricochets off the hard surface, spinal column reverberating with shock. He grabs my right arm, extends it out and across my chest. He grabs my left arm and does the same.

I am bear hugging myself.

He places both hands on my left forearm and presses as hard as possible into my torso, which is planted firmly up against the immovable marble wall. "Owwwwww!" I scream as both shoulders pop while becoming simultaneously dislocated.

I now have two useless arms. All the work to heal both shoulders from so many chaturungas in yoga years ago has been destroyed. From this moment forward, I will have to eat off a plate with my mouth.

I am now Daniel Day-Lewis in the movie *My Left Foot*!

There goes my dream of juggling in the circus, my ability to type, and my ability to share the finger with other unequivocally deserving drivers! Forget ever drinking a beer without using a straw or wiping my ass solo again.

Next he grabs this glove and puts it on his hand. This glove is not your average loofah. It is more akin to pumice-like material. Rough and gritty!

He dips the glove in a bucket filled with soap. He seizes the back of my neck and slings my upper body toward my knees.

Recall that I decided to forego my yoga session that day, and I have been walking the city for numerous hours the last two days. My hamstrings are a wee bit tight, to say the least.

He immediately thrusts me into a deep forward fold. I feel both my hammies and low back pop. *Christ, good-bye ability to walk for the next week*, I think.

He begins vigorously washing my back. More like scratching it with lava rock. Each thrust sends me deeper into the forward fold. Hamstrings are about to sever forever. Low back throbbing with each grinding scrub.

At last, he pulls me back up, once again dipping the bowl in the washbasin and pouring molten lava all over me. Next, he snatches my chin with his hand, holds my head steady, and starts rubbing my face.

Have you ever taken sandpaper and rubbed it against your cheeks? Neither have I! It never seemed to be a good idea to me. He scrubs my face profusely. Forehead, cheeks, nose, ears, and neck!

I think, *I am going to walk out of here looking like Two-Face in the last Batman movie after being exposed to some type of flesh-eating liquid. All people will see are my eyes and the tendons/muscles underneath the skin's surface. I will never get a girl to look at me again!*

After the face exfoliation (a kind term at best), he rubs down my chest and legs. My skin is rawhide.

Thankfully, after about ten minutes, he is done. You guessed it—three more bowls of acid are poured over my head. And, unfortunately, some soap had seeped into my eyes. They begin to burn and I can barely open them.

Think I would prefer to be blinded by the light Bruce Springsteen refers to.

As I am trying to adjust to the blurred vision he vise-grips my left arm and starts lifting me off the bench. What is it with these guys and the super-charged grip thing? Are they trying to prove their masculinity?

The marble floor is an ice-skating ring, I can't see five inches in front of me, and he is leading me across the room. I am going to go down, break my neck for a third time, and never leave Turkey.

We walk over to the giant middle marble platform. Not really walk, more a situation of *him dragging me across the room blindfolded as my legs go this way and that, the ever-present vice grip providing the difference between a safe passage and eleven broken vertebrae. Ever see a parent teach a child how to ice skate for the first time?*

I was the child.

Finally it dawn's on me as to why they man handle people everywhere.

He says, "Lay down on front!"

Now let's all think about this for a minute. Have you ever been to a massage that wasn't on some nice, semi-cushioned table with a face hole in it? Ever? This marble platform is at least four or five inches thick. Only two surfaces are harder than marble: granite and concrete.

"This does not bode well," I mutter.

He begins to cover my body in this bubbly soap. And the massage begins.

As stated previously, women performed all the massages I had the last four months. They all were soft, gentle, and intuitive as to what muscles are taut and what muscles are relaxed, thus which ones to be gentle with and which ones not so much.

He immediately begins to assault my body. Straight into a deep tissue massage, right to the bone, bypassing tenderness completely. No warmup, no body exploration, no awareness at all.

Deep tissue, neuromuscular torture!

A jackhammer comes to mind. Also, he is rubbing across the muscle, not with it. I can feel different muscles move in ways they are not meant to move.

I scream as he hits a tender area below the shoulder blade. "Easy! Slow down!"

He states flatly, "Is good!"

Good for who? A Guantanamo inmate you're trying to ply information from?

He gets to the middle of my back. He puts one hand on top of the other as you would if administering CPR—and then presses down with all his weight at once.

Imagine a bear jumping off a chair onto the middle of your back.

Remember, I am lying atop four or five inches of marble. Every single bone in my spine cracks simultaneously. One entire symphonic back crack!

My chest is pressed against the marble, and I swear to God he caved my entire rib cage in. Both of these anguish-inducing sensations occur at the same time.

A kaleidoscope of Fourth of July fireworks goes off in my brain! I have just received a thousand volts of electricity.

He releases. I arch upward and yell at the top of my lungs, "Oh my God!"

My head and shoulders lift off the table to relieve the pressure on my rib cage. I fall back down to the marble.

No lie, I blacked out. Literally faded into the darkness. Lights out, time to go home to Mom, Dad, and all my deceased dogs in heaven.

Maybe thirty seconds later I come to. He is massaging my legs. I am dizzy, disoriented, and dismayed.

I say again, "Easy!"

He stoically repeats, "Is good!"

"No, not good! Too hard! Lighter!"

My words are absorbed as well as the marble absorbs my spine. Much like a falling tree in a forest empty of humans, no one will ever know if they were actually uttered. All that remains is the crumbled skeleton...

About a minute later he takes his thumbs, places them at the base of my calves, and then drives them upward toward my ass. He presses down as if using a steel rod and runs his thumbs up my calves, over the back of my knees, and then across the length of my hamstrings.

Searing pain goes through my entire lower half. I am a former marathon runner, so tight calves and hammies are a reality for the rest of my life no matter how much yoga I do.

My hamstrings snap like one of Pete Townsend's guitar strings during "Teenage Wasteland"!

Due to breaking no less than twelve bones in my life, I like to think I have a high pain tolerance, or at least more than most people. Pain and I have an agreement—I ignore it, do yoga, smoke a joint here and there, and it occasionally takes it easy on me. Today, pain abdicates our agreement. It frolics over every inch of me.

I get dizzy again.

For the next five to seven minutes, he takes it a little bit easier, rubs all around my calves and legs. *Thank the good Lord above.*

He gets to my feet. I am thinking, *This is almost over, hang tough.*

First, he wraps both sets of thumbs, index fingers, and digits number two around each big toe. And yanks them as hard as possible.

I feel both toes separate from my feet. I imagine they are in his hands right now, and he is holding them up like some type of hunting charm.

He does this with each and every toe. I told you before; I wear a size eleven shoe. I am now an even baker's dozen. Time to buy larger sandals!

At last, at long fucking last he is done!

But wait, you guessed it! He has two more buckets of muriatic acid to pour all over me.

Whatever skin I had left on my anatomy is now gone. I am a walking cadaver for first-year med students to study the rest of my life.

He puts the bucket down. I mutter, "*it's over, praise all the saints in heaven.*"

Nope.

All of a sudden, he slaps the middle of my back as hard as he possibly can. Like I called his mother a whore or his wife a bitch!

I let out a whimper of anguish.

"We done! Good, no?" he asks.

I have no words whatsoever. None.

I am so shell-shocked, I can't speak.

I lay there a broken man.

This is, I swear, exactly how it went down. Minute by excruciating minute! Reaction by reaction, thought process by thought process.

I will not forget any second of it for the rest of my life.

He leaves the room. After what must have been ten minutes, I crawl off the table and drag myself on the floor to the wet sauna room. Here I am, a grown man in his late forties visiting one of the most visually astounding cities in the world, and I am crawling across a marble floor like an infant in front of other grown Turkish men.

Ego and Pride are over in the corner chuckling at the spectacle, pretending we never met. I am too tired to give them the finger!

I lie down on the marble bench, immune to the temperature at this point.

I am immobile for twenty minutes. My mind is trying to come from home planet agony; my body is in a state of shock.

When I can finally move, I go to the cave-like pool area and do yoga in the water for another forty-five minutes—reconnecting every muscle, ligament, tendon, and bone slowly but surely.

When I feel I can walk again, I exit the pool and lie down on the aforementioned marble platform to do some more stretching. Light and easy moves to get the rest of my haggard physique back in order.

I am doing a twist with my eyes closed, one leg across my hips and the opposite arm extended above my head. My spidey-sense starts to tingle.

I open my eyes and guess who is standing over me?

That's right, the dude from the wet room. He looks me over again, raises his eyebrows up and down, and with a twinkle in his says, "You look like shoulder hurt. Want me to massage?"

You gotta fucking be kidding me! After all I have been through, I think. I burst out laughing and then say with a stern voice, "No!"

That's it. I have had enough! I am outta here!

I get up, go to the shower stall, and turn the water on cold. I stay in there for about five minutes. As I towel off in front of a mirror, I notice there is a mirror directly behind me in the opposite shower stall area.

I now have the tattoo I avoided getting my entire life.

On my back is a giant handprint—red, fully visible, and detailed in its five finger outline.

"Son of a Bitch", I say to no one in particular.

I start to giggle out loud.

I shuffle to the outer room, have the attendant wrap me up in two towels, and walk to my locker room like a crippled, broken man. I put my clothes on, take one last look at the place (after all, it is six hundred years old), and walk out the door.

Do I feel better? Hmmm, what do you think? Slightly I guess, but I think it has more to do with the yoga repair work I did afterward than necessarily the Turkish bathhouse factor.

Piece of advice: If you ever think of going to a Turkish bathhouse in Istanbul, maybe rethink that choice. I suggest instead you find the nearest Jujitsu dojo, walk in, hand them $30, and say, "Feel free to kick my ass for three hours!"

You might actually enjoy it a tad more.

Plus, no hand tattoo at the end either.

How can I be upset though?

The whole endeavor was surreal. I can honestly say I got the crap kicked out of me and bear no ill will. I can also say I resembled a drunken, spastic sailor on leave while meandering home in the middle of a sun-soaked Istanbul afternoon.

Sometimes you get what you pay for, others more than you bargained for.

From here on out I am going to stick with the Asian ladies....

RIDING SHOTGUN
WITH THE TRAVEL GODS...

Sometimes you need to let the travel gods take the wheel...

I planned on going to Lombok island, off the coast of Bali, to meet my boy Viggio. That was the plan anyway. You know the saying "Man plans, God laughs," right?

***

So the guy at the front desk of my homestay tells me I can go to a certain pier in town, Sanur, and catch a boat to Lombok at noon. Okay, off I go in a taxi. I get to the pier, where they tell me I am misinformed. The boat leaving from there will not be going to Lombok; that boat left at 8 a.m.

It is now 11 a.m. *Hmmmmmmmm.*

Another taxi driver outside the pier says, "If you want to go to Lombok, we can drive an hour across town to another pier and catch a boat from there, but we have to leave now. Takes one hour to get there."

"Okay, let's go, daddy-o..." I throw my bags in his car and off we go.

His name is Sabbo. Speaks pretty good English. He says, "I am going to drive very, very fast so we can make it on time. Please don't be afraid; all will be fine."

Hauling ass down the highway we go. You need to understand, I don't care what country you travel through in Asia— traffic lanes are just a suggestion at best. More an ideal than a rule.

Thus, we are weaving in and out of both lanes, sliding in between cars, passing motorbikes with literally a foot between our car and them, at least twenty-five miles an hour over what seems a sensible speed limit, passing on the shoulder, passing on the gravel that separates us from the traffic going the other way—we are basically NASCAR-ing it...

In the midst of this action, Sabbo says to me, "Do you know I read palms?"

"Really?" I reply.

"Yes, yes, let me see your palm. I want to read it." He is very earnest.

What the hell, I got time to kill. "Okay, here ya go," and I hold my palm out for him to peruse.

Again, he is driving batshit crazy down the road and now wants to read my palm at the same time. Silently I think, *this may come to be a decision I regret.*

He surveys my hand for a full minute, very diligently. Then he rubs his hand over mine.

"You can get very upset, like arrrghhhhh upset." He clenches his fists, rolls his shoulders forward, and makes the exasperated expression of someone who is about to blow their stack.

"But just as quickly you let it go. Poof, and your anger will vanish. Just as quickly as it came upon you, you can release it. You can let it go. You have learned to do this over the last few years."

Not bad, I think. This is indeed something I have learned to do over the last few years.

He studies my palm again and says, "You are divorced. You were with her for a good amount of time. You loved her dearly, but she not love you the same way."

Wow. That cuts close to the bone. No comment; except to say both you can't make someone love you, and my ex-wife is a lovely person irrelevant of what went down.

It's important to note that I am spending more time watching the oncoming traffic than he is. Seriously, he is driving by some kind of crazy psychic internal GPS.

That alerts him to the exact moment he needs to move the steering wheel an inch so he doesn't wipe out a scooter driver, carrying his entire life's fortune on his shoulders, forever. If not an entire family!

***

The record so far is a family of five on a scooter I was driving next to in Vietnam whilst I was merrily cruising down the road. This is how they get from A to B.

Yep, you read that correctly, a family of five on a scooter. In Saigon I saw a picture on a wall in a bar that had eight people on one scooter. Two kids standing in the tiny front area, Dad driving, another two kids on the seat behind him, Mom sitting on the basket that is affixed off the back of the scooter, and finally, Mom has a yoke over her shoulders with buckets hanging on each side, both holding babies.

Can you imagine this in any Western country?

I once was flying down a backcountry road on Pho Quoc Island at dusk on my rental scooter, and on my right came a dad with his son on their scooter. Mind you, his son was standing up in the front area of the scooter, head bent forward, resting on the handlebars, blissfully asleep. One hundred percent totally passed out, standing up, on a scooter, while his pops just winked at me and left me in the dust.

I was going about 60 M.P.H. They had to be going at least 70 M.P.H. and the kid was simultaneously standing and off flying with Peter Pan!

***

Back to Sabbo, who proceeds. "Ah, but you are going to have two kids. Yes, yes—you will have two children still."

I burst out laughing. "Um, I think you skipped over an important piece of the puzzle—a woman. Shouldn't that come in there before a baby? And this may need to happen pretty quickly as I already told you I am forty-seven; time is not on my side."

"I can't say when or with whom, but you will have two children—this I know for sure," he coolly replies.

"Well, okay then, this is quite the surprise to hear," I retort.

At this point we are approaching a red light. There are two lanes of cars backed up at the light, with scooter drivers in between the lanes and on the outside of both lanes.

Casually, as if summoning the late great Dale Earnhardt, he flips the wheel to the left, goes off, and I mean OFF, road on the left, and flies past essentially four lanes of waiting vehicles, just in front of all the cars starting to cross the street from the left.

A mere .00000000000321 seconds before the light changes for all the vehicles waiting on the left!

Oh, and in Indonesia passengers sit on the left side of the front seat area.

I have no idea how in the fucking world we don't cause a twenty-five-vehicle pileup. I have no idea how we are not T-boned by a car coming from the left. Both my hands are now clenched to the front dashboard.

In the future, if and/or when I ever become wealthy and you want to break into the safe I own, which only accepts fingerprints, all you have to do is find this car and you have my prints. They are indelibly indented in the dashboard from now until car crushing day.

He looks at me and says, "We must hurry to catch the boat." Not a trace of panic in his voice.

At this point I say, "Thanks for the hand reading; let's just concentrate on getting to the pier."

I decide living the next years out is better than having someone simultaneously tell me about them and then promptly expedite my stepping over the rainbow before they happen.

We arrive safely at the pier ten minutes before it is to depart.

Whew! I thank him for the ride, the palm reading, and the conversation. He leads me to one of the eighty-five vendors selling boat tickets. The pier is packed with foreigners and locals, hot as Hades in the noonday sun.

I purchase my round-trip ticket to Lombok Island from a lady friend of Sabbo's.

Sabbo and I hug, say good-bye, and the lady leads me to the relevant pier. She gets me in the line behind about a hundred foreigners and says bye. After eight minutes I get up to the captain, who is taking tickets at the boat entrance.

I hand him my ticket. He looks at it and says, "Oh, sorry, we no go to Lombok today."

"What? I just bought this ticket five minutes ago, and the lady said it was good for the Lombok boat. I don't understand."

"We no go to Lombok today, sorry. This boat goes to Gili Air and then Gili T. You can grab a boat from one of those islands to Lombok if you want, or you can wait till tomorrow. You must make decision now as we leave in two minutes."

"Shit! Well, the travel gods are in control today," I mutter to myself. I decide to keep moving forward.

If there is one lesson I have learned, life is about movement. Keep on moving or you begin the slow march to oblivion. On the boat I go.

I will say three things about the boat ride. First, they stuff approximately two hundred of us in the bottom of the boat with no A/C on a hundred-degree day, then proceed to wait for another twenty minutes before leaving the pier.

All of us are drenched in sweat, smashed up against one another. One giant conjoined moist organism stuck in a steam sauna.

Second, I take a look at the crowd and determine very quickly that Gili T is not the island for me. Everyone going there, identified by stickers on their shirts, looks about twenty-two and ready to party—hard! You can just feel it. Like virgins on prom night!

Not the scene I want right now.

Third, I end up having a terrific conversation with this young couple who met in Thailand and have been traveling together for a while now. We laugh at all the things that happen when traversing anywhere in Asia.

After about an hour the boat pulls up to Gili Air Island. I have had enough of it all at this point and decide to disembark here. Pretty sure I lost eight pounds of water weight sitting underneath. I figure even if I have to wait for a boat, at least I can get some fresh air and a drink in the meantime.

I need to get off the meatpacking boat.

Of course, my backpack is literally at the bottom of the pile in the hull. Thus, I need to climb down in the hull and help the guy move no fewer than seventy backpacks, all weighing about sixty pounds each.

No lie, it is 2,756 degrees down there.

I just did three Bikram yoga classes and 70 squat thrusts in fifteen minutes.

We find my backpack. I am once again drenched in perspiration and no doubt smell like a men's locker room. I jump off the boat onto the deck. The boat pulls away with me standing there—exhausted, bewildered, and clammy.

I survey the action going on just off the pier. Horse carriages are taking people to and fro, I don't hear the normally constant sound of scooters anywhere, and there is this chill vibe to the island.

Something inside me says, *Just stay here; this is where I wanted you all along.*

Okay then. Let's call it a day and find a place to stay.

As I am walking away from the pier, a local approaches me and says, "You need a place to stay?"

Now, usually I would say no. This always happens when you arrive in a new place at a transportation hub, with them getting a cut of the action and often taking you to some random place owned by someone they are related to somehow. This time, due to my tiredness, I say, "Okey-dokey!"

He leads me to this wonderful little home stay that has nice cabins with hot water and A/C, plus a pool. The manager is an affable young man named Jamal. He shows me a cabin, we negotiate a price, and I throw my bags in the room.

After all, what was supposed to be an hour of travel ended up being six and a half hours of travel in 4,376-degree heat, with Sabbo the psychic NASCAR driver, a 200 person sweat lodge, and four extreme CrossFit classes sandwiched in the middle.

I am done.

I go straight to the ocean and take a dip. Do some yoga in the water to loosen up. Lie down in the sand afterward for about an hour. Find a little spot to eat and chill. Meet a really sweet young couple from the States at the pool and chat with them for a while.

Before I know it, nighttime has come upon us and I am pretty darn tired. So I decide to head over to the convenience store, grab a couple of beers, go back to the room, relax on my deck, then hit the sack for an early day.

This entire story comes down to this moment. Thanks for your patience.

I walk out of the store and I hear this strange guitar. If you know me, you know I always follow my ear. Rarely does my ear for music let me down. I see these locals sitting on a pagoda by the pier, playing some tunes and drinking beer.

There is a bongo player, a tambourine player, and a terrific guitar player. Again, his guitar sounds like nothing I have ever heard. I walk over to check this instrument out and soak up the atmosphere.

It is here I meet Septuri and Adi Adi. They are the musicians. Adi Adi is playing what is called a *gambus*. This is an indigenous instrument to Lombok and Gili Air Island. I would describe it as a cross between a sitar and a mandolin.

Very, very sweet-sounding instrument. They are singing songs in the local dialect. The whole scene is lovely.

I ask them if I can sit down and listen. They welcome me with open arms.

I spend the next three hours sitting with them, enraptured by the cool ocean breeze on my skin and the sounds of island music, chatting in between songs, buying them beer, and chuckling with strangers.

As time goes on, one by one, other foreigners and locals begin to sit with us and enjoy all the festivities.

In the end, we have about twelve people hanging about, smiling, talking, laughing, and living in the moment. Septuri is a riot, the joker of the group. Adi Adi is the quiet yet soulful one.

I meet the young lady who will be my scuba instructor for the next three days that night too. And the scuba diving is brilliant. No, outstanding!

I meet locals all over the island, really bond with them. Four in particular I will never forget. I befriend some terrific people throughout my eight days on this magic little piece of land.

I watch sunsets that blow my mind. I mean the most spectacular, magnificent, jaw-dropping sunsets I have ever seen.

I do yoga in blue and emerald-green oceans, ride bikes around the entire island, see some of the most amazing underwater scenery, including giant sea turtles, huge lobsters, schools of rainbow-colored fish, and I receive my best massage so far in Asia.

Septuri and Adi Adi come down to the beach with me the night before I leave. They ask me if I want to hang out. What a gracious and warm compliment.

I become the tambourine man. I buy dinner. Seems fair.

We again hang out for three hours and play music, drink beers, and laugh—now a laughter shared between people who are no longer strangers, but heartfelt friends.

***

So you see, sometimes the travel gods have a different agenda for you. I never got to Lombok. And that is okay.

I took what they handed me and went with the flow. I didn't fight it and I didn't get upset. What was meant to be was meant to be.

Little did I know what was meant to be would be so very special.

I find the more I surrender to the current, the more I surrender to the tides; the more I let myself dissolve into the ocean, the more she takes me where I need to be.

It's damn hard and often frustrating this letting go. You want this, whatever this is for you, but life says, "Nope, not today; maybe not tomorrow either. For that matter—maybe not ever! Then again, maybe I have something better in store for you if you just let me take you on a ride."

More often than not lately, when I give in, she takes me to places, people, and moments that end up being vastly more beautiful, enriching, and rewarding than what my measly plans were.

Thank you, travel gods—no, thank you, God. I know You keep leading me to where I need to be. I am getting better at remembering that Your dream for me is substantially bigger than my dream for me is or even could be.

I have one question: "Where are we going tomorrow?"

SAIGON...

It's bat shit fucking insane here!

This city is a teenager after drinking six Red Bulls and eating four handfuls of gummy bears while listening to Metallica, knowing his parents just went away for the weekend and the next 48 hours are totally unsupervised!

Off the charts with verve, vitality, and vibrancy!

The sheer volume of sounds, sights, smells, traffic, motor scooters, hustling people, food vendors, dogs, construction, and noise is overwhelming at times.

Sensory overload, a cacophony of sounds, people from all walks of life.

Streets are bustling and bursting, vendors of every variation, selling stuff on bikes, in boxes, off the back of mopeds, stacked on top of their heads.

Soups served off the back of bikes, dried fish hanging on racks five feet above the bike frames, grilled pork cooked and served on the side of a scooter, cigarette/candy vendors walking around with those old school serving boxes you see from movies in the 1950's, small carts being pushed around the streets filled with every electronic device known to man, stealthy yet ever present drug dealers, and Vietnamese of every flavor standing in front of their stores beckoning you to come spend money inside.

People packed into street side restaurants and food stands like sardines, eating food cooked right there by the side of the road, imbibing elixirs throughout the meal until the wee hours of the morning, nonstop street action. No lie, at 3A.M. you can find some utterly mouthwatering meals at crowded, lively street front spots.

A culinary symphony!

Truly, my favorite country food-wise to date! Doesn't matter if you are eating from a guy on a bike with a grill off the back, a street-side canopy tent, or a small hole in the wall kind of joint—it is all fantastic! For my money, they are the soup kings of the world!

An astonishing melting pot of personalities, potential, and persistence!

Surprisingly, a drug addict's bucket list destination. I mean, it's a frickin' Communist country and yet you can find whatever you fancy. How is that possible?

***

One day I was walking down the street around 2p.m. and this guy slides up next to me on my right. He quietly asks, "Heroin?" I turn, look at him in shock, look down at my arms in disbelief and stand there somewhat puzzled.

You see, I am wearing a tank top. My arms all fully exposed. Thus, if you looked for even one second, you would see no track or needle marks. I respond somewhat flabbergasted "Do I look like someone who does heroin? Wait, beyond that, who does heroin at two in the afternoon?"

He smiles and retorts without missing a beat, "Heroin addicts do..."

"Hahahaha. Well, you got me there. I guess you are right on that one."

Ever the salesman he moves on and inquires, "How about a horse tranquilizer?"

Again, I let out a hearty laugh. My next reaction is to ask, "Do I look like I have a horse?"

"No, but you can take them yourself."

Inquiring minds want to know more, so I ask, "What for?"

"Feel good for 20 minutes, then sleep for 24 hours."

"Ay yi yi, have a good day pal."

***

Saigon is an exploding metropolis filled with the promise of tomorrow.

Did I mention that it's fucking insane here!

I have never been in a city with such a frenetic pulse.

I remember several occasions where I needed to go back to my room to lie down for a while, allow my mind to unscramble. Honestly, sometimes my brain hurt.

Seriously, crossing the street takes 100 percent focus. It's a real-life, life or death obstacle course!

You have to have your head on a swivel and eyes moving. Cars, buses, trucks, motorcycles, motor scooters, bicyclists, pedestrians, mobile food carts, and animals are around every corner.

When I say motor scooters by the thousands I am wholly understating the magnitude of the motor scooter mania in Saigon. Hundreds of thousands of them on the roads day and night, carrying almost every item known to mankind, all considering traffic laws to be arbitrary notions one can choose to follow or not!

Much in the same way the notion that politicians are elected to serve the people is arbitrarily followed throughout the world.

What this means is that the locals drive their scooters down streets the wrong way in the wrong lane, they cut diagonally across intersections when turning, they ride up on the sidewalks, they have objects protruding in every direction, they cut in between cars, they have upwards of five people on them at one time—am I coming close to impressing upon you how simultaneously chaotic and surprising a walk down the street can be?

You constantly need to be aware, nimble, panoramic, and decisive.

Riding a motor scooter taxi is just, well, "Jesus, please take the motherf-ing wheel!"

Or the handlebars, as it were. And forgive me for swearing too!

Taking a motor scooter taxi through morning rush hour just about made me pee in my pants. I could reach out and touch all the other scooter drivers who surrounded us, all while we were either going hell-bent for leather or coming to a halting stop.

By and large, Saigon is also filled with very, very sweet people.

I had several, and I mean several, Vietnamese go out of their way to help me. One time a motor scooter taxi driver made it his mission to ensure my painting got shipped home. He parked his bike, walked me into the post office, helped me fill out all the forms, went to the counter with me, interacted with the salesperson, and then took me back to my hostel.

The whole trip took over two hours and he never left my side until our job was complete. Yes, I tipped his ass some serious coin for making my life immensely easier.

Tough, hardworking, relentless, honorable, and compassionate is how I would characterize them.

I found beauty, majesty, and joy here that surprised me.

I found the usual frustrations of travel, and the unusual too.

I found unbridled enthusiasm matched with organized bedlam.

I found Vietnam both fetching and annoying.

I found another adventure well worth having experienced.

I found it to be exactly as Bangkok was twenty-five years ago, primed and ready for a whole new world.

Unleashed and untamed; hungry for more!

So nice to see a city ravaged by war finally finding its footing right before your eyes.

I can't wait to see what it becomes.

THANKSGIVING AND GIVING THANKS...

The more I give thanks, the more blessings I receive.

The more I give thanks, the less I carry.

The more I give thanks, the more I let go.

The more I give thanks, the less I need.

The more I give thanks, the more I love without attachment.

The more I give thanks, the less I hurt.

The more I give thanks, the more I see and feel.

The more I give thanks, the less it takes to forgive.

It is through thanksgiving we are transformed to both

More and Less

Of what we truly are

And wish to be...

DO YOU HAVE DEMONS?

I was exceptionally reluctant to publish this piece on Facebook during my trip. I thought that if some friends read it, they would say, "Oh crap, Stan's gone all Marlon Brando/Apocalypse Now on us. Somebody call Martin Sheen, get him down to Vietnam, and bring Stan's ass back home."

Then one night I received the following private message from a friend: "Stan, I relapsed."

This person knew nothing else needed to be said. I understood. I understand because we all have weaknesses hidden beneath our masks.

This person knows I love him/her, warts and all. I am not here to judge. Instead, I am here to sit by your side, with you and your pain.

And so, I decided I would publish it anyway. Who knows, it might simply be drivel. Then again, maybe, just maybe this person can find something in it that helps. Maybe you can also...

***

Let's be real for a minute can we? Each of us has patterns of behavior that interfere with our ability to lead the kind of fruitful lives we all crave. Whether it is anger, fear, hurt, mistrust, self-loathing, no self-belief, abuse, addiction or whatever – we all allow ourselves to be led astray by demons we have yet to conquer.

And every single one of these demons lay within. These are not external forces wrecking havoc on our lives, but issues we have been unable to, shall we say, conquer. Come on peeps, think about it, what are your "triggers"?

What sets you off? What makes your mind go blank, or worse, an explosion of emotions, thoughts and feelings erupt in your head, blinding all rationale thought because you are over-whelmed by the cacophony of dissonance inside?

Before you know it, whatever the situation was that set off the explosion has now gotten worse because you are unable to react the way you have always so desperately wanted to when these moments arise.

Hopefully the following will help you finally figure out how to deal with these issues once and for all. Whatever your partic-ular fiend, may this be of service.

For those who read it and don't buy what I am selling, well, that's okay too. Consider it an allegorical tale. For me it was and is 100 percent nonfiction.

∗∗∗

Without further ado:

Do you have demons?

I know I do.

I am not talking about the mystical, devil, and/or evil spirit kind.

What I mean is do you have habits, behaviors, defense mech-anisms, patterns, programs, or traits that demonize your life? Whenever they rear their head, things get messy.

You behave in ways that don't necessarily make things better. You react to certain situations in such a fashion as to leave you, upon reflection, disappointed with yourself afterward.

You have gotten to the point where, well, you are simply tired of the influence they have in your life. You are over it—done! Yet, for various reasons they keep showing up, stealing your serenity. Pillaging through your peace.

I know how you feel. There are a few demons that, despite my best efforts, I have been unable to stop from influencing my behavior. I, too, am over them.

So I decided I needed to do something about it, once and for all. I took a look at the demons that seem to bother me the most, the ones who cause the most damage in my relationships and in my everyday existence. I decided which one created the largest problems, the one with whom I am most ready to be done.

You see, I know his name well. Therefore, it was easy to choose him first. The way I see it, tackle the biggest right out of the gate. Sort of a David and Goliath philosophy—conquer my toughest foe first, and all others ought to be relatively easier if I succeed, right?

Then I went someplace quiet, where I could be alone and undisturbed.

After clearing my mind for a while, I started to recall many instances wherein this demon had come into my home and caused chaos. My home being the place where my heart, soul, and mind reside.

I looked at the situations and times he showed up, the events that brought forth his presence, the ways I acted when he was around.

I sat with these memories for some time. I said: "It's okay, Stan. Just relive them one more time so you can finally figure this out. Be patient, don't be too hard on yourself; take a sincere and truthful look at each memory to pull out what you need. This is a learning exercise."

I can't say it was fun. But it was illuminating.

Questions such as "Why and when does he show up? What's the common factor? Why does he always seem to get the best of me? Why do I forget what's really important and give him the power to disrupt my life? Why does it never end well and what can I do to put a stop to it?"

Then it hit me. Finally! I got it!

It is me who allows the demon to enter my home, to walk brazenly through the door and start moving my stuff around.

I am the one who affords him the chance to impress upon me his character, to imbue my life with his false charms.

A demon's favorite sandbox is the six inches between your ears.

WTF is wrong with me? How could I be so stupid? How could I give this unwelcome visitor free reign over my heart, mind, and soul? It was and is time for me to stop playing the part of the fool, the foil, and the victim.

Now I knew the face of my demon. Now I could see his tricks vividly. Now I could clearly recognize my shortcomings in this relationship I allowed to fester entirely too long.

Now I was ready to face him.

As my dad said a hundred times, "I don't really care when you learn the lesson, Stan, it's what you do with it once you finally do learn the lesson that is important!"

When in doubt, listen to your parents. They have your back.

Thus, I invited my demon to sit and talk with me.

And indeed, he did. He happily sat down across from me, no more than two feet away. I could see his face; all the detailed features of his countenance. Mostly, I could see that mischievous smile of his.

I could hear his thoughts: *Well, this is interesting! Considering I usually get the best of you, I can't wait to see why you invited me here now. It's not when I usually show up. You have piqued my curiosity.*

He communicated all of this without saying a word. I could see it all in his eyes. He came ready for a battle he thought he would win, as he had done so many times before.

The skin on his face tightened, and his steely eyes closed to a squint as he readied himself for an onslaught.

I said: "I invited you here because I wanted to thank you."

The look of surprise on his face was priceless.

"I want to thank you for the lessons you have taught me. For the ways you have exposed a weakness, a flaw in my character. For all the times you brought out the worst in me. For all the times I had to clean up after OUR MESS."

He started to stammer. I cut him off with the sweep of my hand.

"That's right, as with any teacher I must be grateful, appreciative, and respectful of the lessons you have imparted for my benefit. Because of you I have grown. And for that I can't be angry. Growth in any form is good, no matter how painful the process."

I could see he was befuddled. I honestly doubt he gets thanked often, if ever. His eyes were growing dimmer. His hold on me was weakening.

I was literally killing him with kindness. Ha, how poetic!

I continued, "Now that I understand these lessons, my role in their outcomes, and what you are all about, well, I have no more use for you."

This was delivered with total indifference, with an equanimity that had no emotion; a calmness in my heart that was impenetrable. I felt nothing for him beyond simultaneous gratitude and nonchalance.

I was truly over him. We were done.

We sat for a bit longer, as if he wanted to be sure. I kept looking him straight in the eye, rooted in my resolve.

Once I knew he knew for sure, I said, "Again, thank you. I hold no ill will. Now you must go. We have nothing further to discuss. Wherever it is you go, I do not care, but you are no longer welcome here. Good-bye."

His power over me was finished. He knew it and I knew it. He looked befuddled.

At this point I started praying and thanking God for helping me vanquish my enemy. I began ignoring the demon sitting across from me and pondered how I was going to enact change due to this new freedom.

To be honest, I am not sure how much longer he sat, but I do remember looking up as he was walking away, head down and shoulders slumped. I recall how he looked back one last time just to be sure, and I simply laughed, waved him off, and went about constructing my plans.

The rest of the day I felt emancipated.

But wait, folks, the story does not end there.

You see, like all demons he was tenacious. Sure enough, the next morning I heard a knock at the door to the house wherein my heart, mind, and soul reside.

I knew who it was.

I said, "I told you yesterday, you are no longer welcome here. Go away. I have no need for you anymore."

He paused for a second, slowly realizing I was not going to allow him to get me worked up. Again, I was done with him. With that I could hear him walk away slowly.

Ha, another attempt averted, I thought. *Keep it up, Stan*. The rest of my day went amiably.

I will be damned if, on the second day after our conversation, I heard a foot land on the front porch. I thought, *This guy doesn't give up easily, does he?*

Before he could even knock on the door, I said, "Nope, don't even bother. We are done. Move along. I have things to do."

And he left again. Another good day was notched on my belt.

Day three after the talk, I was inside my home and I heard the front gate to my property open. It creaks as all wood fences do over time. I didn't even have to look out the window to see who was outside; after all, I had not invited anyone in today.

It was a family day.

I shouted calmly, "Not sure why you keep coming around, but I will repeat what I have said numerous times now. Our business is finished; our relationship is over! Move on down the road, and make it quick before I send my dog after you. And trust me, my dog is not as kind as I am."

Yes, I got a guard dog. Couldn't believe I hadn't thought of it before since I am an animal lover.

Who better to task with the job of chasing off nefarious characters? Who better to help ensure your home is safe and secure? All dogs are loyal to their master if he treats them well.

And I knew what dog to get—my beloved German shepherd, Brandy. I asked her to come back from that eternal dog park in the sky and protect my house, as she had done so many times before.

She crossed over the rainbow years ago, yet joyfully resumed her protective role in my life. Whether it be the physical or spiritual realm, she always has my back.

I suggest you get one too—great way to relax when at home, knowing your pal is out front ensuring all comers know they have to go through him or her first. Turns out demons are scared of animals, who can't be tricked—what a bonus!

***

Do you understand where I am going with the dog metaphor here? What I found is it's imperative I develop an attunement to the signs which begin to develop that show me my old demon is approaching again.

I need to implement a strategy whereby I analyze the initial feelings, the physical, spiritual and mental manifestations that come forth when those moments arise that start heading me on a crash course with my demon.

For me, my old dog represents being on guard. Being aware in the keenest of ways how the demon approaches me so I can not only prepare my new reaction, but begin to dissuade his presence from the very onset of his appearance anywhere near my psyche.

✳✳✳

Day four and early in the morning, I heard Brandy barking. You know that low, guttural sound they make when they sense something or someone is not to their liking?

He wasn't even near the house yet, probably down the road some five hundred feet or so. But my dog could smell him, and I could too. Remember, I have known him for years. Of course I can smell him.

This time, in my mind I told him, "You need to find a new neighborhood, pal. Because from now on I am leaving the front gate open so my awesome dog, Brandy, can roam the streets and head off strangers before they come close.

"You want to mess with me, you need to go through her first. I said it before, I will say it again—we are done!"

With that he turned around and walked off in the other direction.

I now see that our demons are willful, determined, and possessive. They do not give up without a fight.

You must continue to reinforce your message, without emotion, until they understand beyond a shadow of a doubt your relationship is over. You must stay vigilant.

I can't wait till a month from now. If I keep practicing what I have learned, I may very well have him aimlessly wandering the streets of some far-off land, confused and saddened at the loss of his old foil.

And that suits me just fine. For once, I can accept the reality that another being's sadness became my joy.

I didn't steal from him; I didn't beat him up or berate him.

All I did was thank him, release him, and banish him. All I did was accept my part in our relationship, forgive myself, and look to the future. Unfettered, unabashed, and undaunted. I am ready to face my next demon.

If I have my way, one by one they will fall. Sooner rather than later!

After all, I have some living to do...

Peeps, you have all the power necessary to vanquish the enemies inside you. You have a deep well of strength and willpower; all you have to do is dip the bucket down into the water and drink up.

Your peace is patiently waiting for you.

What are you waiting for...

Let's go slay some demons shall we?

BREAKING PROMISES MADE
UNDER THE BRIDGE...

And why it is necessary at times, however painful!

Friendships, at least true-blue good ones, are sooo hard to form. Finding a friend who is both a generous giver and a gentle receiver is, well, like, so damn rare!

Too many people lose sight of the value of friendship—the dedication, work, loyalty, and understanding it takes often being more than a lot of folks can seem to muster these days.

Which makes it even more difficult when past friendships no longer serve the present you! Especially ones you made long ago under the bridge that carries us all from our youth to adulthood.

And with remorse, with actually knowing the death of anything that was once good is indeed a grievous occurrence, you decide it is time to walk away from the relationship.

It just plain sucks!

In another piece I reference an article in *Vanity Fair* magazine I read regarding the author's long relationship with The Rolling Stones, along with where the band has come to now in both their careers and interpersonal relationships.

His summary of the present situation was the following:

"The Stones began as a gang, which is why we loved them. Friendship. Brothers under the bridge. But by the time I'd come around, they'd broken into warring camps...

"At the center of that gang were the Blood Brothers, Mick and Keith. Their friendship was rock 'n' roll. The songs being written together only amplified that point, for what is more intimate than co-writing. But what happens when that friendship dies? What does it do to the music?

"But I think the death of the friendship explains the loss of the mojo... Without the friendship, there was no band. Nor love, nor music.

"Keith believed Mick had sold out to the forces of reaction that once busted and hounded them in England. Keith's the friend who won't let you forget the promise you made under the bridge."

I love that line: Promises made under the bridge.

That is exactly what they were. You promised you would be there for one another forever. You promised to keep not one, but many secrets. You promised to hold them up when they couldn't stand on their own. You promised your friendship would never end.

At the time, you sincerely and truly meant every word.

But now it is years and years later, and both your lives have gone in drastically different directions. Both of you have taken beatings, been served up some tough dishes, and had others cut you to the bone.

Both of you have also experienced various joys, successes, and blessings.

These experiences have carved out new people, it seems.

You look at this person in your mind's eye and say to yourself:

"I love you and what we used to share. I will always fondly remember the honest love that existed at one time, the memories that bring back smiles and laughter. I will forever cherish those moments we were there for each other.

"But I no longer feel like I can be myself when I am with you. I really don't think you understand or respect who I have become. Which is fine. Really, it's okay.

"I have certainly grown in different ways than you may have expected. My choices may be suspect and/or questionable to you. But I do feel I am a better, more caring and well-rounded person than I have ever been before. And for whatever reason, you don't see it. Therefore, it is time for me to move on. To shed influences that reduce me, filling that void with ones that expand me.

"Trust me, this is very, very difficult for me because I work incredibly hard at building lasting relationships. But let's be honest, the house of friendship we built is more an ancient structure than a modern classic.

"It's time we both went on to other, more promising and enriching projects."

And you begin to weep! The pain of goodbye, even when done for all the right reasons, can still cut to the bone.

Over the last few years, I have had to do this very process. With people I have known for many, many, many years. These were people I cherished. I adored. I shared tough times with.

I shared the days of my youth with some of these characters, continuing into our young professional days and all the way until middle age.

And it kills me! Rips my heart apart and stomps on my spirit.

You know what has happened in many cases? You lose your old-school boys or girls to adulthood.

Watching as responsibility, accountability, distance, family, and a whole slew of other distractions take over, whittle away at their ability to remember what is important—friendships. The bond you shared. The feeling nobody understood you like they did. The promises under the bridge!

The saying goes, "Old friends are the best friends." So, it is tough to lose those you care for so much to what you consider a mirage, a false dream—a bill of goods not worth the price.

The bill of goods I refer to is today's version of happiness: the more you buy, the happier you become.

Consumption equals happiness. Busy equals fulfilled. Facebook equals friendship.

Watching T.V. is easier than reaching out and listening. Your phone is your lifeline.

I am not even talking about assessing blame here. Heck, it takes two to tango. Each side is guilty. That is why there is no fault.

It just happened. You don't see the world from the same viewpoint anymore. You don't view each other in the same light as you used to. You don't really make new experiences anymore as much as talk about the past ones most of the time.

Recently, as referenced above, I let go of some such relationships. For varied and different reasons, they were no longer serving either party anymore. They were cold.

If I were to be honest, I no longer felt they even really knew me anymore, let alone had my back. And in real friendships, you have to know they have your back. Otherwise it's a fraud. A relationship that, while nice to have, needs to be understood for what it is—an acquaintance!

If a friend can't see the real you how in the world will they know when you are backed into a corner or your back is up against the wall; which in either instance requires reinforcements to show up in the form of those who will stand right by your side?

> Life is kind of like a party. You invite a lot of people, some leave early, some stay all night, some laugh with you, some laugh at you, and some show up really late. But in the end, after the fun, there are a few who stay to help you clean up the mess. And most of the time, they aren't even the ones who made the mess. These people are your true friends in life. They are the only ones who matter.
>
> ~ Author Unknown

Well, the ones who matter are the people who see the beauty in me. The effervescence. The grandeur, charm, and sincerity in me. The random, sometimes unpredictable, yet pleasantly surprising in me. The gentle, caring, and concerned in me.

The undeniable heart and splendid soul that is me!

Thus, I need to focus my attention on them. Maybe find some others out there who better see, understand, and appreciate my loving friendship. I know they exist because I know I exist.

I have heard their similar cries. And recently I have felt the touch of a few that left me yearning for more.

Saying good-bye is usually tied to a feeling you are leaving something you wish could be around longer. Imbuing the process with a sense of loss.

Then there are some good-byes that bring with them freedom. Freedom from a past that no longer defines you. Freedom from a day or days long ago that have no relevance today, which is the only day that matters. Freedom from a time-capsulated prison in which you no longer wish to be shackled.

There are good-byes that sap your spirit, but need to be done so your spirit can continue to rise. Rise above the muck and mundane to a different place.

A place where the new you sees the old you, smiles, and says, "Go ahead, the promises made under that bridge needed to be broken so you could cross over a new bridge. Now you are on the other side. Let's see what we can do over here today!"

If that friend ever really and truly did love you, over time they will come to terms with the same reality you did. Reality being the fact life was pretty darn kind to give you that friendship when you needed it!

One of the best aspects of positive memories is they age rather well, much in the same fashion as wine.

So raise a glass to old friends, hallowed and treasured broken promises, and discovering new lands after crossing over the bridges yet unknown.

Let go, my peeps. It's time. It's okay. Often it's necessary!

Your new friends are looking for you...

DID SOMEONE SAY WHITEWATER RAFTING?

Down the biggest river in Bali?

I'm in, 'cause, well, ya know, I am a thrill seeker.

I turn to Alex and say, "We gotta do this!"

She looks at me with trepidation in her eyes and replies, "I am not so sure on that one, Stan. I am a little intimidated by the idea."

Okay, fair enough.

So, over the next two days, I slowly cajole her, gently nudge her, professing "all will be well." I talk of my past experiences doing it and try to ease her fears.

I book the trip for two at the front desk. A great guy we met in Seminyak named Matt M. says he will do it with me.

The night before he tells me he can't go as he double booked; he wanted to go see a healer in Ubud and had forgotten he already made an appointment.

I say to Alex, "You can't let me do this alone. Come on, we will have a blast, and I promise I will keep you safe."

Finally, she relents and responds, "Okay, I am in. Let's do it."

The next morning the driver from the rafting company picks us up, tells us it is a two-hour drive to the starting point, and off we go.

The drive up is splendid. We go through all these winding backcountry roads with tight hairpin curves. Scooters and trucks and cars squeezing by each other with an inch to spare!

Did I mention there are no traffic laws in Bali? I am not kidding, there are zero laws governing driving. No rules of the road. No speed limits. No signs that say don't do this or don't do that.

No traffic laws—can you imagine?

On our drive up to Ubud, I ask the chauffeur, "What is the speed limit here?"

He replies, "If you can't make the turn without going off the road or hitting another driver, you are going too fast. That is the only general rule."

Makes sense to me.

You need to understand, entire families travel by scooter.

I have seen the equivalent of a Chevy pickup truck bed filled with items somehow affixed on top of a scooter.

I have seen no fewer than six five-gallon water jugs, full, weighing forty-five pounds each, arranged on a scooter, driven by a sixty-five-year old lady who also had a three-foot-high stack of palms on her head.

I have seen eight-year-olds drive scooters better than Jackie Stewart at Le Mans. That's right, kids drive scooters every day on the roads too.

Again, eight-year-old kids driving down the highway next to you... And it's all cool!

In America they can't even get into the front seat of a car until they are seven!

Guess what, it all works out fine.

Like I said, there are no laws. And these kids seem to understand if they crash the scooter, they have destroyed the family vehicle. They take the responsibility seriously.

Only the foreigners drive like idiots here.

Then again, only the foreigners act like idiots here. But that is another story.

Honestly, it's safer to drive the streets here than in any Western country. By a long shot!

I digress, back to our journey.

We drive for two hours through rice paddies, hills, and small towns populated with tiny huts all over—we are enthralled by the rural spectacle of Bali's countryside.

We watch Balinese folks slaving away in billion-degree heat to harvest the rice. We are humbled by their work ethic. Every one of them has a smile on their face.

We arrive at the starting point. Alex sees there is a dam with a twelve-foot drop just above the launch area. She gets a little nervous. I assure her all will be well, the guides are trained, and they know what they are doing.

The rafts are smaller than what I am accustomed to, with room for only four passengers along with the guide in the back.

As we are stretching out, getting warmed up and fitted for our life vests, we notice this Chinese couple. Young kids, early twenties. The girl appears, how shall I say, frail. The boy tall and lanky.

You guessed it; they will be our partners on the boat.

The young lady comes up and introduces herself in broken English. Good for her. She is making an attempt to be friendly.

She explains to us that they did the trip last year. She says, "It did not go so well the first time. I have trouble. We are back to try again."

Alex and I look at each other; we are thinking the same thing. *What does she mean when she says, "It didn't go so well"?*

What happened last time? Why is she here again if she had a bad experience?

Well, we both applaud her for getting back on the horse, so to speak.

Our guide comes over and introduces himself. "I am Okee. Just call me Okee, okay? Today we have fun. Have you done this before? Where are you from?"

He is a jokester. We like him immediately. He and I have some fun back and forth. Alex and I take some pics before the start with our gear on. She does a pose with an "Oh my god, what am I doing" look on her face.

I have to go to the bathroom. As I am walking to the wash closet, as it is coined here, I pass by our female Chinese companion. We smile. She gets two feet past me and SCREAMS!

I turn on a dime. "What happened? Are you okay?"

"Dragonfly!" she states with a shudder. She is visibly shaken.

"Um, what do you mean?" She is standing there in somewhat of a cowering position. "Did it attack you or something?"

"No, it just flew close. I am scared of dragonflies."

"Really?" I say without thinking. "You are scared of dragonflies? They are harmless, good for eating mosquitoes. They can't hurt you."

"Oh, I am scared of mosquitoes too."

"Well, he flew away so you should be okay now."

I turn to go relieve myself and think, *Sweet Jesus, who in the world is afraid of dragonflies? Did she just say she was afraid of mosquitos? No, that can't be right.*

This will prove to a harbinger of things to come.

The head of the rafting crew gives us all a safety speech with directions as to how we are supposed to act, the commands our guide will give us, and what to do if we fall in the water—general stuff that is mostly common sense.

At last, we board the boats. The guide looks at the Chinese couple and us; he immediately puts me in the front on the right. This is so the Chinese girl is seated between us in a front-to-back-of-boat sense, thereby having the two strongest paddlers covering the right side.

He takes a look at Alex and the Chinese guy and puts Alex in the front on the left. Evidently, he thinks Alex is stronger than the Chinese guy. Again, the Chinese guy is taller than me, yet skinnier than Alex. The guide ascertains the boat will be safer with Alex and him sandwiching the Chinese guy on the left side.

I silently chuckle!

Before we launch, the guide shows us how to hold the oars. You take one hand and grip the oar about halfway down; you take the other and place it directly on top of the oar, palm down.

The Chinese girl can't quite get it. She grips the oar five different ways with her top hand, backward at one point. I turn and show her exactly how to do it. She looks at my grip on the oar and says, "I can't do it. I don't understand."

Sweet Mother Mary and Joseph, I think. She has no physical dexterity whatsoever. She can't even grab a stick from the top with her palm while holding the other portion of the stick halfway down.

This is going to be interesting.

Off we go down the rapids.

I would say the rapids are a two and a half to three out of five on the rapids difficulty scale. Not incredibly challenging, but a heck of a lot of fun. Alex is hooked immediately.

Within five minutes she is giggling, screaming with delight, and smiling from ear to ear. I look at her and say, "Well, what do you think? Was I right?"

She grins and gives me a high-five. All is well.

Next thing we know the Chinese girl SCREAMS AGAIN.

WTF? We turn around and she is cowering in the middle of the raft. "Mosquito!" she says. Ay yi yi.

We console her; say it will be okay. Her hubby rubs her leg where the mosquito landed.

You have to understand, the rapids require split-second reaction time. If the guide says, "Forward," you have to dig the oar in the water and start rowing so he can get the raft going in the right direction. If he says, "Back," you must paddle backward hard so he can turn the raft to face the rapids.

If you don't react quickly, his job is brutal in terms of trying to get the raft to hit the rapids facing the right angle so the water can do more of the work and we all take less of a beating by not crashing into waves at the wrong trajectory.

Alex and I are in "all hands on deck" mode, digging deep with each command and working hard to follow his orders. Muscling our way through.

Every time we turn around, the Chinese girl has either lost control of her paddle, is in the middle of the raft, or has a look of bewilderment. I don't want to sound harsh here, because it isn't that big a deal due to the manageable water levels, but she is useless. Incapable! Dead weight on the raft! Her hubby isn't as bad, but he has to spend most of his energy consoling her.

At one point, you guessed it—she lets out another SCREAM. Again, we turn to see what happened.

She is in the middle of the boat, crouched down, with hands over her head and the oar dropped in the water.

"Butterfly!" she states with a shiver.

"Let me get this straight. You are afraid of butterflies?"

"Yes, very!" she states earnestly.

This time neither Alex nor I can contain ourselves. We bust out laughing.

How in the world can you be terrified of butterflies? I mean, for Christ's sake. A fricking butterfly!

Later Alex and I agree we feel empathy for her husband. We can't imagine what she is like on a daily basis at home. Not to mention, if you are afraid of every single thing that flies, why in the world are you on a rafting trip through the jungle? Where is the logic in that? What is the point? Why put your-self through the experience? I just don't understand.

How beyond understanding are this young lady's multiple neuroses?

Yes, for the rest of the trip, she screams every few minutes, ducks down into the boat, and cowers. At another spot we come into contact with some plant leaves as the raft crashes into the shore. Sure enough, she freaks out and screams again. Apparently, she doesn't like it when plants come into contact with her skin.

The raft guide is befuddled. He keeps rolling his eyes and giv-ing Alex and me the "I can't believe this" raised hands gesture whenever we turn to see what has terrified her again.

***

I can only guess she is trying to conquer her fears on this trip seeing as how she already went through it once, so for this fact alone she deserves praise. Despite all the joking I do here this element about her character is not lost on either Alex or myself.

I stand up and applaud anyone looking to defeat his or her demons, as you well know by now.

Nonetheless, the river and scenery are brilliant! We are deep in the jungle, surrounded by huge rock walls. There are at least forty waterfalls. We rafted right under twelve.

We see rice paddies galore. Giant trees with vines stretching some fifty feet down to the river—Tarzan would have loved this place.

We see locals bathing in the water naked because that is how they get clean. We respect their privacy at every turn.

We crash into stone walls, go down rapids backward, descend rapids sideways, get stuck between rocks, and flow through areas where the plants are fifteen feet high and the rapids are only five feet wide.

Alex and I work overtime to help the guide. We are wiped out by the end of the trip, totally exhausted! My right arm and her left arm are numb by the time we climb off the raft.

At the end of the trip, we have to walk up these stone steps to the top of the valley. No lie, a thousand steps. Remember the scene in *Kill Bill* when Uma Thurman has to carry a yoke of water buckets up those stairs to her master's compound? Pretty much the same.

As a side note, Asians love enormous, steep, thigh-crushing staircases! Invariably they appear at every magical temple/monastery you want to see. I can hear the ancient ones saying, "We are going to make you earn this visit to serenity, whether you like it or not!"

Alex and I have to take a break twice on the way up to catch our breath. I am no slouch when it comes to being in shape. By the same token, I don't regularly climb mountains everyday either. Man, are we tuckered out.

Meanwhile, the guides are bounding up the steps like deer, in flip-flops no less, carrying four deflated rafts on their heads and laughing at us for being winded.

It is all capped off with a scrumptious buffet of Balinese food served to us while looking out over terraced rice paddies, watching the irrigated water flow down to each paddy, feeding the crops.

Curry soup, sautéed vegetables, peanut chicken satay, cucumber salad, roasted potatoes and a spicy sambal sauce. Spectacular! We are so hungry and the food is so good, we both go back for seconds.

As we sit there sipping our coffees, soaking up the astounding beauty surrounding us, we feel elated. Filled with gratitude for such a surreal experience. Forever thankful the good Lord makes such amazing places on this gorgeous planet for us to enjoy.

I will never forget the smile on Alex's face when we hit the first rapids. Pure joy!

We say our good-byes to the erstwhile Chinese duo, tip the raft guide, walk up to the car, and at one point or another fall asleep on the ride home.

Neither of us will ever forget the day! For the exhilaration, for the grandeur of nature, for the Balinese hospitality, and for the nutty Chinese couple!

Suffice it to say, Alex can't wait to get after the rapids in Colorado or Utah...

MUEZZIN DUETS...

When staying in Muslim countries one of the first things you need to adjust to is the daily call to prayer. Muslims pray five times a day according to the basic tenets of Islam.

Entitled *Adhan*, it's called out by a *Muezzin* from the mosque five times a day, traditionally from the minaret, summoning Muslims for mandatory (fard) worship (salat). A second call, known as iqama, (set up) then summons Muslims to line up for the beginning of the prayers.

The timings of these prayers are spaced fairly throughout the day, so that one is constantly reminded of Allah and gives opportunities to seek His guidance and forgiveness.

Muslim call to prayer (Ezan) is chanted six times a day. The exact time of the Ezan changes each day due to rotation of the earth, revolution around the sun, various latitudes of the earth's locations and daylight savings time.

The timing is based on the following ideals: Two hours before dawn (Fajr), dawn (Tulu), midday (Zuhr), Afternoon (Asr), Sunset (Maghrib) and right before last light of the day (Isha).

The key player in this whole process is the Muezzin. This is the person appointed at a mosque to lead and recite the call to prayer for every event of prayer and worship in the mosque. The muezzin's post is an important one, and the community depends on him for an accurate prayer schedule.

The professional muezzin is chosen for his good character, voice and skills to serve at the mosque. The call of the muezzin is considered an art form, reflected in the melodious chanting of the adhan. In Turkey, there is an annual competition to find the country's best muezzin.

Historically, a muezzin would have recited the call to prayer atop the minarets in order to be heard by those around the mosque. Now, mosques often have loudspeakers mounted on the top of the minaret and the muezzin will use a microphone, or the muezzin recording is played, allowing the call to prayer to be heard at great distances without climbing the minaret.

The key change talked about above is how they now broadcast the prayer call via loudspeaker. Ha! Loud is seriously a gross understatement. In some towns, you can hear it a mile away. If you happen to be staying close to the Mosque, it can be as loud as a rock and roll concert.

Again, five times a day some dude sings songs in a language you don't understand from a loudspeaker so the whole town can hear him. The first one occurs before dawn. Meaning, no matter who you are and/or where you are in town, you are going to hear this random guy sing to you every day.

Did I mention Super-duper loud?

Absolutely no need for an alarm clock while here!

Now, Arabic is a language that can be both melodic and lyrical, and at other times somewhat ear-splitting too. It has a high pitch octave/range that when sung can sound transcendental, just mellifluous. It can also sound slightly irritating.

It all depends on the quality of the singer's voice. Some guys are just out of this world beautiful, some are "maybe they should pick another guy for this" quality.

We all have attended a Karaoke night gone awry.

When in Istanbul I stayed in an area called Sultanmeht; basically the old town area of the city. I slept in a hostel no less than 1,000 feet from both the Blue Mosque and the Hagia Sofia. Which meant I would hear the prayers sung twice during each appointed time in the schedule.

Usually the prayer goes on for about 10-15 minutes. Thus, I would hear two different guys sing for almost a half hour as one would sing from one mosque, then the other would follow. Five times a day means I heard them sing each day for a total of two and a half hours.

On two occasions they did something unique. They sang together. Well, they sang back and forth really. One Muezzin would sing the first verse, then the other would follow with the second, back to the first guy for the third verse, over to the second guy for the fourth verse and so on.

It was intoxicating! Spellbinding. Ethereal. Priceless.

One time while heading back to the hostel at dusk I stopped walking around, sat down on a bench with the Hagia Sofia and the Blue Mosque standing as bookends on either side, in front of a fountain with this dazzling light show, and simply listened.

Tagged yet ownerless dogs roaming the streets, kids with parents marveling at the fountain colors, men laying down their carpets to kneel on for prayer, kiosks busy selling cold drinks/snacks to passersby along with the random street buskers scattered around plying their trade for spare change.

As the dueling Muezzin's sing I begin to lose focus on my surroundings, their voices are so melodious I lay my head back on the bench to fully relax. Enraptured, I close my eyes, allowing their voices to whisk me up and away to the clouds. Floating, I was transported to a place where only music and notes fill the air.

No gravity to hold me down, I thought, *this is what heaven must sound like.*

I have attended certain concerts in my life that stand out, hold special space in my memories, for the virtuoso performances of the person or bands involved. Music has the ability to touch the deepest parts of our souls and linger there long after the melody has stopped.

If I close my eyes today, months later, I can still remember exactly how they made me feel for those utterly precious 30 minutes. Floating away I go, the Blue Mosque to my right and the Hagia Sofia to my left, with their glorious domes and Byzantine architecture, carried off on prayers sung in a foreign language by two men infusing every word with beloved devotion to their faith, conveying a message that imbues me with hope still.

Those 1,800 seconds were better than every single T.V. show I saw in the last year. More melodically pleasing than easily half the music concerts I have ever seen in my life. Far more captivating than three quarters of the museums I visited.

A transfixing and transcendent half hour to say the least!

When I returned to my hostel I asked the manager if he happened to know what they were singing about for the dusk Adhan. He replied, "I have no idea. None of us ever have any idea. We don't speak the traditional language anymore. They all sound the same to me."

Funny how what one person hears everyday, and takes for granted, can leave another person, hearing it for the first time, both astounded and forever thankful to have heard it at all.

Some men I have never meet sang songs in a language I don't understand with meanings that totally escape me who had no idea I was even listening somehow took me to a place I could never have gotten to on my own.

How nutty.

BELIEVE...

You must believe to Receive.

That's it.

There is no trick to it.

It is that SIMPLE.

Believe in your majesty.

Believe in your beauty.

Believe in your strength, your willpower and your tenacity.

Believe you can be more if you set your mind to it.

Believe life is DESPERATE to give you what you want.

Because, guess what? It is!

Think about it. You have made it this far.

Somehow you have managed to make it down the road to this point.

Somehow you have landed on your feet time after time, right?

Sooooooo, Believe!

Now, go out and make it happen. Let your belief carry you. Let your belief push through problems, overcome obstacles, and refuse to relinquish.

The greatest gift we have is our belief, and it's also quite often the first one we misplace.

Find your belief.

It is there, beneath the surface

Patiently waiting for you to awaken it.

Once you do, nothing will ever be the same.   I promise.

Dream big, Believe bigger

Then Receive the Best!

A COMMUNITY OF SPIRIT...

We all want a sense of community.
"But where is my community, the community for me?
The community that accepts who I am?" We ask,
"Does it exist? Will they love me?"

The answer is yes, to all the above. And,
They await you at the banquet table.
They too are looking for you, with the same questions.
We are all the same, wanting to love and be loved.

A community of lovers searching for the feast
Serving up nourishment, grace and bounty.
First, empty your cup
Of passion, desire and want. Pour it all out.

Dip your feet in the puddle and dance.
For only when you are empty
Will your cup be filled to an overflow.
A well with no bottom you are.

Shut your eyes to the images
That feed your worries and anxieties.
Open your mind to the dreams lying dormant
Beneath the surface—yearning to manifest!

Stop clenching your fists; holding tight to that which
Does not serve. Release what you clutch
And watch what you cherish.
Fill empty hands with abundance.

Listen for the Voice, that soft whisper
Amidst the noise. He speaks when there is
No more dissonance. Clearly, truthfully
Without guile!

At night, worry comes to your door.
Hear the knock, but do not answer.
Think of what you love. And,

Console your heart with thanks.

Do not eat from fear's tree.
It is bitter food without nutrition.
Instead, taste of the vine
That bears fruit from friendship.

Lovers will come and go,
Some may stay forever. Yet,
There is only one true love
He that made you from dust

Why do you stay bound
By your own thoughts, words
And a past long since gone?
Freedom awaits your company.

Be still. Surround yourself with nature.
Stop talking and start listening.
In silence you will hear
The echo of your friend's heart.

Let go. Forgive. Praise.
Serve. Give more than take.
Revel in the splendor that is
The unfettered and unequivocal Self.

To thine own self be true!
It's all you can do.

Your community of spirit
Will find you
As soon as
You find YOU!

We long for your arrival.

FOUNTAINS OF YOUTH...

I have been carrying one book with me on this trip that I have read no fewer than four times. Incredibly insightful! It's called *One Flash of Lightning, A Samurai Path for Living in the Moment*, by Stephanie JT Russell. I highly suggest you find a copy.

There is a term relevant to the subject, *bushido*, which essentially means "the way of the warrior." When you think about it, we are all warriors. Warriors of Light, fighting the good fight to lead honorable, noble, and meaningful lives!

I am particularly fond of this passage:

> Bushido is fluid as a stream, sweetening the creative flow and bathing the warrior in cool awareness. Firmly grounded in integrity, the Samurai must yield to circumstance as a fern responds to morning dew.

> Like water wearing away river stones, adaptability erodes fear and releases the wonderment of innocent awareness. From this purity of mind, principle can ideally shape itself in harmony with the moment at hand.

> But new circumstances are a tricky portal to the unknown. To enter unfamiliar turf with confidence, the Samurai cannot be enslaved to preconceived ideas of right and wrong. He/she must bend to the facts as they are presented in the here and now. And even for great Samurai, a strange predicament may be loaded with terrifying uncertainty and isolation.

> This dilemma underscores the Samurai's vow to endure loneliness with grace. He/she must go within and gather the resources to find fresh answers and suitable actions. To banish his/her doubts, he/she must uncover new reservoirs of flexibility.

The process can be painful. His/her instincts may contradict the successful results of past experience. He/she might wrestle with the fear of public reaction to his/her unusual choices. But the challenge compels him/her to innovate, tap untested skills and deepen his/her trust in the unknown.

Adaptability is the fountain of youth and the tutor of wisdom.

It exposes the Samurai's own resistance to change, and calls him/her to end old patterns that don't serve the moment. The freer he/she becomes, the more attuned he/she is to the world with all its fleeting sparks of vitality.

He/She uncoils, loosens, pours his/her being into the hidden nuances of life—and proceeds unhindered into fair, truthful and relevant action.

Fantastic, no?

I mean, read this again. Heck, read it three times. Let it sink in. Read each sentence slowly. Follow the connections.

I am fond of saying, "Yoga is the fountain of youth" to all who inquire about my practice. At the end of the day, yoga is about adaptability. So I can concur with the premise here.

Life is this difficult, crazy, and frustratingly precarious balancing act between feeling like nobody in the world really understands you—therefore, you are standing alone—and simultaneously overcompensating by trying to please too many, thus getting lost in the crowd.

We all battle with the internal yearning for true and sincere companionship while knowing the only way we will ever find peace is digging deep within ourselves.

Change and death are the only two constants in this life. The best way to find the balance mentioned above is to adapt.

To be supple, to banish doubts and release old habits.

To surrender!

But first you must take the long journey to the depths of your heart.

You must unshackle yourself from the worry of the unknown, from the attachment to what others think, from what society tells you is relevant versus what your heart is softly whispering in the recesses of your mind/heart/soul.

You must stand alone, find your own version of nobility, truth, and importance.

When you do so, the chains fall away.

You are no longer a prisoner of the programming.

You are free to run wild with the wind, because you are finally one with the wind. Able to go whichever way the wind blows, because you don't care about the direction.

You take what you are given and you run with it, happy to simply be in the moment, while still existing in that moment on your terms, vibrating with your own frequency. The frequency that always eventually emanates from love.

My dear Warriors of Light—yield!

Flow like water downstream. Get to the bottom of your river. All rivers are tied to one another. All streams come from the same source. All paths end up at the same place. And both that source and that place are You!

Your radiance.

Your undeniable evanescence!

Your inherent ability to respond with whatever is necessary to whatever is needed in the moment.

Without fear, regret, or remorse.

With boldness and courage!

With all the power residing in you responding to any obstacle life presents.

All obstacles are lessons. And all lessons can be learned, absorbed, and responded to with vigor.

Your bounty is as endless as the universe. You have everything you need inside.

You are, indeed, 100 percent limitless.

You are the student and the teacher at the same time.

You are everything and everything is You!

Keep on fighting the good fight, dear warriors; I promise you will find victory.

Today, tomorrow, and forever!

AN EXPENSIVE NAP...

Yesterday, I had the absolute best four hours of sleep thus far on my journey, and maybe in the last seven years. I was in a luxurious black hole of deep, restful slumber. Actually beyond restful, it was catatonic. I think I went to another universe.

Unfortunately for me, it was the most expensive nap in my lifetime!

Ha! What can you do? Life is such a paradox of learning how to take the good with the bad, all with a grain of salt.

Or in this case, a hefty credit card balance. And maybe a large portion of chagrin!

Let me explain.

It was time to leave Istanbul, Turkey. I had been there for eight days. I saw so many flabbergasting, brilliant, historical, and breathtaking sights, it blew my mind.

This place lets history unfold in such a way as to leave you speechless. It's Constantinople for crying out loud!

The multiple 1,000+ year-old buildings and structures, the cobblestone roads with their steep ups and downs, the statues and towers, the palaces and mosques, the underground cisterns and aboveground aqueducts, the super-friendly people and the con artists—it all combines to present a cornucopia of experiences like no other place I have visited.

I walked more kilometers than I can ever recall in seven days' time. Hours upon hours of random wandering around city streets with no maps, downloaded apps, or directions! Just saunter down the road, take a left here, take a right there, or keep on moving forward—whatever my gut told me to do.

Sure, some days I went out with an objective. Especially when I was with my friends Constantine, from Greece, and our erstwhile butterfly, Celine, from France.

We gave Celine the nickname because as much as both Constantine and I tried to have at least one of us watch over her—she would somehow manage to flutter off for a few minutes without leaving a trace. We would stand there looking around and all of a sudden she would appear at our sides, out of thin air!

She was a sweet, earnest, and articulate young Parisian.

Constantine was this energetic, affable thirty-something man with a warm smile. He was yet another of my heroes on the trip in terms of the adventure he was undertaking. He was on a two-year journey to ride his motorcycle over 230,000 kilometers through approximately fifty-eight countries.

I mean, some people dream, some people dream big, and some people dream huge, right?

He had been preparing for over two years to embark on this massive logistical test of the human spirit.

We were the three amigos for three days.

Constantine and Celine seemed to be more intent on visiting certain landmarks than I was, which was fine because I was glad to be in their company.

We made a good trio. The conversations were both light-hearted and yet sometimes took a turn into *meaning of life* territory; the personalities gelled well, with nobody trying to necessarily lead or follow; and we all seemed to truly enjoy the perspective each brought to the group.

I really enjoyed the fact that they were open to leaving the hostel on a few occasions with no agenda or purpose. "Let's get lost and see what happens" would be our motto.

This is rare, I have found, when traveling with others. So many times the people I hook up with have a place or thing they need to see or do—an objective for the day.

Which is fine. I can go with the flow for a while. Sooner or later though, I find they leave and I am on my own, or I feel the urge to break away. I guess that is the paradox that is me, both social seeker and lone wolf in one man.

It's always been that way. At times I crave the group, the friendship making, the bonding, the laughing, and the shared experience. At others, I need to go off and do my own thing. Be the guy who shuns company and looks to explore the world on my own terms, with the only company being my thoughts.

We are all complex creatures with divergent, seemingly contradictory characteristics, no?

I mean, don't most of us have times when we say, "Man, how can I have so many wildly opposite traits, quirks, and tendencies? Am I crazy or just slightly schizophrenic? How will I ever balance it all out without either alienating everyone I know or myself?"

Nonetheless, this is who I am. Dichotomous is the best word at the moment.

Back to the story, Stan, you are probably thinking.

So, both my friends left before me, which is always hard because I become attached to people. Especially if I find them kind-hearted, funny, and intelligent: indeed, they both were in their own way. Just good people from different countries out in the world, searching for the same wanderlust as I was, trying to find that magic carpet ride!

Trust me, if it is carpets you want, there are a thousand guys to sell you one in Istanbul. All with a sly way of trying to engage you in conversation before the eventual *come visit my store* pitch arises.

My favorite is when they approach you with a piece of paper and a bunch of English words on it. They pretend they are working on their proficiency and ask you to help them pronounce the words.

Somewhere along the line they innocuously segue to the sales pitch. Like too many other times in life, knowing who has the magic carpet and who is selling tricks can be tricky.

Dang, I got off track again. Sorry, folks, but it happens.

I was talking about walking the streets, if you remember. Together, on several days we walked for no fewer than eight hours, with breaks in between for an hour or so at the hostel. Even before they came and after they left, I would saunter the streets for hours at a time.

That is my way. I don't understand the whole *Lonely Planet*, *Backpackers Guide* thing. I really don't. Look, they are great as guideposts. They provide a lay of the land and a "sights to consider" infomercial that certainly helps.

The problem is everyone ends up following them without hesitation. To the letter and too often, if you ask me! Why do I feel this is more a negative than a positive, you ask?

Because everyone becomes a sheep, doing the same thing everyone else is doing, led by the shepherd that is the book-writing committee. You end up at the same sights as all the other travelers, doing the same things as all the other travelers, having the same experiences as all the other travelers.

Where is the authenticity in that? Where is the adventure?

Where is the singular occurrence that leaves you speechless, befuddled, or bewitched?

How do you interact with the locals in a genuine way that isn't staged?

When does the randomness of travel intersect with your trip, leaving you a better person because you went with the flow as opposed to following the same path that has already been beaten by others?

Do me a favor, go ahead and use those travel books as a means of research, planning, and bearing.

Absolutely, go see some of the famous places; they are famous for a reason. Participate in some of the suggested activities because they are, indeed, a blast.

But once you get to the land you want to visit, put the book down, walk out of your hostel/hotel/guesthouse, and get lost.

I mean it.

Get completely, totally, and utterly lost.

Take a bunch of lefts, then a bunch of rights, then go straight for a while, then turn down a random road.

I can assure you this: After having gone this route sooooo many times, almost without fail it ends up bringing about the best days of my trip.

I swear, it rarely fails me!

Write your own story, people. Make the trip entirely yours, leave your own mark, find a stranger and forge a bond. It may only last a short while in terms of time, but it will linger forever in the recesses of your heart and soul.

Well, what do you know, I have now successfully gotten off the beaten path of my own story three times now. Life imitates art, which imitates subject matter.

Let me ask you, have these literary off-road trails been worth the digression? I hope so.

Okay, so after all this walking around Istanbul, after all these hours on cobblestone streets that are uneven, hilly, and filled with wonder—my body was really tired.

After having my mind blown way more than I could have imagined, on way too many days in a row, I guess I was exhausted beyond what I realized.

I spent the last day mailing off presents to friends, and stuff to my buddy in California, where I would be staying upon my return. I wanted to lighten my load backpack-wise and ensure some of the items I had picked up along the way as souvenirs got back to the States safely.

For once the endeavor was easier than I thought it would be, considering the post office peeps barely spoke any English.

I quickly ducked into a barbershop, got a haircut. Albeit way shorter than I had expected because the barber, after having been told to "shorten a little" took out the shears and proceeded to cut my hair almost to the scalp on his first sweep.

Oh well, summer haircut before the summer, I guess.

After that I went back to the hostel, grabbed my stuff, and proceeded up to the roof.

Whenever I am about to go on a long flight, I try to get a quality yoga session in to open up my low back, hips, and hamstrings. This helps me survive the hours of sitting erect required in chairs literally designed by the descendants of those who invented the first medieval torture devices.

Except for first-class folks, who get to fall asleep in essentially La-Z-Boys! No wonder they all look rested when exiting the plane and the rest of us common folk look like the walking dead.

The rooftop of the hostel was glorious. The sun was shining bright. The rooftop overlooked the Bosphorus River as it led out into the Aegean Sea, and I saw giant ships making their way to far-off lands. There were birds flying above and the sounds of the streets below.

I had it all to myself.

Before I started my session, I took a moment to thank the good Lord above for such a spectacular stay, telling Him how nothing good happens but by His grace. Asking Him to join me as I flowed.

Then I had a fantastic practice. Just nailed it. Everything in my body opened up and released. I was ready to go.

Quickly I washed myself down, changed clothes, said goodbye to the hostel boys, and was off to the tram. On the way I grabbed my last Turkish doner sandwich with a Sprite, gobbled it down, and snagged my token for the rails.

Within forty-five minutes I was at the airport. Two and a half hours before my flight, no less! Sweet, I could relax as I went through the airport shakedown.

I got my ticket, checked my backpack, made it through customs, and had an hour and a half to spare. Went and bought a coffee with two pieces of baklava. Sat down to enjoy them for a half hour, people-watching as one does whilst waiting at airports. Finished it all up and felt great. Sauntered over to the gate and was sitting twenty feet from the desk a full forty-five minutes before the flight was scheduled to leave.

I read a *Vanity Fair* I had purchased to catch up on the world. All of a sudden, I began to feel tired. *Stay awake, Stan. Make sure you get on the plane, and hopefully you can pass out on the flight for once.*

I focused on the article again. A few minutes later I looked up and saw they had changed the flight time; it was now delayed another hour.

Crap! I was really hoping to board the plane and get on to Morocco. *Oh well, grin and bear it for a little longer.*

As I continued to read, my eyes started to blur. I felt this heaviness envelop me like a warm blanket on a cold winter's day. My body began to ache a tad, and my legs started to tighten.

This is strange, I thought. *I did four handstands at the end of my yoga routine along with some shoulder stands; plus a few other inversions and heart openers. They always energize. Give me an extra boost.*

But I felt really, really tired now.

I took out the water I purchased and had a couple of big swigs. *Get some fluid in me,* I thought. I put the magazine down because maybe that was making me tired. I placed my head on my hand, which was supported by the armrest underneath.

I was slowly fading to black.

Maybe I will lie down on the floor over here by the window, only ten feet from the front ticket counter in the terminal. Take a quick catnap. No doubt I will wake up when they get on the loudspeaker and announce it is time to board the plane.

I went over and stretched out on my back, using my pack as my pillow.

Nine hundred and ninety-nine times out of thousand, I have this crazy ability to wake up when I need to. I haven't had to set an alarm in over ten years. If I tell myself to get up at 5 a.m., bam, I am up at 5 a.m.

Never fails.

Also, I can invariably tell myself to relax but stay aware, knowing I must listen for some type of calling to move on with my day. I swear to you, it is uncanny yet virtually foolproof! *Virtually* being the operative word this time.

Let me digress one more time, this time on purpose.

I was the *only* Caucasian in the entire terminal. The only fricking white man or woman waiting to board this plane! I had light brown hair and green eyes and was wearing a bright teal shirt.

All the rest of the folks were of Middle Eastern or Turkish descent—dark-skinned, black hair, and 75 percent in typical Middle Eastern garb with all the resplendent robes and head wraps.

The lady at the terminal counter saw me at the ticket counter before customs. We smiled at each other as I entered the terminal area, a smile of recognition that we were meeting again. I figured if, for whatever reason, I nodded off and didn't hear them call for boarding, she would certainly come over and shake me.

Still, I tried to stay aware. I tried to keep my senses attuned. But slumber, like fog rolling in over the San Francisco Bay, overtook my body and mind.

At some point in time, I was out.

Now, we have conveniently returned to the beginning of my tale.

I passed out hard.

Gone.

I cannot remember having slept so soundly in a very long time. The deepest of REMs experienced in maybe ten years.

And nobody woke me.

Nary a soul came over and nudged me.

Not a person interfered with my comatose state.

I woke up—get this—four hours later!

Delirious. Confused. Disoriented.

But astonishingly well rested! Refreshed! Rejuvenated! No aches, no pains.

But... It... Was... Four... Hours... Later...

Son of a bitch!

I popped up. There was an entirely different set of people in the terminal. A new airline attendant was behind the desk from another airline than the one I was taking. The TV screen above the counter read "Paris, France." My mind starts racing, *What the heck time is it? Where did they go with my flight? Where are all the other passengers? Sweet Jesus, this is a totally different carrier on the screen.*

I went to the counter and asked the lady about my flight. She said she had no idea, as she worked for a different airline. I needed to go to the info desk. Frantically, I ran over there, waited for a person in front of me to finish his conversation, and handed the lady my ticket. She looked it up and said...

"Ummm, sir, your flight left about three hours ago. You are a bit late. I am sorry to say you missed your flight. You must now go to the transitions department, get a stamp to re-enter Turkey, and go retrieve your bag."

"Fuck! Son-of-a-bitch!" I said.

I was stunned. Staggered. Shocked.

What is she telling me I have to do again? I tell her I don't understand. "Can you explain again?" I ask. She does so and points to a sign that says "Transitions."

From this point on I will spare you most of the details except a few. I was mentally berating myself for falling asleep. I was confused and lost in a foreign airport, going through a process I had never gone through before and dealing with people who spoke the barest of English.

They sent me to and through the bowels of the airport where not one single person could or would try to speak English.

I was unequivocally upset and frazzled.

When I finally got to the counter for the airline in question, I immediately recognized the guy who originally greeted me in the ticket line when checking my passport. He looked at me and said, "What happened, you missed your flight?"

"I know. I don't understand. I was at the gate. I was ten feet from the boarding counter. I never heard the announcement."

"Impossible, I made the announcement myself. I walked around the terminal at least five times calling all passengers," he coldly stated.

I said, "How did you miss me? I was right there, ten feet away from the check-in counter. I was the only Caucasian. You knew who I was, and you knew I had checked in. Why didn't you call my name? How could you not see me if you walked around five times?"

"Doesn't matter. Not my fault. I am sorry. We are closing now. You must call airline or go online and book a new ticket," he said flatly. Then closed the door on me.

Customer service at its best.

A foreigner in a strange land in a random airport who missed his flight, and he couldn't care less. Just another day at the office, and the office was now closed. Time to go home and have some Turkish coffee with baklava.

Suffice it to say I riffled off a few unkind words as he was shutting the door, furthering our already bad diplomatic relationship. To no avail, but it allowed me to let off some steam for a moment.

I walked outside and over to the end of the departure dropoff area, plopped my
bags on the ground, and crouched down, head in my hands. A mixture of anger, confusion, reality, disappointment, self-flagellation, and disarray ran through my mind—clouding my ability to think.

I actually bummed a smoke to try to calm my nerves. I sat there for about twenty minutes doing my best to regroup. After doing so I realized I had no choice but to go to the nearest semi-affordable hotel (remember, no hotels near any airport are cheap) and figure out what to do in terms of leaving Istanbul.

It is what it is, brotha, I told myself.

Talking with a Turkish businessman who spoke fairly good English, I was able to determine there was a hotel just a tram stop away. Having no desire to go all the way back to my hostel to save money, I decided I would accept the financial punishment and grab a nice room.

On the way to the hotel, I realized I had also booked two nights via Booking.com for my initial stay in Tangiers.

Double crap, now I was out another $80.

So, let's tally up the damage.

A $420 plane ticket, $80 in bookings for Tangiers, another $95 dollars for the room that night, and approx. $70 in food and drinks. (After all, I needed a few Jack and Cokes when I got to the room to quell my nerves.) We are talking just shy of $600.

Annnnnd, I needed to book a new flight for the next day.

Somewhere.

But guess what? I felt fantastic! Like I said, despite all the angst over what happened, my body was juiced from such a good sleep.

To save myself any further embarrassment, I am not going to add the price of the new ticket to this particular story. Let me just say it wasn't that horrible.

Okay, okay. The new ticket was another $360. So that brings the tab to just shy of a grand large. For a nap on a dirty carpet!

Not the most ideal value proposition.

Further, based on what happened, the attitude of the airline, an email to a friend, and my gut, I felt like Morocco was not meant to be this trip. The travel gods, while allowing me one of the best naps I can ever remember, also doled out a very expensive lesson. That made two such occurrences in Istanbul for me.

Make no mistake, I shot a cannonball-sized hole in the ship that was my budget. Not happy about that in any way, shape, or form.

You are never too old or too experienced to have life hand you some castor oil and say, "Drink up, sonny boy, you still need some purification."

Thus, now you all know the story of the simultaneously most exquisite and most expensive four hours of sleep I have ever had in my life. And it happened on an airport floor of all places.

There have to be some angels in heaven laughing at the irony of me spending $1,000 to sleep on a carpet in Istanbul when there are ten thousand Turkish people trying to sell you a carpet for $1,000 every day, all day.

Go figure.

***

Today, I sit on a plane headed for Madrid, Spain, with a connection to Seville. Booked the ticket at 11:00 last night. Randomly, a friend posted on FB he was going to be there, and I have heard nothing but good things about the southern parts of Spain.

Guess what? Next to me is seated a young lady from Madrid. She informs me that in Seville this weekend there is a wonderful festival called La Fiere.

"It is the *biggest* party in Spain!" she declares. "It's all about fun, street food, and dancing. The ladies wear long, traditional flamenco dresses with flowers in their hair; the men dress up in classic horse-riding garb, food and wine are served all day and night; and the entire city of Seville lets loose, moving to the groove of the live flamenco music. You are going to have a great time."

For the record, it was nuts. One of the best "the entire city just goes off" party scenes I have witnessed. Super-duper fun.

Who the hell knew? Most assuredly not me when I missed my flight yesterday, nor when I purchased the ticket late last night. Something in my gut said go to Spain.

Additionally, Portugal is right next door, which many travelers on this trip have raved about.

You can't beat yourself up too long in life.

You smack yourself around a bit, you maybe even chastise yourself for the financial gaffe, you log the mistake in the books, you try to accept what went down without bitterness, you find the positive in the experience wherever it lies (good pun, no?), and then you must let it go.

Got to keep moving on in this life. Can't let mistakes slow me down. Nor should you. There is too much living to do, and it's living fully I came to do on this adventure around the world.

Pay the price of admission and get on with the ride.

Most importantly, laugh! Wholeheartedly! Loud and proud! Own it!

How can I not?

Seriously, don't take it all so seriously. I speak from experience when I say I am 100 percent confident I will screw up again. So will you! You aren't living if you aren't making a mess of things every so often!

Boy, did I make a mess of this one. But, as I said, best nap of the last ten years easy. And now I go to a dance festival in the streets. Good and bad, yin and yang, win some and lose some—whatever!

It will work itself out in the long run.

One day I will get the money back. If not, I paid for one heck of a memory.

Until dementia sets in, that is...

By then I may be the one wearing a red and white polka dot Flamenco dress.

I AM NOT HAPPY WITH WHO I AM, AND THIS IS OKAY...

"Abandon Any Hope of Fruition" is the name of the chapter I am reading in a book entitled *Start Where You Are. A Guide to Compassionate Living* by Pema Chodron.

Immediately, I am drawn in.

I live on hope. Next to God, it is nourishment for my soul.

> Pema continues: One of the most powerful teachings of the Buddhist tradition is that as long as you are wishing for things to change, THEY NEVER WILL. As long as you want yourself to get better, you won't. As long as you have an orientation toward the future, you can never just relax into what you already have or already are.

Wait a minute. We are always taught to strive to be better. To be more. To set goals and work hard toward bringing them to fruition. We are supposed to constantly improve ourselves in this life, no?

> One of the deepest habitual patterns we have is to feel that now is not good enough. We think back to the past a lot, which maybe was better than now, or perhaps worse. We also think ahead quite a bit to the future—which we may fear—always holding out hope that it might be a little bit better than now.

> Even if now is going really well—we have good health and we've met the person of our dreams, or we just had a child or got the job we wanted— nevertheless there is a deep tendency always to think about how it's going to be later. We don't quite give ourselves full credit for who we are in the present.

Ha! No shit. How many times a day do I let a situation from my past occupy my thoughts today? How many times do I look to the future when I will have my life together? How many times do I beat myself up for the things I feel I should be better at?

> In one of the first teachings I ever heard, the teacher said, "I don't know why you came here, but I want to tell you right now that the basis of this whole teaching is that you're never going to get it all together." I felt like he had just slapped me in the face or thrown cold water over my head.

> There isn't going to be some precious future time when all the loose ends will be tied up. Even though it was shocking to me it rang true.

> One of the things that keeps us unhappy is this continual searching for pleasure or security, searching for a little more comfortable situation, either at the domestic level or the spiritual level or at the level of mental peace.

OMG! She is right. I can't tell you how long I have been trying to get my act together. Constantly harping on my own deficiencies, my less desirable features—my weaknesses.

Entirely too many times have I mentally spanked myself for not being the person I want to be! Like I need to be fixed or something; broken and in need of repair. Finding fault everywhere I looked: with myself, my thoughts, my behavior and even finding fault with my inaction.

As if on cue, the next paragraph reads:

> Many people feel wounded and are looking for something to heal them. To me it seems that at the root of healing, at the root of feeling like a fully adult person, is the premise that you're not going to make anything go away, that what you have is worth appreciating. But this is hard to swallow if what you have is pain.

Tell me about it. When you are in deep, personal anguish, platitudes often seem banal and trite, like bumper stickers on a car.

> Dr. Jon Kabat-Zinn, a Buddhist practitioner and author of *Full Catastrophe Living*, says the basic premise is to give up any hope of fruition. If there's some sense of wanting to change yourself, then it comes from a place of feeling that you're not good enough.

> It comes from aggression toward yourself, dislike of your present mind, speech or body; there's something about yourself that you do not feel is good enough.

Again, this is soooooo contradictory to our concept of the self-improvement process. But think about it. The minute you start fixating on your "issues" is the minute you also tell yourself you are inadequate.

> That's the main thing. As long as you are wanting to be thinner, smarter, more enlightened, less uptight, or whatever it might be, somehow you're always going to be approaching your problem with the very same logic that created it to begin with: you're not good enough.

I am not a good enough friend. I need to be a better mom. I am entirely too impatient. I need to lose twenty-five pounds to be more attractive. I am never going to be the person I want to be. I am afraid to change. How many of us have these thoughts running rampant in our brains?

No matter what version of "I am not" or "I need to be" haunts your every day, if not multiple versions, they all have the same root issue—feeling inadequate. Incomplete. Insufficient.

Every "I will never" is the unseen riptide that pulls us further from the shores of acceptance and serenity. It is this very deep-seated feeling of "I am not good enough" that has us all drowning in an ocean filled with images of who we should be as opposed to floating buoyantly in the backyard pool of who we are.

> Buddha means "awake," it is not someone you worship. Buddha is our inherent nature—our Buddha nature—and what that means is if you are going to grow up fully, the way that it happens is you begin to connect with the intelligence that you already have.

> If you are going to be fully mature, you will no longer be imprisoned in the childhood feeling that you always need to protect yourself or shield yourself because things are too harsh. If you're going to be a grown-up—which I would define as being completely at home in your world no matter how difficult the situation—it's because you will allow something that is already in you to be nurtured.

There it is again; we have all the answers. Further, we have all the questions too.

Which means if I recognize something about myself, good or bad, I need to awaken to this awareness. I don't need to immediately analyze it, diagnose it, and then stack it into some categorical description of who I am and how it relates to being the best or worst me.

Why not simply open up to this awareness about myself, see what happens over time as I continue to ponder its existence and ascribed meaning? Instead of taking a stance that confers or passes judgment upon my discovery, why not skip right over this habit, allowing both to relax on the couch for a while?

> Anything that you can experience or think is worthy of compassion; anything you could think or feel is worthy of appreciation.

Honestly, does anyone beat you up more than you? Maybe it's about time we finally embraced the philosophy that compassion begins at home, and home is your heart, mind, and soul. A happy home is a compassionate home, no?

Think about it another way. No matter where you go, there you are.

Since we have all heard the above platitude, let's spin it around.

No matter where you are, there you go.

By "there you go" I mean there you go spinning the same tangled web of perceived inadequacy despite being in an entirely new, exotic place.

You simply can't get away from yourself. There is no escape. I can choose to imprison myself in thoughts of inadequacy or I can choose to free myself with thoughts of kindness.

We are prisoners of our own shackles and the holders of the keys to those shackles.

It is our relationship with us that is the determining factor regarding which role we play in our relationship with awareness.

> If one would enter into an unconditional relationship with oneself, one would be entering into an unconditional relationship with Buddha.

Meaning, an unconditional relationship with awareness! With acceptance! With compassion! With inadequacy! With doubt and fear!

With me… Today… Now… As I am! Totally unequivocally, undeniably, unhesitatingly, and incomparably incomplete…

> That is why the slogan says, 'Abandon any hope of fruition'. Fruition implies that at a future time you will feel good. There is another word, which is open—to have an open heart and mind.

This is oriented very much to the present. If you enter into an unconditional relationship with yourself, that means sticking with the Buddha, the awake and aware you, right now on the spot as you find yourself.

Right now today, could you make an unconditional relationship with yourself? Just at the height you are, the weight you are, the amount of intelligence that you have, the burden of pain that you have? Could you enter into an unconditional relationship with that?

Life sometimes feels like it is more about deconstruction than construction. It is this uncovering of layers—layers within the recesses of our mind that have been built one upon the other to form this structural arrangement in our psyche. Layers which, in the end, only build houses of cards.

There is a quote by an unknown source: "Maybe the journey is not so much about becoming anything. Maybe it is about un-becoming everything that is not really you, so that you can be who you were meant to be in the first place."

We are all so very adept at building constructs that deny, obfuscate, cover, bury, distract, and demean the very real and indisputable, yet entirely human, false truth we keep believing in—that something, someone, or someplace will fix me.

Giving up any hope of fruition has something in common with the title of my previous book, *The Wisdom of Escape*. "No escape" leaves you continually right in the present, and the present is whatever it is, whatever mood you happen to be in, whatever thoughts you happen to be having. That's it.

If you can't go anywhere, if you can't run to anyone, if you can't buy anything that alleviates you from the reality of being you—there is no escape!

And that is fine. Really, it's okay. What the heck! Sometimes it's better to go with the tide than fight it.

If I can't escape myself, then I may as well accept myself. While I am at it, I may as well stop trying to be something I am not—complete. Figured out. Together. Whole.

What I am is wholly ready to stand in the center of my incompleteness. Aware, now more than ever, I am going to leave behind a bunch of loose ends. Let a few stay untied. Who knows, maybe if I leave them alone, they will tie themselves together, weaving a whole new fabric to my day that surprises and delights as compared to the days when I tried to stitch everything up nice and tight. I mean, how many times does that really happen anyway despite my best meddling efforts?

I am aware the closest I will ever come to completion is when I completely devote myself to the moment before me.

> Whether you get meditation instruction from the Theravada tradition or the Zen tradition or the Varajana tradition, the basic instruction is always about being awake in the present moment.
>
> What they don't tell you is that the present moment can be you, this you about whom you sometimes don't feel very good. That's what there is to wake up to.

I think I am pretty much done trying to fix me.

Why? Because I am not broken!

What I am is here. Trying to figure out how in the hell to finish this piece. Accepting the fact that the ending may disappoint. I may not be able to come up with the right way to resonate with you. I may fall short of the hope inspired earlier in the piece. Heck, there is a very real possibility this whole piece sucks...

But I am still going to put all my heart into coming up with something worthy. I will spend hours thinking about how to get the ending "right."

My writing may indeed be more boring than watching paint dry. I may see you in the streets of some random city in some far-off land, outstretched hand with palm up, demanding a refund for your purchase. I am cool with it.

Why?

Because I gave my heart and soul during the effort to write every sentence of this book, I found, however fleeting the moment was, you could feel complete.

Think about it. Anything done with all your love is complete in and of itself.

When I give all my heart to an endeavor, it manifests the best of whatever I am at that moment.

It also happens to be the best example of the best way I can be the best representation of my purest self.

If, by chance, we happen to meet on said random street in said far-off locale, after you tell me my book was only useful for propping a window open, you may be inclined to ask me, "How are you doing otherwise?"

I think my new stock answer will be "Incomplete, and happy to be so, thanks!"

DESTINATION ADDICTION...

A friend posted the following quote the other day:

"Beware of Destination Addiction...

A preoccupation with the idea that happiness is in the next place,

The next job

And the next partner!

Until you give up the idea that happiness

Is somewhere else,

It will never be where you are!"

Excellent, no?

Happiness is standing right next to you at all times, peeps,

Just waiting for you to hold its hand and wander down the road.

Stop thinking the next place, person or possession

Will fulfill you.

Start believing you are the source of your happiness.

Begin each day saying I am complete. I am beautiful. I am worthy.

I am more than enough. I am all I need.

One of my favorite pastors used to say,

"People can, at best, complement you.

Only God can complete you!"

I have said this many times, we are all divine.

We are all Magic. Majestic. Magnificent.

Made from God to manifest God.

We are the very best creation has to offer.

You are only as happy as you choose to be,

Not just a byproduct of what transpires each day.

So, instead of letting what happens determine your joy,

Be your joy.

On this day start anew.

Wake up; gently grab happiness by the hand

And say, "Let's you and me have fun today!

Let's saunter on down the path and see what

We can find together."

No matter who or what comes across your path,

Happiness will still be right by your side

All you have to do is let it.

FIND YOUR SPOT...

I was utterly blessed to be able to practice yoga at a very special spot every day for eight days while staying in Ubud.

It overlooked a valley filled with layered rice paddies, farm animals, and humble thatch huts.

The sun would rise over the rice paddies, shining God's love upon me.

The birds would sing me a chorus as they swept over the morning dew.

The river below would set the rhythm for my movements as I flowed in synchronicity with nature.

The insects would share their vibrations with mine, lifting me to higher levels.

Even the roosters would add their nutty voices to the mix, letting the world know it was a new day brimming with opportunity.

Every question you have or didn't even know you needed to ask... Every answer you are searching for or weren't even aware was out there... Every solution you can't find or never even knew you needed yet...

...can be found on your yoga mat. Or by sitting alone in a splendid setting.

When you listen to the world, it gives you every question and all the answers; it tells you there is beauty everywhere; it tells you that you are beauty manifested, personified, and magnified.

You just have to take the time to listen!

Do me a favor, my most amazing friends, sit yourselves down and let the world whisper sweet nothings into your ear as only a true lover can.

You may be surprised to discover the golden nuggets of wisdom contained in sweet nothings.

It starts with you cutting the connections to all the noise and finding that certain spot where you can let your mind wander.

It's a funny thing how the more you let your mind wander, the closer it takes you to where you belong.

The sooner you find your spot, the sooner you find you!

NAKED IN HOLY WATERS...

Yes, you, too, can fly off to distant islands, visit revered grounds, partake in ancient customs—and have thoughts like the following travel through your mind:

I just mooned at least forty Indonesian families, all their ancestors since the beginning of time, and about three hundred Hindu gods while standing in thousand-year-old sacred Indonesian water gardens. Crap, my next twelve lifetimes are screwed.

At another point this dandy of a soliloquy ran screaming to the forefront of my cranium...

OMG, my sarong is gone. WTF—where is my sarong? It is floating away. I am now standing naked in a national shrine, providing small children, mothers, and grandmothers a lunar eclipse in the middle of the afternoon! That's it, I am going to Indonesian jail for indecent exposure and desecration of a national treasure.

Yep, see the world. Expand your horizons. Step out of your comfort zone.

And inadvertently draw the ire of multiple Hindu gods whose wrath will be brought down on your family for generations to come.

Ah, I love travel. Makes you realize embarrassment has no boundaries, prejudices, borders, or passport requirements! An equal opportunity enabler; all you have to do is wear a sheer sarong with no underwear to a holy spring and then bow under freezing cold fountainheads, carved to look like demons, a total of almost eighty times whilst wading in frigid waters barefoot, with little rocks jabbing away at your feet like reflexology ninjas.

Add in about 150 locals there to receive purification, blessings, and relief—well, what you get is a perfect way for yours truly to have a cultural experience that is at times comical, spiritual, magical, and delightful.

Let me explain the situation that brought about all these thoughts and feelings.

One of my favorite afternoons in Bali was when our new friend Matt took the gang out to see some of the sights in and around Ubud. Matt and his girl had been living on the island for a few months now, so they had gotten to know the lay of the land.

After taking us to several very neat sights—driving up into the mountains to see massive volcanoes, touring an Indonesian coffee farm, walking through a traditional hillside rice paddy farm—we finished the day at a sacred temple.

There were six of us in the minivan. A great crew of fun and funny people!

The grounds were constructed out of stone. As with everywhere in Bali, incredible carved statues abounded all over the property, ranging from two feet tall to forty feet tall.

When we first walked onto the grounds, we were greeted by an enormous statue of a Hindu god, standing easily forty feet high. The statue was impressive, imposing, elaborate, and detailed. Huge trees provided a cool canopy cover for all the tourists and locals. The place had a decent-sized crowd, but not too over-whelming.

We paid our nominal entry fee and went inside.

We first entered a huge courtyard lined with giant stone pavers and enclosed by ten-foot-tall stone walls. There were a few shrines interspersed amidst the open space, each with a statue depicting some Hindu god surrounded by offerings, flowers, and burning incense.

As with most temples in Southeast Asia, while strolling the grounds we were ensconced in the scents of serenity. Flowers of every color were strewn about the grounds, offerings of beauty that combine with the smell of sage, lavender, and such to create a steady, reassuring calm.

From this area we then walked through a stone archway to the sacred water gardens. Families were everywhere. People were in the gardens, sitting cross-legged on stone plateaus, praying; kids were running around giggling...

***

Before I go any further, I think it's a good idea to give you some history about the place. Not only will it help you understand the temple's importance in Indonesian history and how it is set up, but I hope you find the story interesting too.

Tirta Empul temple is a Hindu Balinese water temple located near the town of Tampaksiring, Bali, Indonesia. The holy springs are located at **Tempak Siring Temple.**

Balinese people have come to this temple for more than a thousand years to bathe in the holy water for healing and spiritual merit. The temple is dedicated to Vishnu, another Hindu god named for the supreme consciousness, Narayana.

The temple compound consists of a *petirtaan,* or bathing structure, famous for its holy spring water, where Balinese Hindus go for ritual purification and healing. The temple pond has a spring regularly supplying fresh water; the Balinese Hindus consider the water to be *amritha,* or holy.

Tirta Empul means Holy Spring in Balinese.

Tirta Empul Temple was founded around a large water spring in 962 AD during the Warmadewa dynasty (10th–14th centuries). The name of the temple comes from the ground water source, named Tirta Empul. The spring is the source of the Pakerisan River.

The Jaba Tengah is the most famous part of Tirta Empul temple. This section contains the two purification pools, or gardens. The water in the gardens is believed to have magical powers, and local Balinese come here to purify themselves under the twenty-three fountainheads, elaborately carved from stone, that line the edge from east to west and feed the pools.

The main pool area is a long, rectangular pool carved of stone, filled with koi, and fed by the sacred spring via thirteen fountains, spouts, or showerheads. The other pool area is separated by a stone wall into two spaces: one with two more spouts, and then a pool area that contains six spouts.

After solemn prayers at an altar-like shrine, worshippers first make an offering at a different shrine. The offering is a small basket handwoven from palms holding gifts such as flowers, oils, incense, and herbs. Then they enter the crystal-clear, cold mountain water to bathe and pray.

The water from the first spout is not to be touched as it is reserved for the gods alone. Spout 13 is meant for purification purposes in funerary rites, therefore also left alone. With hands pressed together, you bow under the gushing water of the second spout, perform the requisite prostrations, and carry on to the twelfth.

When you arrive at each spout, you are to lower your head underneath the water three times while praying to God, your parents, and your ancestors. Next, you are to fill your cupped hands and swallow some holy water three times. Each time praying for healing, a loved one, relief, and so on! Finish each sequence at each spout with a profession of thanks, as evidenced by kneeling under the fountainhead one more time.

The spouts/showerheads are not merely for cleansing the physical body, but also the spiritual body. Bali's language has a deeply entrenched spiritual aspect; they call this process of external and internal cleansing *ngelukat.*

Each spout of the thirteen spouts in the first pool has an association with a color, certain physical and/or spiritual body parts, emotional states of being, and the like. The two spouts in the middle pool have to do with curses and oaths. The six spouts in the last pool are for either serious diseases or future life dreams.

The myth behind the curative and purifying spring tells of a Balinese ruler, known as Mayadenawa, who defied the influence of Hinduism and denied his subjects religious prayers/practices. The legend goes that this eventually angered the gods, and in a war campaign, god Indra sought Mayadenawa's subdual.

The hide-and-seek tactics of Mayadenawa fleeing Indra's troops occurred at various places all over the region, from the rivers Petanu to Pakerisan, and up to the north of Tampaksiring.

Hence, the names of the sites and natural features all reflect an episode from the tale, such as Tampaksiring—*tampak* meaning "feet," and *siring* meaning "sideways," depicting an episode when the fleeing king left his footprints up the hill.

It was here that through his magical powers Mayadenawa created a poisoned spring from which Indra's exhausted troops drank and succumbed. Indra noticed the dire condition of his men and thrust his staff into the ground where a holy purifying spring spurted out, curing the troops—even bringing some of them back to life.

This escapade became the legendary background to the holy spring of Tirta Empul, as well as the holy days of Galungan and Kuningan, celebrated by the Balinese Hindus.

Okay, now you understand where we are, what the history and the meaning of the place is, and why it is so sacrosanct.

***

With almost all temples in Asia, you must bring a sarong to cover certain body parts. As always, women must cover more areas than men, Matt had told us. We needed to bring our own or we could rent one there.

Not realizing exactly where we were going or what we would be doing, I assumed we would either need to wrap the sarong around our shoulders or wear it around our waists as we toured the site. I did not know we would be going into water.

Thus, due to the fact that it was a thousand degrees out, I grabbed a sarong I bought that was extremely lightweight and sheer, more suited for covering your mouth in dusty areas or as a scarf on breezy nights. Plus, I loved the colors.

It was not necessarily made for adequate screening of body parts in a public setting.

Also, I have a confession to make. I gave up wearing underwear. It was too annoying, took up too much space, and it was too hot in Asia to bother.

Well, turns out we were all going to throw our clothes in a locker and wade into Indonesian waters, both in a figurative and literal sense. We all changed, strapped on our sarongs, and gathered by the water's edge. As we were trying to absorb the scene, a local man approached us and asked if we would like an explanation of what to do.

"Absolutely!"

He proceeded to relate what I have already described as far as the required intentions with which we approach each fountainhead, the relevant prostrations we must perform, the recipients of our prayers, the types of prayers, and what-not.

It was great. He made us all feel welcome and excited to participate in a ceremonial process dating back centuries. Fully informed travelers now, each person gently slid down into the water.

First thought jumping forth:

Holy shiiiitttee... This water is cold. I mean frigid. And we have to stand in line behind every fountain while waiting for about fifteen people to do their part? You mean I have to dunk my head under these spouts flowing with frigid waters some seventy times? Sweet Jesus, is this a Navy SEAL initiation ceremony? We are going to be in this water for an hour!

Second thought emerging from the depths:

OMG, my sarong is merely a thin veil. Even wrapped around me twice, now that it is wet, the...veil...is...lifted! My sausage, despite all my hopes, is most probably not going to be looked upon as a deity by these fine people.

Third thought rampaging forward:

Well, it's so damn cold in here, there most assuredly won't be much to see!

With every step I took toward the fountain, my sarong wanted to float to the surface. Before I even got to the first fountain, I realized the next hour would be an anxiety-riddled ride as I tried to avoid being locked up for desecration of holy lands.

This meant, as best as possible, I had to keep the sarong pressed between my knees while I performed any prostrations or moved to the next fountainhead.

However, as mentioned above, the floor of the water garden was a bed of small rocks rounded to various degrees of smoothness. I guess the idea is while you are being purified, you may as well receive foot reflexology treatment. This makes the journey from one fountain to the back of the line in front of the next fountain a tricky proposition.

The first time you perform all the rituals at the fountainhead, you are trying to make sure you do it all right. You are acclimating to each frozen dunk under the fountain, then figuring out how much water to ingest, and finally initiating your last bow. Then you secure your sarong and carry on.

Recall, you basically have seven physical steps/actions to follow that coincide with a supposed mental and/or spiritual step. The water is freezing, there are nine people behind you waiting and you have to do this same process for another twenty-one fountainheads.

At the end I genuflected under the fountain, which released my sarong from captivity between my legs, and it aimlessly floated toward heaven. Quickly I secured it and shoved it back between my knees.

I moved to the second fountainhead. As I gingerly stepped across the rocky floor of the garden, I thought:

Whose brilliant idea was this? These rocks on the bottom feel as if the gods are trying to extract valuable intel from me. Every step unleashes an internal debate as to which is worse, the pain or the cold.

I think it was while in front of the third fountainhead, when bending to one knee for the last part of the process, a koi fish brushed my inner thigh. I said to myself, *Brings a whole new meaning to the term "fresh fish"! Now where the fuck is my sarong?*

Somewhere in the middle of it all, I started to accept the circumstances, manage my sarong as best as possible, and give myself over to the experience.

I embraced everything: the atmosphere, environment, and historical significance the sacred gardens offered, earnestly devoting my thoughts, emotions, and prayers to friends, family, and future.

I altered my focus to the beauty of the surrounding grounds, the joy I saw in so many of the locals, the spectrum of age groups in the waters, the reverence displayed by the people in attendance—and in doing so the entire adventure became more profound.

When you take the time to thank your parents for all they have done, to thank your friends and family for all they have given, to offer up heartfelt positive wishes for their lives, to thank God/the Universe for all you have been given in this life, to ask for blessings to be bestowed upon the people you love along with your own life, to appreciate how special the moment you are living, you can't help but be transformed.

By the time we were done, I felt vibrant. Alive. Humble. Buoyant. Joyful. Everyone in our crew was ecstatic. We smiled, hugged, and laughed at our good fortune for having participated in such a unique cultural endeavor.

We went back to the lockers, grabbed our clothes, and changed. As we were exiting the locker area, the man who explained the process to follow approached Matt and asked for a "contribution."

"Ah, Asia, nothing comes without a string attached, even at a holy site!"

We all pitched in. It was the proper move, and he did make our experience terrific!

Some of the ladies wanted to hit up the shops, and others wanted to saunter the grounds for a bit. I went around to the backside of the temple for picture taking and happened upon a monk giving a talk to a large group of pupils. While neat to see, unfortunately, I could not understand a word.

After a half hour I began making my way back to the van. As I was walking out of the compound, a lovely elderly lady dressed in all white struck up a conversation. She was from the city Katu, visiting with a group of friends. Her English was decent. We chatted about where I was from, if I liked the shrine, and if I had enjoyed my time in Bali. It was nice small talk.

I saw Matt approaching us from the parking lot and said, "Hey, brotha!"

Now, you have to understand, Matt is about six feet, two inches tall. He has a full beard. A sizeable, stocky dude!

The lady turned to me and asked, "Is this your girlfriend?"

Matt and I looked at each other, paused for a second, and simultaneously burst out with laughter.

"If it is, he needs a shave and I need to see an eye doctor!"

Without missing a beat Matt retorted, "And I need to spend a lot of time with a psychologist!"

Now, whenever Matt sends me a message, he includes the tagline "Your girlfriend without benefits..."

Can't make this stuff up.

Thankfully, I was able to manage my sarong issues and stay out of Indonesian prison. While I mooned several hundred, I would like to believe the gods seemed to take it all in stride too. That being said, as to whether future generations of family are cursed, I am unable to report yet.

At the very least, I hope I left a distinct impression on a 'fresh' koi fish.

GRACE PERSONIFIED...

At 4:00 one morning in September of 2015, my mother, Dottie Crossland, was finally, mercifully, brought home. May she be sitting at the Banquet Table, in the presence of her precious Lord, family, and friends, celebrating her astonishing spirit.

I share this with you because she is so much a part of why I went on this walkabout. Her presence manifested itself numerous times in various odd, yet specific ways on this trip. And, her spirit imbued so many of my experiences it feels relevant I address the subject.

Before her passing, my mom suffered from severe Alzheimer's. This entire process took ten years to play itself out.

Ten years of watching this beautiful, compassionate and fierce woman slide into decay, the house that is her mind and body crumble one painful brick at a time. Each brick not just crumbling away, instead, vanishing into thin air, leaving holes in the walls, floors and roof.

Brutal. Gut-wrenching. Horrifying. Crushing.

Outrageously, offensively and cruelly unfair! These are the words to describe what I witnessed at a glacial pace.

3, 650 days it took for her to finally reach blank slate status.

I can't imagine watching anything more painful for the rest of my life.

It.... Fucking... Sucked...

But we do what we are called to do. My job was to see it through till the end, personal feelings be damned. And I did.

So, you can understand why I was pretty much done with everything and everyone. Beyond all the ways life had kicked my ass over the last eight to ten years, this situation in particular really had me questioning the point of, well, anything.

I was super pissed God took her mind and wiped it clean. Erasing her whole life; leaving her an empty, useless shell! No past, no present and no future. A void.

Thus, before I let myself fall completely into the abyss of "Who the fuck cares?" I used my last lifeline: Travel.

In order for you to understand the amount of soul searching I was after this time around the world I felt you needed to know the main reason why I felt soulless.

Further, I wanted you to get a smidgen of why she had a rather large imprint on my mindset.

Can I share just a bit with you about her? There is a story a little further in that is very relevant because it's not only pertinent for us all to remember, but it was reinforced on my little expedition a bunch of times.

My mom carried herself with a certain grace. Not in her gait or the way she physically moved, but more so in the way she stood above the fray. It was like she learned a secret when very young: If you recognized that your own dignity was all that mattered, everything else would fall into place.

I suppose it came from her character. She had impeccable morals. Her ethical compass always knew which way was up; all other directions were distractions until you found the truth. And the truth for her was quite simple—follow the words in Red.

Her faith in Christ was unshakeable. It sustained her through every and all circumstance.

It's taken me forty-seven years to learn how to be faith in action, not just in word. She somehow managed to manifest it with every step long before I set foot on this planet.

She stood her ground on concepts such as compassion, kindness, civility, decency, and forgiveness. She was elegance personified. She always knew exactly what to wear for every occasion, with an exceptional eye for the "appropriate"! When she walked into a room, other women knew this lady had class!

My mom could cook like nobody's business too! You know that one friend whose mom always made awesome meals and you wanted to stay at their house for dinner after school? Well, that was my mom.

My dad was funny. He was a jovial person with an infectious laugh. Generally, a happy-go-lucky guy. Most folks really enjoyed his company.

My mom was witty. Witty people are such a joy because their humor is based on brains. She could turn a phrase, twist an expression, throw out a double entendre, or simply put a whole new spin on the conversation wherein you could not help but bust out with laughter. This gave her an amazing ability to put things in perspective in one sentence.

On too many occasions I watched her put someone, including me, firmly in their place while still leaving their dignity intact. The line was delivered, and in slow motion, you or they would realize, "Well crap, that about sums it up, doesn't it! Not much else to say is there now."

And thus, it was time to move on, absorbing the grace of her delivery and the wisdom behind the words. People would thank her later for deftly reminding them of what was important. This is a gift few learn how to master.

Simultaneously, I saw her on that rare moment where she'd had enough of some fool's nonsense deliver that line in such a way as to drop them to the canvas. There was simply no point in getting back up.

When truth is delivered from such a strong moral presence, you best just scurry on down the road. I mean, what are you going to do, make more of an ass of yourself?

And yes, she was tough. Tough, in my book, is someone who can withstand the slings and arrows of this life and somehow endure with a smile. And an open heart. She had a smile that stretched far and wide, a heart that was as big as the ocean.

When it came to the people in her life, well, loyalty called her up to make sure they were "representing properly."

But you know what most defined her?

Empathy.

She was one of the most giving souls I have ever had the pleasure of watching in action. Her benevolence was unending to any and all in her circle. Always checking in with her friends, relentlessly trying to find the perfect gifts, she had a huge soft spot for the elderly, to the point where we took in several older folks because she wanted them to have family. And she gave to the poor like it was second nature and more of a gift to her than them.

As for me, well, I guess The Giving Tree, by Shel Silverstein about sums it up.

Pure hearts seem to recognize that in giving they become more full, more human, and more complete. Therefore, they do so with an ease that breaks down barriers, that builds instead of divides, that allows the receiver to see they are loved.

My mom's ability to give love freely, without wishing for anything in return, was staggering in its display.

One last thought, in the first few months of my life, I was incredibly blessed. Some woman I have never met had the courage to carry me inside her womb. To feed and nurture me, allowing me to grow and blossom.

To become life!

Then she promptly gave me up. What an astounding act of selfless love. I mean, WTF, how amazing a gift was that?

Whoever you are, wherever you are, whatever the circumstances were—thank you! I can never adequately repay you for such a favor.

Three months later I was swaddled up and taken home from the Cradle Adoption Agency in Evanston, ensconced in the bosom of two very special people. These people became my parents. I became their son.

They gave me every single thing a son could ever ask for—unequivocal love, unending support, unwavering faith in my abilities, and the chance to see the majesty this life has to offer.

So you see, my first mom gave me life. My second mom showed me how to live it! In every way possible, she was BEAUTIFUL! Thank you for letting me share and honor her life for a moment.

My mom would always say, "By the Grace of God!" It had a plethora of meanings simultaneously.

By the Grace of God, I live, love, and learn. Because of the Grace of God, I am blessed with family and friends. From the Grace of God, I have abundance. Through the Grace of God, I will have many good times. With the Grace of God, I will have fewer bad times. And if I do have bad times, well, it is By the Grace of God I will get by until the good times come again.

Following her lead, it is indeed by the Grace of God I have all of you in my life.
If I may, I want to share the last message my mom imparted to me. Well, it was more of a reinforcement of a mantra she made sure I understood on many occasions.

It was about three years ago. As usual, I was there on the weekend visiting her at the nursing home. At this point, she was 98.5 percent off in the Land of Oz mentally speaking. I mean, she was pretty much lights out, maybe able to string together a few random sentences. No real ability to follow more than a few basic short sentences from me.

So, we were sitting there chatting, repeating the same conversation every two minutes. This would usually go on for about two hours. Yes, we would have the same three-question conversation literally 250 times in two hours.

Except this time she looked at me and out of nowhere asked, "Are you seeing anyone?" with a sparkle in her eye.

I looked down, like every kid does when their mom asks them a question they don't really want to answer, and said, "Well, not really. I'm still licking my wounds over my last business endeavor, and my confidence is a little shook. I don't feel like I've got my mojo working right now. Just haven't tried…"

All excuses, if we are being real. I was feeling sorry for myself. It happens to us all, right?

She raised her hand and slapped it on the table. It startled me. She fixed her gaze on me, eyes narrowing, and said:

"I didn't raise you to sit on the bench. It's about time you got back in the game and step your ass up to the plate, don't you think…?"

I was staggered. I looked left, then right, then down. I shook my head; looked up at the ceiling as if catching God's eye, and busted out with laughter. I mean, what can ya do?

Like I said before, she could sum it all up in one sentence. So I picked my jaw up off the table, secured it back into its socket, and said, "Okay, you are right! I will get on that, I promise."

She smiled. And with that she went drifting off to the Land of Oz again. I can honestly say she did not remember any of the conversation nary two minutes later!

That night I went home and signed up for a dating site—got in the game. Shortly thereafter I met a woman and we dated for two years. It didn't work out in the end, but really, who cares? I was in the game again. Taking a swing.

How amazing! Think about it: How right was she?

It doesn't matter if Nolan Ryan is on the mound—Are you going to get off the bench?

It doesn't matter if you are both nearsighted and farsighted, which means you're screwed 'cause you can't even see the pitch coming—Are you going to pick the bat up?

It doesn't matter if this is your first at bat, first game, or you're a grizzled veteran—Are you going to step into the batter's box?

It doesn't matter if you struck out your last at bat, went zero for four in your last game, or haven't had a hit all season—Are you going to take the bat off your shoulder?

It doesn't matter if the count is three balls and two strikes, the bases are loaded, and the tying run is on third—Are you going to swing at that pitch if it's anywhere near the plate or are you going to watch it sail by, leaving your fate in the umpire's hands?

No, if you truly want to live, you will say: "Who gives a crap, I am going for it. Consequences be damned!"

If you truly want to be in the game, you are going to boldly swing away.

If you want to feel that pulse-quickening adrenaline rush, which lets you know you are still, indeed, very much alive, you are going to put aside everything negative that ever happened before and step into that singular moment.

If you want live today, right here and now, you are looking out at that beautiful green ivy in Wrigley Field and saying, "That is where I am going, baby!"

At the end of the game, who cares if you struck out? Hit a single, a triple, or even a Grand Slam?

All that really matters at the end of the day is that you swung the bat.

Period!

Whether you live a long life or a short one, it's not about the results of your at bats; it's the fact you got into the batter's box in the first place. It's the quality of each swing put forth, not what happens after the swing.

For my mom, victory lay in the dignity of the effort. The valiant effort to wake up, get in the game, pick up the bat, and take your cut at the next pitch!

Do me—and my mom—a favor, folks, if you would be so kind. Whether it is today, tomorrow, next week, or next year— swing for the fences as often as you can.

The more swings you take, the more vibrant your life will be.

Thanks for listening.

COMPLETING CIRCLES IN SPAIN...

Often, you never really know when you have impacted another person's day or life in a deep, profound way do you?

Yesterday, I got to share with a friend how he did so for me.

And I, for one, am thankful I had the chance to thank him, thus completing the circle.

Let me explain by going back in time a bit.

As I have mentioned, I lost my mother last September. Alzheimer's is a cruel disease. The process of watching her die was exceptionally difficult.

It's cool; I have dealt with everything and come out the other side of the entire grieving process stronger, more whole than ever before.

Nonetheless, there was some unfinished business. To date, I had been able to personally thank many of the people who stood by me during all the tribulations such an event brings forth.

Except one last guy!

I was at a yoga retreat the weekend her final demise began.

I met a fun yoga teacher named Wade.

To make a long story short, I had to exit the retreat early due to the dreaded 'phone call' we all see in the movies. Since I was running a booth there I had to go back and retrieve all my stuff a few days later. I ended up taking Wade's class when I arrived back at the retreat because I needed something to grab a hold of, give me some grounding after spending two grueling days in I.C.U. with my Mom.

I pulled up to the parking lot, immediately changed my clothes without saying hi to anyone and slid on over to his session. I plopped my mat down and just sat there, pretty much numb. Not really talking with anyone cause I was too tired, too weary and too afraid of stealing his/her joy from the weekend's activities.

The class begins. Wade let's everyone know he is going to take it easy on us because all attendees have done several classes a day for four days now. He has another lovely lady teaching alongside him and this very sweet DJ/guitar player performing while he teaches.

He warmed us up with some exercises and got us into heart openers; poses that stress front body opening, back extension and expansion. I started laughing because I am the opposite of everyone else, wound as tight as a band of gypsy's. Oh well, can't do anything about it now.

Next he had us partner up. He instructed everyone to assist one another into deeper versions of back bends, our hearts stretching wide open to the skies. I am dying here from being so taut, but holding on as the lady assisting took me further into chest opening poses that make my rib cage feel as if it will burst open.

We finish with the partners. Wade sits us down, starts talking to us while exchanging comments with his female teaching partner. At some point in the middle of his talk I lay back down and, you guessed it, started crying like a baby.

Damn heart openers! He took my heart and sliced it open, thus opening the gates to my love flowing like a mountain stream.

Somehow, after a bit of time, I regain my composure. I sit back up. This time I have a smile on my face. I was able to let go, release and relax. Wade has us stand and separate into two groups on each side of the floor space.

He and his companion teach each group different chants. Once each group has them down, he has us start to clap to a 2-count beat and begin our different chants. We walk towards one another, eventually joining groups and chants into one big amoeba of song and dance.

People are hugging each other, smiling and kissing on the cheeks. A lovely experience!

At the end, Wade's guitar-playing pal has us join in singing a kooky song about a monkey in the zoo and how we all, at times, are monkeys in a zoo. A light-hearted way to remind us all life is a jungle so let's swing from some vines.

The whole session was splendid!

When it ended, I was calm. Relieved. Serenity was my cloak.

I was set free from anguish.

I was surrounded by complete strangers, and yet, ensconced by love.

Today it's nine months later and I am off on this crazy round–the-world endeavor to rediscover my joy for life and people. By chance, Wade and I are both in this fair city of Seville at the same time for different purposes. After a few hiccups, we were able to meet last night and catch up.

Actually, it is the first time we have ever had a lengthy con-versation.

Amidst watching a fantastic Flamenco guitar/dance show, and I mean a dazzling performance, Wade and I were chatting away; reveling in our good fortune to be in such an amazing city, surrounded by such vitality. We were both in great moods; exhilarated at the bounty life offers.

If you ever get the chance, please do catch a show with a professional Flamenco dancer, they bring it! Especially if accompanied by a Spanish acoustic guitar player. Powerful, sexy, passionate, energetic and soulful are few ways to describe what these particular dancers bring to the floor. Foot stomping, heart pounding force! Way cool to see in person.

Sitting on benches at a long table with his good friend, Karen C., and other fun people, laughing and drinking the night away, I tugged on his shirt, asked him to come close and said,

"Let me share something with you I have been meaning to say for awhile."

"It starts with 'Thank You'!"

Briefly, I shared this whole story with him. I finished by adding, "So my dear yoga teacher friend, you never know who you are affecting when you stand up there in front of everyone. What they are going thru, the weight they carry at any given moment. From the bottom of my heart, I thank you again for that afternoon class on a Labor Day weekend."

He looked at me and said, "Are you kidding me? I had absolutely no fucking clue Stan!"

"You just made my night. Sometimes we forget how lucky we are to be doing this for a living. I am fairly exhausted from leading this group in a far away land, speaking multiple languages, ensuring everyone is ok and having a good experience. You just lifted me up again."

"Thank you for sharing this with me, I really do appreciate it my brother!" he states with a smile. We hugged and went back to enjoying the night. Nothing more needs to be said. As I said at the beginning, the circle is complete.

Strangers no more, family from now on!

Last circle is now closed. My thank you efforts have been brought to an end.

We all have an affect. We are all part of the constant, unending cause and effect. We all are too often unaware of the ways what we do can lift another at the very crucial moment they needed that lift.

We are all inspiration, enthusiasm and consolation.

We all have the power to change lives, alter emotions and spread love whilst being totally unaware of another person's pain, sorrow or anguish.

Just by being radiant, caring beings. Just by doing our best each day to be positive, considerate and respectful of those we come across.

Life is so precious, beautiful, tragic, inexplicable - yet it's poetry is woven with the fabric of love that can never be taken for granted, replaced or forgotten if you take the time to cherish the moments and the people who help make them.

At times my heart sings a song of joy for having been blessed with so many incredible people throughout my years on this planet. There is no greater splendor than that of friendship and family.

I travel alone these days, but every day and with each step the love of those who previously walked by my side during portions of this path that is my life always walk with me. So, in essence, I am never alone.

And neither are any of you if you think about it.

> There is a secret medicine
> Given only to those who hurt so hard
> They can't hope.
> The hopers would feel slighted if they knew.
>
> Look as long as you can at the friend you love,
> No matter whether that friend is moving away from you
> Or coming back toward you."
>
> ~Rumi

May all your cups spill over with the abundance of fond memories for shared experiences and the love received in your lives – even when those around you had no clue how much you needed it, but found a way to provide it nonetheless.

It is amazing how the light of love can reflect your way from the most unexpected places.

May it too shine upon all of you, as it0 did for me, in your moments of need.

May you also shine your love far and wide; you never know who needs a light at the end of the tunnel.

Could be the person next to you right now.

Maybe say hi to them. Ask if they need a hug. WTF, what do you have to lose?

You could actually be the very person who gave a hug when someone was desperate to receive one.

Trust me, I know what it's like to be on the receiving end.

You might even end up in Spain, watching an incredible performance, at a table with ten people, drinking Sangria's and being thanked for one simple act of kindness, or leading a particular yoga class.

Now you know the odds are actually quite good it could happen to you too.

Isn't it about time we all took responsibility for picking each other up as opposed to waiting for any particular government, church or company to do so?

Pick up your phone and use it for something old-fashioned, to extend an olive branch.

Get out there, take the time to look around and initiate some circles. Or maybe there are a few you have yet to complete. Do it!

I have a feeling you will love what happens when they finally come full circle.

ARE YOU TOUCHED BY A SENSE OF DIVINE LUNACY?

Considering how much life is made up of this panoply of the absurd, how can one not be touched by a sense of divine lunacy?

I am not talking about lunacy in the sense of the definition most equate in today's times. I am not referring to being crazy. I am talking about lunacy in the sense of a spoonful of frivolity, a smidgen of irreverence, a dash of eccentricity, and a heaping handful of humor.

Let's face it—so much of what happens every day makes no sense! There is no logic to events that transpire, no rationale that can sugarcoat the randomness of what occurs.

People, places, and circumstance crash into one another, and we are left with this feeling of WTF just happened? You can try to figure out who, what, or why, but at the end of the day, we often just shake our heads and mutter, "I can't believe the crap that goes down in my life."

Right? You sit there, alone at night, wondering what stars aligned in such a matrix as to leave you with this mess of a day on your hands.

Someone does this or that to you, something occurred that threw your day into a grinder and spit out a weird kind of goulash. Inedible, distasteful, smelly, and stomach-turning!

Then, on other days, the universe conspires to bring you serendipity.

Everything goes better than according to plan. Everything gels in such a way you are left speechless, as if life handed you a golden ticket. You now own Willy Wonka's factory!

From one day to the next, your luck changes as quickly as a cat's affection. Yesterday you were the mouse, today you are catnip, and tomorrow you are the litter box.

So, what can we do? How can we deal with it all? Where do we turn for answers? When will it all even out and allow us to get a grip on things?

The answer is never!

Thus, instead of trying to figure it all out, why not allow yourselves to simply laugh at it all like a jester in the king's court? Why don't we look at it from the perspective of madness that is not characterized by being nuts, but can best be described as understanding we have no control.

We must simply find the wit, the joke, the charm, and the release that comes from lunacy.

When you are a lunatic, you let go of attachment to control, the plans, players, situations, and outcomes. A lunatic manifests better than anyone the "come what may" attitude we all strive to attain.

And a divine lunatic realizes that despite all the above, it is in the yielding to the moment that the essential truth of all things, of that specific moment, becomes evident.

Never fear, today's truth may be tomorrow's illusion.

The divine lunatic goes with the flow. The divine lunatic accepts every moment because he/she realizes that, at any moment, all moments may cease to exist.

A divine lunatic says, "Right now is all I have. This very moment is it!"

Everything else is a distraction. Everything else a mirage, a dream, or a yearning! Everything else is a preconceived notion, a perspective formed and based more than anything else on where you stand geographically in the world. Shaped and molded by who raised us, what community they raised us in, which religion we were taught to put our faith in, what books we read, and how wrapped up in our heads we are.

The divine lunatic understands all of the above is the joke we play on ourselves. And we are the teller of the joke, the story line, and the punch line. Sometimes, we are the butt of the joke too.

The best jokes are the ones that are not made at the expense of others, but illuminate a truth. Provide relief. Make us laugh instead of cry at the reality of life.

So screw it!

From now on, you may just as well revel in the joke. Immerse in irony, frolic in frivolity, and skip to the beat of silly.

You may just as well find the hypocrisy, the absurdity, the randomness, and the acceptance. You may just as well become the joke and the jokester, thus ensuring you at least have fun. No matter which side of the joke you end up on.

You may just as well laugh like a lunatic. Divinely inspired by the fact you may never know what needs to be known until after the fact, long after the outcome has been determined.

Be careful—facts, these days, seem more a product of what you are trying to validate than what is actually there.

At the end of the day, nobody has the answers. Nobody truly knows why this or that happens. Nobody can for sure, definitively, say this is the way it is.

> *"Above all, watch with glittering eyes the whole world around you because the greatest secrets are always hidden in the most unlikely places. Those who don't believe in magic will never find it."*
>
> ~Roald Dahl

The only choice we have is to listen to and follow our hearts. For our hearts never lie. They never lead us astray, adrift, or alone. They never deny our existence. They never, ever let us down.

Go ahead, when life hands you your ass on a platter, laugh your ass right off the platter. It's a heck of a lot better than crying, no?

Go ahead, find the inherent beauty in each moment. The complete idiocy, stupidity, and cleverness of each event as it unfolds. The utter unfathomable goofiness of your day!

Peeps, give it a try today. Embrace your divine lunacy.

Let it imbue and embroider your day.

Let it overtake your needs, wants, and desires.

Let it set you free from your wish to know.

Wisdom is realizing you can only choose your attitude. How you react. What emphasis and significance you place on each moment.

Wisdom is the knowledge you know nothing beyond what your heart says is real to you.

Wisdom is realizing a joke is being played on us all if we take shiiiite too seriously.

The wisest jesters understand some riddles have no answers. Nor do they always need to be solved!

There are twenty-six letters in the Roman alphabet. Just remember, if plan A doesn't work out, you have twenty-five more letters to get through.

So chillax and enjoy the day. For tomorrow will unleash upon you a whole new joke. You can, for sure, be sure of that.

Then again, what do I know, I am just a lunatic!

DRAW CLOSE TO ME...

I ask Him, "Please draw close to me, touch me."
He tells me, "I am here, in every moment.
I am the sun, the moon, the stars & the ocean. I am the sand
underfoot & the wind caressing your skin. I am the blue sky.
I am in you & you are in me. We are everywhere, you & I."

I reply, "I understand, but I don't comprehend."
He responds, "I am the flowers & the trees.
I am the laugh of a young child, a mother's love & each
breath.
I am beauty in all things. I am divinity & humanity.
I am in you & you are in me. We are everywhere, you & I."

I inquire, "So if I look for beauty in all things, I will find You?"
"I am there in despair and pain, grief & sorrow.
I am prosperity & peace, joy & exuberance.
I am harmony & agony. I am tragedy & bounty.
I am in you & you are in me. We are everywhere, you & I."

I plead, "How do I please You? How do I manifest You?"
"I am thanks & praise. I am love absent judgment.
I am the fragrance of life. I am forgiveness & benevolence,
I am the music in awareness. I pray for you & all you love.
I am in you & you are in me. We are everywhere, you & I."

Crying, I say, "But I am not worthy. I have failed You many
times."
"I am majesty & so are you. I am the best in you as you are
in me.
I am your father, your brother & your friend.
I am proud to call you family. I love you each day in every
way.
I am in you & you are in me. We are everywhere, you & I."

On my knees, tears flowing, I utter, "Thank You. I love You too."
"Never forget, I am purity & you have been washed clean.
I am the heart & soul of life; thus, you are too.
I am with you always & you, forever, are with me.
I am in you & you are in me. We are everywhere, you & I."

I humbly beseech, "How can I repay You for such wisdom?"
"I am charity, kindness, compassion, empathy, gentleness.
I am serenity in forgiveness, the inspiration for hope,
I am the grace in humility & understanding. I am the rock & the water.
And so are you. We give & therefore live—together!

"I am in you & you are in me. We are everywhere, you & I."

MY MAGIC MAN...

As you walk down the path of life, through all its twists and turns, its alleys and back streets, its hills and valleys, its never-ending ways of getting lost—it has a way every once in a while of bringing you to an intersection wherein, all of a sudden, there is an old friend standing at the same crossroad.

Yesterday was such an occurrence.

Out of nowhere my Iranian friend for life, my brother from another land, posts, "Who is in Istanbul?"

Holy shit, I think. *No way. My Magic Man is here right now. This is too good to be true. And it appears he is with the woman he told me so much about in Thailand.*

He shared with me how she had captured and captivated his heart. How she was something he had never before experienced. How he could not stop thinking of her despite being in a foreign land, experiencing all it had to offer. He could feel the connection all the way across the globe.

***

We met on Koh Chang Island while staying at Yuyu's Guesthouse. My boy Mark, our adopted little Sistah Stacie, and I loved this family so much because of the way they ensconced us in their familial embrace. One evening Yuyu and Yusef, the owners, decided to throw a party with a DJ.

About an hour into the evening we are having a great time. Spiced rum drinks abound, the sand beneath our feet, ocean waves cascading onto the shore, fantastic dishes made of King Prawn shrimp, calamari, scallops and Mahi-Mahi (all seasoned with so many different Thai flavors and herbs) along with upbeat electronic dance music to have everyone's heads bopping.

Out of nowhere comes this cool *"Cat in the Hat"* type character dancing up to our table. He is pumping his fists, stepping to the beat, weaving this way and that way with a mischievous Cheshire cat grin spanning ear-to-ear.

He is wearing what I can only describe as a pied piper's hat, a Fedora, with a single feather stretching aloft from the brim. He is of dark complexion and has a goatee. Not a thick goatee, nor a short and tight one, but one of those elegant style goatee's where the hair is thin and silky. He has a stately handlebar mustache.

He has a Chartreuse velvet vest on with no shirt underneath and sinewy arms. On one arm there has to be 30-40 bracelets of every material variety: clothe, bead, stone, leather, bamboo and so on. He is wearing baggy cotton shorts that stop just below his knees.

Without missing a beat dance-wise he introduces himself as "Farhad", says he is from Iran. His carefree, 'come what may' attitude permeates the air. He has a certain lightness of step, a whimsical energy emitting from every pore.

As you can guess, Mark, Stacie and I fell in love with the character that sooner or later became known as 'The Magic Man'. We spent four days hanging out, drinking way too many espresso's while playing backgammon, sharing joints and talking about the things that make us the same as opposed to those that make us different.

Sometimes you meet a person and you have conversations that just take both of you to another level, a new paradigm. Farhad and I had several of these.

The guy was an absolute gem. We even made a video together to share with all my friends back home where we talked about how people all over the world want the same things — A life filled with friends and family, a sense of belonging, the need to be recognized as individuals and the fact most of the world is kind.

We agreed ice cream is the best medium for peace. It was both cheeky and a great public service announcement.

On our last night together, Mark and I gave Farhad a wonderful bracelet before we left, seemed to be the evident choice. He added it to his collection with effusive praise and a warm hug for us both.

We partied until the wee hours that night and said our good-byes with heartfelt good wishes. Mark and I left the next morning at 7a.m.

***

I never even contemplated when I would see him again. Five years, ten years—who knows? And here he is in the same city without either of us planning it out.

I post back, "My main man. My Magical Man! My dearest of friends, I am here. We must gather again."

And we do. Once again it is very special.

He opens his hotel door and we immediately hug for literally two minutes, not saying a word. Just letting our hearts feel each other's pulse, speak their language.

We have the richest of conversations. We share our hearts, our thoughts, our dreams, our perspectives on the world and all its beauty.

We bond even more deeply than when we met in Thailand. We go further into the recesses of our soul, opening up and giving freely to each other.

I see him with even more clarity and he sees me with even more appreciation.

And his woman, Nina, is simply the rarest of gems. An exquisite diamond. A splendid creature! She is gorgeous. She is sweet. She is compassionate. She is astonishingly wise.

She reminds me of my mother in countless ways. A soul not often found in this world. Somehow floating above the turmoil; dancing with the angels!

And this brings a warm feeling to my heart. To meet and see my mother again, manifested in another. To know she is with me, everywhere and always.

I revel in their love. I find radiant joy that my friend has found such a counterpoint to his immense, wide, and vast spirit.

I tell him so.

He says, "Thank you so much for sharing in my happiness. For rejoicing in my exhilaration. That is the mark of a true friend."

I return, "You are my Magic Man!"

He replies, "I only mirror you, Stan. I only reflect what you shine upon me. I simply give back to you what you share with me."

That is how it should be, no?

We give without expectation. Without judgment. Without guile.

With honest and true sincerity. With love and affection.

Lo and behold, the world gives it right back. And I didn't even ask for it. It returns to me what I gave away freely.

I am thankful beyond words, my dear friends Farhad and Nina. Your bounty is a gift I can never repay, but will always do my best to try. Peace, love, prosperity, blessings, and luck to you both.

I began the piece by talking of meeting old friends at cross-roads. Every once in a while you come across someone, and, despite having just met them, you are *sure* the two of you go all the way back to the beginning of time.

I have no doubt Farhad and I have been pondering the meaning of life since life itself began.

All it took was meeting him in this lifetime to be reminded of what we have shared in past ones. And to remind me how much I treasure friendships that transcend time. As I always say, "There are no good-byes. Only the hope we meet again on down the path, at yet another crossroad."

Until then, see ya, my newfound long-lost old friend.

VICARIOUS MESSAGES...

More than any other messages my parents imparted to me, the two most important ones they repeated over and over and over again were the following:
"You can do anything you put your mind to" and, "We believe in you."

They relentlessly pounded these statements into my brain. No matter how bad I 'screwed the pooch' or how many times I fell down, these words were as ubiquitous in our home as water flowing from the tap.

Ingrained!

I can't thank my parents enough for their diligence in reinforcing both.

"Good for you Stan", you are probably saying. "Why tell us?"

Well, on this trip I had the pleasurable company of many young women, mostly in their early twenties. It's been uncanny to be honest.

Hold on a minute, before you go down that road let me say this: I have been intimate with one and only one woman. It was with a lady much closer to my age. We shared some very special time together.

Back to the story... I would like to believe they have found my energy to be non-threatening.

I had no agenda to get in their pants. I made no attempts to use my position as an older man to gain favor.

Nonetheless, they kept showing up at my side. For one reason or another, they opened up to me. Make no mistake; I valued what each and every one of them had to share with me.

They have all been a blessing. I truly mean that. A friend said to me the other day as I related all of this to her "Well that seems to be one of the ways you were called to service on this journey."

Fair enough, I thought.

So many of these young women had positive, attractive and worthy characteristics.

Except eventually the same subject came up with a fair number of them. And it bummed me out at times.

Deep down, many of them suffer from a lack of belief in their self worth. They question their value. They can't see their own splendiferous selves through all the bullshit society throws at them.

Whether it was their father, a past boyfriend, the media, the culture they were raised in or their life experiences – something caused them to lose sight of their power.

Something was missed in their upbringing that should have served as positive reinforcement. Someone told them something negative that stuck with them, in the furthest recesses of their minds.

And it left them longing.

Longing to be recognized for who they are. What they bring to the table. How inherently valuable they are. Why they are absolutely vital. Why they should be cherished. How gorgeous, beautiful, lovely, breathtaking and amazing they are.

I sat with them and started reinforcing what I saw from an objective eye. What they already knew but seemed to have forgotten, misplaced, lost or maybe never possessed.

I asked them to recognize how strong they are. How powerful they are. How cool they are. How bold they are. How adventuresome they are. How we need them to be the best they can be because, at the end of the day, they make us all better.

I kindly asked them to stop beating themselves up. I requested they forgive themselves, let go of the 'slings and arrows' from the past that pierced their hearts. I implored them to stop listening to the outside world and start listening to the divinity within.

Sometimes, I would beg them to realize how super-duper awesome they are.

I tried to get them to stop focusing on the negative drumbeat in their minds, to start speaking kindly to themselves, with uplifting words of encouragement and inspiration. I reiterated how they needed to tune society out if that is what it took.

And tune into what God/The Universe/The Spirits have in store for them.

I always ended it by saying the following, "Once you realize how astonishing you are, how truly beautiful you are, how utterly captivating you are then nobody can ever take that away from you. You are incredible and don't you ever, ever forget it. Don't let anyone steal this realization from you."

I continued, "You are fantastic. Stop doubting it and start believing it with all your heart, soul and mind. People are going to try and steal your belief, trick you into thinking another way or use you for their own purpose."

"But don't you dare let these things happen anymore! You must put a stop to it. You must embrace your inner magnificence even if nobody in your life seems to recognize it."

"Because it is there, it is real and it is yours."

Some would respond, "But I don't feel that way. I don't see myself the way you do. I don't know how to hold back the dam, so to speak."

I replied, "Fake it till you make it! Wake up everyday and spend five minutes looking in the mirror, reinforcing what it is you already know about yourself. Speak out loud words that lift you up, words that treat you with kindness and words that empower."

"Sooner or later, something will start to take hold. You will begin to sincerely see and adore your worthiness. You will begin to shed doubt and fear, replacing it with confidence and strength. You will become what you always wanted to become – a woman standing on her own two feet, firmly rooted in her evanescence."

I have had this very conversation at least two dozen times.

Don't get me wrong; I for sure met a few that were already there. These young ladies have dug deep, done the work and come out the other side both better and stronger. They found their foundation upon which to stand.

Further, throughout my life I have had the good fortune of being exposed to intelligent, strong, tough and benevolent women.

In business, yoga and my personal life, some of the most incredible women cared enough to impart their wisdom to me because they saw that I had no concern for the gender of the message provider.

I simply wanted to learn at their feet.

These people and memories give me hope. I am grateful to have the encouragement. They serve as power sources for me to draw from and use in other conversations as examples.

My Mom had a great saying, "Behind every good man is an even better women!"

As stated previously, she had a great way of summing shit up in one sentence.

As sure as I am standing on terra firma in Bali, the next century will be the century of the woman.

You ladies are gathering steam. Gathering together and fighting back! You are no longer taking crap, swallowing your pride and letting things go on they way they have any longer.

You are standing up and speaking out. You are holding our feet to the fire, and it is burning them. We need to feel that pain, as you have all these years. How can we know you until we understand your story?

I see women lifting us all to a more civil, rationale and caring society. I see women these days showing us a new way. Leading with dignity, compassion and sensibility

I, for one, am delighted they are finally taking their rightful place in not simply our homes, but also our workforces, communities, and societies. I am proud to watch as they shatter so many of the molds previously forced upon them. Throwing each mold in the garbage where it belongs.

To all the women I know – thank you for putting up with me. I appreciate your patience. It's a quality I am learning to develop with much more gusto than we have to date.

Ladies, I love you and I believe in you! Please take the words my parents were so very kind to chisel into my brain and make them yours, as if they were talking to you too. Vicariously embrace their loving support in your life, indoctrinate your thoughts with their voices.

Heck, guys too. If you did not and/or do not have someone or some people telling you this use my parents too. Trust me, they would love it.

Every single one of you, and I mean every single one, are exquisite. You are the very best of us.

> "I think women are foolish to pretend they are equal to men.
> They are far superior and always have been.
> Whatever you give a woman she will make greater.
> If you give her sperm, she will give you a baby.
> If you give her a house, she will give you a home.
> If you give her groceries, she will give you a meal.
> If you give her a smile, she will give you her heart.
> She multiplies and enlarges what is given to her.
> So, if you give her any crap, be ready to receive a ton of shit."
> ~William Golding

DAD'S GOT YOUR BACK...

If you haven't figured it out yet, I am Christian by faith. But I equally adore Buddhism. I can say with honesty I don't really care what your faith is because I believe they all spring from the same well.

What's more, if you are an atheist or even agnostic I am cool with that too.

My faith is where I hang my hat when it's time to come in from the cold. It not only works for me, but also sustains my heart when weary from carrying the weight of my particular world.

When you take the time to study various faiths from around the world, going back to the beginning of time, you discover that the message of all of them is virtually the same, quite often word for word.

What's more, when you study the prophets that have appeared on earth from the beginning of time, no matter what faith or philosophy they ascribe to, almost every single one says the same thing...

There is indeed a Divine One, we are all connected to and descended from this Divine One and all of us can talk with this Divine One at any point and time during our day.

I have not only chosen to agree with them, but found their truths to be, well, factual.

The great Paramahansa Yogananda, a highly revered yogi who was the first to bring the practice to the U.S.A. and founded the Self-Realization Fellowship in Encinitas, Ca., around 1920 says in his book, *"In the Sanctuary of the Soul"*:

> Faith, or the intuitive experience of all truth, is present in the soul. It gives birth to human hope and the desire to achieve... Ordinary human beings know practically nothing of this intuitive faith that is latent in the soul, which is the secret wellspring of all our wildest hopes.

Faith means knowledge and conviction that we are made in the image of God. When we are attuned to His consciousness within us, we can create worlds. Remember, in your will lies the almighty power of God. When a host of difficulties comes and you refuse to give up in spite of them; when your mind becomes 'set', then you will find God responding to you.

Faith has to be cultivated, or rather uncovered within us. It is there but has to be brought out. If you watch your life you will see the innumerable ways in which God works through it; your faith will thus be strengthened. Few people look for His hidden hand. Most men consider the course of events as natural and inevitable. They little know what radical changes are possible through prayer.

If all this is not your cup of tea, the next portion of this chapter piece might not jive with your sensibilities. Then again, as stories go, you may appreciate the twist provided by the author for it's literary keenness.

In no way, shape and/or form am I trying to proselytize. As Tom Petty says, "You believe what you want to believe, but ya' don't have to live like a refugee!"

The following is taken from *The Pilgrimage*, by Paulo Coelho:

When the Son of God descended to earth, he brought love to us. But since people identified love with only suffering and sacrifice, they felt they had to crucify Jesus. Had they not done so, no one would have believed in the love that Jesus brought, since people were so used to suffering every day with their own problems.

Do you know what Barabbas means, Paulo? Bar means son, and abba means father.

The intentions of the Divine Glory were so wise!

When Pontius Pilate made the people choose, he actually gave them no choice at all. He presented them with one man who had been whipped and was falling apart, and he presented them with another man who held his head high—Barabbas, the revolutionary. God knew the people would put the weaker one to death so that He could prove His love.

And regardless of which choice they made, it was the Son of God who was going to be crucified.

Personally, I love this amazing twist that I never knew before...

Humans may have thought they were getting the best of God, but all along He had the deck stacked to ensure the outcome that was best for the very ones trying to subvert His cause was still protected.

"Man plans, God laughs" is how the saying goes no?

Quit suffering on your own.

Quit thinking, *I have no allies.*

Quit thinking, *Nobody really cares about me.*

Quit getting down on yourself.

Somebody does and did, so much so He gave the ultimate sacrifice.

Somebody was so smart He knew how to ensure His will was done, no matter what the people chose.

Remember, His love for you is so enormous, so unending, so complete, so utterly genuine, so without guile, so infinite that YOU were who He was thinking of so long ago when He set His plan in motion.

He did it for us...

How spectacular is that?

So we could know and understand what He knew all along.

Nothing is more powerful than love.

Nothing can defeat love.

Nothing can hold love back.

Nothing, and I mean no thing known to man, can stand in the way of His love for you.

Not even death.

Wake up tomorrow with exhilaration!

Give thanks and praise for the love He has always had in His heart for you.

Greet the day with insurmountable confidence knowing your Father, your Dad as it were, will never, ever let you down.

He has your back, front, top, and bottom.

He has you covered every which way.

He has you ensconced in His provision, protection, and prosperity.

Whenever you think you can't, don't forget He already did—for YOU!

Dads are the best...

MANIFEST MAGNANIMITY...

There was an incredible Vietnamese Buddhist monk named Thich Nhat Hanh.

His story is beyond inspiring. I can't suggest strongly enough you acquire some of his books and take the time to learn about his life. His ability to combine courage with compassion was uncommon.

The following excerpt is taken from his book *The Novice*:

Kinh Tam answered:

It is because I have learned and am applying the practice of inclusiveness that I am able to avoid falling into suffering and reproach. Practicing magnanimity brings us away from the shores of sorrow and over to the shore of freedom and happiness.

Paramita means crossing over to the other shore.

The Buddha taught:

Those who are caught in cravings
are no longer clear-minded,
Which causes them to inflict pain and humiliation
on us.
If we are able to magnanimously persevere,
then our hearts and minds will be at peace.
Those who are self-indulgent
do not abide by moral conduct,
which causes them to slander and harm us.
If we are able to magnanimously persevere,
then our hearts and minds will be at peace.
Those who are ungrateful tell lies about us.
The gardens of their minds are full of the weeds of
vengeance,
which causes them to treat us unfairly and
unjustly.

If we are able to magnanimously persevere,
then our hearts and minds will be at peace.

When we truly practice looking deeply, then we
have a chance to understand better and be more
accepting. Our hearts naturally open up, becoming vast like the oceans and rivers.

In understanding the sorrows and difficulties of
others, we are able to accept and feel compassion for them, even if they have caused us difficulties, treated us unfairly, brought disaster
upon us, or unjustly harassed us.

Due to desire, vengeance, ignorance and jealousy, people have made numerous mistakes and
caused much suffering to themselves and others.
As we become more inclusive, our hearts and
minds will be at peace.

Being magnanimous does not mean suppressing
suffering; nor does it mean gritting our teeth and
bearing things with resentment or even resignation. These reactions are not inclusiveness or
magnanimity and cannot take us over to the
other shore.

We must practice deep looking and contemplation in order to understand and cultivate loving-kindness, compassion, joy and equanimity.

In cultivating loving-kindness, we offer happiness; in nurturing compassion, we relieve others'
suffering; practicing diligently strengthens our
inner source of joy; and developing equanimity
helps us let go of all hatred, prejudices and
entanglements.

When our heart is filled with loving-kindness,
compassion, joy and equanimity, its capacity
becomes boundless, immeasurable.

With such an expansive heart, immense as the wide open sea, those blatant injustices and suffering cannot overpower us, just as a small handful of salt cannot make a great river salty.

Wow! How spectacular, huh, peeps?

Go deep, my friends.

Cultivate loving-kindness.

Nurture compassion.

Practice and fill your hearts with joy.

Find equanimity.

Manifest magnanimity.

Make your heart as boundless as the oceans so that nobody, and I mean nobody, can replace the love you carry with hate, pain, and sorrow. *Boundless*. What a great word. Simultaneously referring to the lack of chains and limitless possibilities.

Worry not what others say about you. Cast aside all the comments you have received that hurt you. Pour the salt from these transgressions into the ocean, your immense and immeasurable heart, and watch them dissolve away, blend into nothingness.

Your peace is there for the taking.

Your serenity is waiting on the other shore.

Your love is as infinite as the universe.

Plunge deep into the ocean that is your heart, and I promise you will find the scenery is as beautiful as the Great Barrier Reef, as astounding as the Milky Way, as awe-inspiring as the most brilliant sunset on earth!

To be truly free is to live with a wide-open heart, able to give love away without any thought as to the consequences.

Take every hurt, every slight, every bad memory you hold on to, imagine each one as a grain of salt, then release each into the ocean of your heart. If you need to, release them all into God's ocean of forgiveness. Watch them all dissolve into the infinite capacity of the Universal seas.

For a grain of salt can do nothing but disappear when dropped into an ocean of magnanimity.

There is an ancient story about a boy made of salt. He traveled across the land trying to find out where he came from. Finally, after many years he comes to the shore of the ocean.

As he steps further into the ocean he begins to dissolve, exalting in the knowledge his home and family are the sea. Now he can be one with his past, present and his future.

Through magnanimity we can all dissolve, and thereby become one, with our home and family.

ONE LOVE...

Gili Air Island, more than any other place thus far, was about the locals. Brilliantly beautiful people who are happy every day just living the small island life. And it is a small island. You can walk around the entire perimeter of the island in forty-five minutes.

Located off the coast of Bali, it has an old-world charm I hadn't experienced since the time I lived on a remote island in Thailand twenty-six years ago.

Most of the locals have lived there all their lives. Or, as I found out, they move away for a while and eventually return home.

I met this man while walking down the street one day. As I approached his shop, he looked up from a sign he was painting, saw me, and immediately broke into a Bob Marley song.

"One loooooooovvveeeee" he sang out loud, in a baritone voice with a huge smile on his face.

Before he could move to the next line, I sang out loud right back to him. "One heaaaaarrrrtttt" with a huge grin on my face.

Next, we joined voices and finished the lyric. "Let's get together and feel all rigggggggghhhhhtttttt."

We both laughed with gusto.

He fixed his eyes on mine and said, "My man, who are you and how are you? No foreigners ever sing back to me. You are in my heart already. Welcome to Gili Air Island, my home. Where are you from?"

I introduced myself and gave him the specifics. I asked his name. He told me. It was something ridiculously long and barely possible for me to ever recite properly in his dialect.

So I said, "Brother, that is too much for me. How about I simply call you One Love?"

"Perfect, I will then call you One Heart!"

"Done!" I said. And we both laughed.

For the next week, every day when we saw each other, we would sing out our names to one another. All the people sauntering up and down the sand paths by his booth would stop and listen to us with smiles on their faces as we hugged one another at the end. We would embrace, perform the obligatory "bro shake" and visit for a while.

He was always, and I mean always, in a fantastic mood. Always had a kind word and always grinned from ear to ear.

For nine straight days this was my morning greeting. Not a bad way to be welcomed on an island halfway around the world, eh?

Why don't we all start putting a little extra effort in the way we greet people every day? A little extra pizzazz, zing, and energy!

What if we tried to specifically be nutty, kooky, or zany? How much more fun would it be to say hello? How many people would end up hugging you because you made them laugh, smile, or feel special?

Let's make greetings salutations again. Moments when we shower others with appreciation for coming across our path today!

Celebrations of the mere fact you and the benefactor of your salutation got the exquisite opportunity to breathe fresh air for one more day.

And do so together!

Come on, go out this day and greet a random person with a heartfelt, exuberant, and joyous hello. See if something magical occurs for you both.

I am anxious to hear about the results.

ONE, AND ONLY ONE, CHOICE...

"Get busy living,
Or get busy dying!"
   Andy Dufresne, *Shawshank Redemption*

If you decide to get busy living, keep in mind one very impor-
tant fact.
You have one, and only one, choice.
Your attitude!
About everything: religion, politics, relationships, career, fam-
ily—whatever!
When you really peel the onion,
The only choice you have
The only miniscule amount of control you have is
Your attitude!
Wanna know how to get your attitude straight?
Add a G and an R to the beginning of
Your attitude!
Peace, my friends...

FIND YOUR PLACE...

On a little island off the coast of Vietnam I found my own sanctuary, Phu Quoc Island. I adored staying there.

I sat at the same spot every day, three times a day for nine days straight. Sitting on a giant boulder, meditating, soaking up the sun, watching the waves roll in, and reveling in the wind against my sunburnt skin. The boulder was hidden behind some giant boulders, out of sight from beach walkers, so it was generally just the occasional fisherman and me.

It's amazing what things you can learn if you just listen to the world. And drink up the splendor.

This view is forever etched in my mind. I can close my eyes and see it all.

Sitting under the Southern Hemisphere sky, star constellations I hadn't seen in twenty-six years, waves softly flowing around the rocks, always a steady, cooling breeze—it was my oasis!

Much like the Irishman in *Braveheart*. "Yeah, but it's my island..."

I cried for hours there when I received the news of my friend passing away. I laughed the next day thinking about all the great talks, times, and truths we shared.

I did some of the deepest soul searching in my life.

I prayed extensively for many, many friends, wishing upon them all blessings, health, prosperity, and joy.

I forgave myself, and others, once and forever.

I did some of the best writing of my life.

I found a totally new understanding of what grace truly is. How divine we all are. Why the masks we wear are so useless.

In his book, "*In the Sanctuary of the Soul*", Paramahansa Yogananda tells us:

The Sanskrit word for faith is wonderfully expressive. It is *visvas.* The common literal rendering, 'to breathe easy; have trust; be free from fear', does not convey the full meaning. Sanskrit *svas* refers to the motions of breath, implying thereby life and feeling. Vi conveys the meaning of 'opposite; without'.

That is, he whose breath, life, and feeling are calm, he can have faith born of intuition; it cannot be possessed by persons who are emotionally restless. The cultivation of intuitive calmness requires unfoldment of the inner life.

When developed sufficiently, intuition brings immediate comprehension of truth. You can have this marvelous realization. Meditation is the way.

Meditate with patience and persistence. In the gathering calmness, you will enter the realm of soul intuition. Throughout the ages, those beings who attained enlightenment were those who had recourse to this inner world of God-communion.

Go within the Self, closing the door of the senses and their involvement with the restless world, and God will reveal to you all His wonders.

It is amazing how many answers you receive when you sit down, shut up, and just listen.

Seriously, who doesn't want to experience 'the gathering calmness' and/or 'enter into the realm of soul intuition'?

Go find your oasis, settle your mind and see what turns up. Take your time.

I promise you won't be disappointed.

Come on peeps - give it a try! Heck, if it has worked for sages since the beginning of time we ought to at least give it a shot right?

If you are not at peace, if serenity is as far from your mind as the other side of the earth from where you stand, what do you have to lose?

Maybe look at it this way, what limitations are you fighting so hard to hold on to and why do you clutch them so tightly?

If you are ready to finally let them go, and thereby effortlessly breathe the intuitive truths of this life, don't you owe it to yourself to give meditation a serious effort?

IT'S HARD WORK TRAVELING ALONE...

I swear, it really is.

I can hear you all the way over here saying, "Cry me a river, Stan!"

It is exhausting. Frustrating. Time consuming.

You create matrix charts on paper. You have notes written on napkins. You are always trying to either write down or print out stuff just in case, for whatever reason, you can't get Internet access where you are landing. Not all airports offer free Wi-Fi.

You spend hours scouring the Internet. Looking at all kinds of websites. Booking, Hostelworld, Agoda, Trivago, Travelocity, Trip Advisor, Lonely Planet, Arbnb, and a slew of airline sites.

You read reviews. And I mean you read reviews. You go three to five pages deep to see what the general consensus is because you can never, ever put your faith in only a few reviews.

Every time you go to a new place, you have to figure out logistics: How am I going to get there, via bus, train, plane, automobile, transport service, tuk-tuk, rickshaw driver, or scooter? What is the schedule of said transport vehicle? Is it in English? Where is the stop/station/airport in relation to where I think I want to be?

Whether by plane/train/bus, you need to consider cost, time frame involved, loss versus gain in time of travel and time allotted to spend in said location, level of comfort said vehicle offers, layover aspects, and word on the street about safety factor of chosen transport method.

Some of these trips can be more than thirty hours when you include time getting to the airport, time at the airport before the flight, layover time frame, arrival time, and transport time to sleeping location.

My advice: Always try to fly direct, or with one relatively short layover maximum if possible. Pay more for the time and energy saved. It's worth it.

Cramped seats, sleeping in airports, long layovers at airports that charge outrageous rates for stuff, waiting outside bus stations in blistering heat for three hours—it is always flat-out draining the day you travel, so make the trip as quick as you can.

How will I arrange transport from drop-off point to end destination? Oh, and where does said end destination leave me in terms of how it fits in transport-wise to the next location?

Now, where am I staying? What is the price range for a hotel versus a guesthouse versus a hostel versus an Arbnb? Does the part of town I want to stay in affect prices due to popularity?

If I choose another location that is more cost effective, is public transport accessible and easy to use? Can I just taxi it around? Will that negate the savings of the out-of-the-way hostel?

What is the quality of the reviews on the places I am looking at? Do they have dorm rooms or the opportunity to have my own room? Is the staff rated as friendly and knowledgeable?

Do they offer a breakfast? That can affect the hidden value of one place over another. Can they arrange pickup from said drop-off point? What is their check-in time? What is their checkout time?

Here is always a good question to try to figure out: What is the normal/fair cost for getting from the airport/train/bus station to my accommodations? Meaning, how do I not get ripped off by the almost universal overly aggressive taxi guys who hound foreigners the minute we exit customs?

What are the websites that are more "ear-to-the-ground" websites in terms of up-to-date things to do in the area you want to visit? Beyond the typical Tripadvisor and Lonely Planet, are there any sites or blogs run by people who were just there in the last six months?

Can I get a good night's sleep in the place I will be resting my head? Is it known as a party hostel? Am I in the mood for that? Is it located on any type of bar/restaurant strip? Am I sharing a bathroom or do I have my own?

Do you get the point? Can you see how maddening it can become? Especially when you are the only person dealing with it every time AND you are moving every three to five days.

Crap, I have slept in over ninety beds the last six months. I feel like a gypsy in search of the perfect "Fuck, I am exhausted. Tell me you have a good mattress instead of those damn plastic/vinyl-type hospital mattresses because too many young drunk travelers pissed on the good ones?"

Trust me, once you are north of forty, a good night's sleep is tantamount to pleasant next day's adventures.

Seriously, I made a few concessions very early in my trip. One of the main ones was that I would try to get a private room whenever possible and/or unless I felt I had overdone it money-wise, thereby needing to get back in line with my prospective budget.

I tried on several occasions to deal with the dorm room factor. To mix it up with the budget traveler, to have a chance at meeting more people (both male and female, as many hostels in foreign countries offer mixed dorm rooms), to expose myself to a wider variety of personalities—and almost every time it drove me nuts!

People come from all walks of life. People come from all over the world. Everyone brings a different perspective to the table about what is or is not acceptable behavior.

People are arriving from and departing to exotic locations at goofy hours. People of all ages, lifestyles, nocturnal habits, and drinking habits are all living in rooms, with bunk beds, that house anywhere from eight to sixteen people.

Suffice it to say, people make noise, arrive late, leave extremely early, unpack or pack at odd hours, push their limits or push the limits of the city they are in, or just want to connect with friends or family back home at crazy hours 'cause that is how the time change works—and it all shows up in your room at one point of the night or another.

There is always somebody creating a ruckus. Along with that, many bunk bed structures make all kinds of funky noises as the other 'bunkie' either climbs in for the night and/or rolls over during the night.

And get this: Based on my own entirely unscientific yet real-world experience, one out of four people snore. It's a moth-erf*@king fact! The range, volume, and supersonic capability of each particular snorer varies, but rarely did I come across one who did not have the innate ability to both snore outra-geously loud and sleep like a baby who just breastfed from whoever you think has the greatest boobs ever.

So, I can honestly say I never, not once, achieved a good night's sleep in a dorm room in a hostel.

For the record, when my buddy and I were traveling through Bangkok early on, both in Chang Mai and on the island, we stayed in some pretty damn funny places. Some were surreal in terms of random stuff happening, and some were surreal in terms of roosters starting to crow at 4:30 a.m. and there being nothing you can do about it.

For three days we stayed in this shack, and I mean hovel, at this particular guesthouse because we loved the owners so much. At some point, a cat climbed the
wall from the outside and trampled all over our bags/bed/clothes. It even pissed on my buddy's backpack.

For three nights we listened to what had to be World War III in the geo-political feline landscape that makes up Koh-Chang Island. I mean at about 4:30 each morning, it was like Nor-mandy outside our shack. These cats came to brawl, and brawl they did.

I have never heard such feral and ferocious cat sounds in my life. They were bloodcurdling and simultaneously hysterical all at once. It was a symphony of horrifying, screeching, hair-raising hilarity.

I mean, there was nothing you could do but bitch for a minute, then laugh at the absurd nature of the civilized society you just came from versus the jungle nature of where you were now.

And you were not sleeping for a while!

Every city has bus and train stations. This is indeed a good thing. That being said, you are usually worn out from what it took to get you there, and now you must fix your eyes on an entirely new map, always in a different language, to get to your place.

You are carrying a backpack that weighs about fifty pounds, along with a daypack that has your "most valuables" in it, and you have to figure out how to get a ticket from the machine.

Oh, did you grab some local currency when you arrived? What's the conversion rate and how much should you grab at the airport, knowing they always give you a bad deal?

Assuming it only took a half hour to do all that, you have your ticket, you made it through the turnstile, the train finally comes, you board, it is crowded, and now you need to become hyper-vigilant about not getting pickpocketed or find a bag go missing.

Forget the fact you have just been spit out of the travel vacuum, shriveled and beaten down by seats made for inmates at San Quentin Penitentiary, and all of a sudden you are on sensory overload due to this entirely new and completely foreign city—you still have to process stuff.

By the way, how is your stomach feeling after all that crappy food the last twenty-three hours? Or, what time is it where you just arrived? When was the last time you had decent food? Is it still a decent hour whereby you can find an open restaurant?

Mind you, all of this is before you actually get to the city/town/village wherein you then have to wake up the next day, still groggy from your travel endeavors, and start figuring out how to do all the stuff you think you want to do, plus what you just heard about from the other travelers staying at the hostel while eating breakfast.

Again, you have maybe half a week to see all the sights, do all the activities, and eat all the food. The planning for the next leg then starts all over again around day two or three, while you are still trying to enjoy the last few days in your current location.

Or, you can just wing it when you land.

I know, it sounds crazy. But you can pull it off and be quite surprised as to the outcomes. This is especially true in Asia. Just about everywhere you disembark from whatever form of transportation you took, there will be exceptionally eager beavers waiting to escort you to a brother's/sister's/cousin's/friend's place.

I have done this many, many times—just trusting in the travel gods. Like I said, my success rate was very good. And if you don't like the place, just move.

Imagine doing all of this every two or three days for over six months straight. On top of it, you are packing and unpacking your bag all the time. Locking it up and unlocking it ten times a day to grab something you need. Rushing to catch some transport to some other transport. Making sure you have all the tickets, or confirmation numbers, or e-ticket scans, or hand-scribbled in another language receipts that could actually say "tourists are assholes" and I wouldn't know it.

Make no mistake; some parts of the world are not as technologically advanced as others.

You find yourself walking up to a ticket taker with a tiny piece of paper in your hand that has illegible writing on it, hoping it doesn't read: "Uncle Jim, check out this schmuck I just fleeced. Love Wong."

"It is what it is!" truly becomes a way of life.

I haven't even brought up the whole conversation overload factor.

Think about it, every day for 180 days you are meeting new people.

Not just one person, not just five people, usually anywhere between ten and twenty-five. Every day. Morning, noon, and night!

Throw in language differences to the mix. Maybe add a tad bit of alcohol, three to four late nights per week 'cause you're in "so and so, when will this happen again?" Top it off with the locals you meet those days too, and you can get literally sick of talking to people.

Not kidding, I remember hiding at some hostels in the corner with a book covering my face just so I could be alone for a day or two.

Is seeing the world worth it? I mean, how can you not say yes to that? It is amazing. Beautiful. Awe-inspiring. Astounding. Mesmerizing. It leaves you with such a sense of wonder.

But it also drains you bit by bit. The energy required to sustain a constantly moving caravan is significant, if not relentless in its requirement. The variety of environments, foods, sleeping arrangements, time changes, language differences, and so on, combined with their effect on you, is daunting in terms of consistent effort to say the least.

When you travel in this fashion—bring your A-game. Along with a lot of patience!

Everything in life has a price. These days you can pay as much as you can afford to remove many of the hassles from the endeavor. The more you do though, the less you are challenged and the more you leave chance by the roadside.

If you travel to be inspired again, why would you leave beside the road the very character you want by your side on the road less traveled? Where is the fun in that? The challenge?

Like so many other aspects of life, the pain-in-the-ass process required to travel in such a way ends up adding so much satisfaction to the overall story. Especially when gazing back through the lens of fondness later on in life.

I am telling ya, travel wears you out. But it's a beating I can take.

LEAVING NATURE NATURAL...

While in Ubud my friend Alex scored us the best Airbnb place ever!

The resort was amazing, gorgeous, pristine, preserved, serene, and peaceful.

Above all else, it was natural.

The grounds of this resort were the most beautiful I have ever seen:

In the middle of a jungle, overlooking terraced rice paddies with an attention to architectural and natural purity.

Enormous trees everywhere, fantastic foliage all around, flowers blooming in nooks and crannies, paths that meander past statues, shrines, and solitary spaces.

Fountains, small waterfalls, baskets filled with offerings, and incense wafting in the air at all times.

Pools built on the ledge of the hill, bathtubs built into the side of the hill overlooking the river, massage rooms next to the river with open windows, and lounge chairs on every level of the eight-story encampment.

Astounding!

I had the pleasure of sitting with the owner for dinner one night. He is a martial arts master. Lovely man. He has lived on the property for over thirty-five years. For twenty-five of those years he had the entire place all to himself. Plus extended family members.

I asked him with a smile, "You couldn't keep it to yourself anymore, could you? You had to share this beauty with the world, right?"

"Yes," he replied. "Not fair to be so selfish. My father would disapprove. He trained me to give with love!"

It took him eight years to build the place.

An architectural and engineering nightmare! Self-imposed nonetheless.

A feat beyond maddening I imagine.

Why is that?

They did not destroy one single tree.

The directive to all involved was to preserve every bit of natural setting possible. By his estimate, it added over four years and $2 million to the project. And well worth the effort I say!

He offered, "Everything must remain as God intended it."

Blessed beyond measure, awed to the point of silence—we were stunned as to our good fortune.

I love it when I come across people who take the long road, overcoming maddening difficulty, huge expenses, and endless grief, losing all kinds of valuable time in the process—just to ensure the right thing is done.

People who say to themselves, "This place of majesty will stay so. I will preserve all the inherent goodness already in existence here. Then I will openly share this place of beauty with the world."

Makes me happy to know people like him exist.

Makes me think Mother Earth might still believe in us too.

Makes me realize not all people and places have a price.

This is a very good thing to know these days.

Despite what you read and hear seemingly all the time, not everybody has a price.

MOM TAKES A TIME-OUT...

I made a new friend in Seville, Spain. Her name was Ursula, from Germany. A married mother of two, she was walking the road to Santiago.

It was her last night in town, so we met at the hostel and went out to the La Fiera festival. We had such an enjoyable time together, wandering around, marveling at the crazy atmosphere, bumping into each other a hundred times as we took in all the sights.

We laughed, were captivated by the costumes, danced to flamenco music, and even managed to sneak our way into a few of the private tents for some free beers.

I loved her attitude.

Even though she had kids and a hubby at home, she still needed to complete her own dreams, to recharge her batteries. Stay energized about life after giving so much of herself to the ones she loved.

She talked about how, when she was younger, the opportunity was not there because of the time and effort it took to be a good wife, mother, and community member. Later, she realized she was limiting her own happiness by always giving to others, not necessarily taking care of herself.

Her tank was running empty; she was drained. Maybe even becoming a tad resentful.

We all know the adage about not being able to take care of anyone without taking care of ourselves, right? How many of us actually pay heed to the sentiment?

How many of us give and give and give until there is nothing left inside? Until we no longer recognize ourselves because we spent so much energy giving to others, we lost our identity in the process?

We look in the mirror and see a reflection, but it is indeed one we are wholly unfamiliar with.

A stranger in our own skin!

So she made a change. About eight years ago she began taking adventures on her own with the encouragement and blessings of her entire family. Since then she has accomplished multiple long-distance hikes, meaning twenty to thirty days' efforts, in different countries through rough terrain, all by herself.

Each time she came back more full of life! More full of wonder, inspiration and, most importantly, love. More complete and therefore better equipped to fill the roles she truly cherished.

After all, what's a more privileged role than being the rock of a family?

I thought many of us in the same situation could garner inspiration from such an adventurous and intelligent person. Someone who realized if she didn't make a change, she might well vanish.

At least her dreams might fade away into oblivion. If we don't have dreams, we aren't truly living, are we?

For that matter, how would her kids learn to reach for the skies?

A mother, whenever possible, wants to not only share with her children the ways of the world, but also how to fully take advantage of them.

Sometimes you have to leave your life behind, let the ones you love fend for themselves, and walk your own path—all so your passion can remain alive.

In doing so, you can then give freely to those you love when it's time to do what needs to be done.

It is in service we find the true meaning of life, of what it means to be humane, to live with an open heart. Let us not forget we must be of service to our own hearts in order to be of service to all the hearts contained therein.

Safe travels, dear lady. I hope you find what you are looking for on this journey. Until we meet again, see you on down the road to revitalization.

IT'S ABOUT THE SPIRIT, NOT THE NUMBER...

I am in line at the local grocery store. I need to stock up for tomorrow, as the entire island of Bali shuts down to relax on Nyepi Day.

As I am daydreaming, a mature gentleman gets in line behind me. "Hi!" he says, bringing me back to the moment. "Where are you from?"

I tell him Chicago, and then ask, "How about you?"

"Well, I was from Canada. Now I am a citizen of the world. I am a backpacker like you."

"Awesome. How long has your journey been so far?"

"Been on the road for nine years," he states.

"Wow. That's fantastic!" I reply. "Mind if I ask how old you are?"

He looks at me and grins. "I am seventy-four years young. I have been just about everywhere. The world is a fascinating place."

My new hero!

Travelers come in all shapes, sizes, colors, creeds, and faiths. And age groups.

Why? We all have the same wanderlust for this magnificent planet circling the sun. You are never too old to go on a new adventure. Nor too young or naïve!

The road less traveled always has room for one more intrepid seeker of mystery and mayhem.

There are no age requirements when it comes to those who hunt the magical moments.

The only requirement is a willing heart and an open mind.

I met many "seasoned" travelers who readily admitted they were well past their primes, their "salad days" miles behind them in the rearview mirror, exploring and living in foreign lands, giving up all they knew to start fresh.

Each one echoed the same sentiment: "I am not done sucking this life dry!"

I met this beautiful woman, Laura B., in Banos, Ecuador, who while in her forties was riding a BMW motorcycle from the top of South America all the way to the bottom on some of the most challenging and rugged terrain you can imagine.

Take a look at a map and check out all the countries she passed through, all the crazy altitudes she ascended. Back-country dirt roads with chopped up terrain, mud infested valley paths, boulder covered mountain passes with drop offs to certain death three feet away and all kinds of crazy city streets in between.

All by herself on her little horse, as it were. This is after having already ridden through most of North America and then all of Central America on another motorcycle in past years. This girl is tough!

Even more so, she displays a will power that is both stunning and inspirational to everyone she comes across. She has posted all kinds of videos literally baring her soul for all who care to read. Here is the kicker; she is an old soul with a terrific sense of humor. Just warm, loving and brave.

I met another lovely young lady in her mid-thirties while staying in the Valley of Volcanoes, a place I describe later, who was as cool as a cucumber. I mean she emitted this super tranquil, take life as it comes vibe.

She had a smile that lit up the room and was full of life.

She also had not been home in over fifteen years. That's right, she had been on the road for over 5,475 days straight. Holy shit! Mucho respect Senora.

Talk about odd jobs: everything from hard labor on multiple farms in multiple continents, crewing boats and ships of all sizes, teaching kids of all languages and a crazy array of other random yet story-filled endeavors to make a buck and survive. Made me feel as if I have done practically nothing with my life, and I have had a lot of careers!

She simply carried with her a good attitude, a love of wonder and the willingness to do whatever was necessary to get to tomorrow. She blew me away with her understated grace, wisdom and soulfulness.

I meet a guy on Gili Air Island who happened to have a really sweet mountain bike. I asked him why he had such an expensive bike on this remote island while we both waited in a Doctor's office for different reasons. He replied, "Well, I have ridden that bike over 285,000 kilometers over the last 7 years."

"Wait. What? Did you say 285,000?" I ask incredulously.

"Yep. I have covered all of Africa, all of Eastern and Western Europe, all of Southeast Asia, part of Mongolia and part of China." With that he shuts up and smiles at me.

I say, "Sweet Jesus, you take the cake. By far the most adventuresome escapade I have heard so far on my trip. Let me buy you a beer, I have to hear more."

Heck, last summer one of my good buddies allowed his daughter, at the ripe age of thirteen, to travel all of Europe by herself. No adult companionship.

Of course, she had a Euro-Rail pass and folks waiting in every city to welcome her, but much of the job of getting from A to B was in her hands. Think about that, a thirteen year old spent 90 days traveling Europe all by her lonesome. Fucking awesome!

All these people had the same spirit, the same yearning, and the same unquenched desire to see/experience something different. The unknown. That which lay beyond the comfort zone!

What makes their fires burn so bright with passion? I think it best to let an expert chime in on their behalf as he seems to have summed it up well enough years ago.

> If you are going to try,
> Go all the way. Otherwise, don't even start.

This could mean losing girlfriends, wives, relatives and
Maybe even your mind.

It could mean not eating for three or four days.
It could mean freezing on a park bench.
It could mean jail. It could mean derision.
It could mean mockery – isolation.

Isolation is the gift.

All the others are a test of your endurance,
Of how much you really want to do it.
And, you'll do it,
Despite rejection and the worst odds.

And it will be better than anything else
You can imagine.
If you are going to try, go all the way.
There is no other feeling like that.

You will be alone with the gods, and
The nights will flame with fire.
You will ride life straight to perfect laughter.
It is the only good fight there is.

~Charles Bukowski

REPORTING VERSUS LIVING...

I was reading an article in *Vanity Fair* on a flight last week about the relationship of a writer with the Rolling Stones. Essentially, as a young reporter for *Vanity Fair* magazine, he was assigned to go on tour with the Stones for almost two years.

I know, right? What a fantastic gig at the ripe age of twenty-six.

Without getting into the article too much, he did say something that struck a chord.

The author was addressing how at some point during the tour, he realized he was focusing so much of his attention on being the reporter, he was forgetting to take in the overall grandeur of the experience.

To not only report the events as they occur, but also remember to live in them first.

Participate in the endeavor. Inhabit the moments with all your awareness. Be an active contribution to the environment as opposed to a reporter recording events.

He said, "I'd been too busy trying to pay attention and do a good job to notice the surrealism of the experience."

Why did this resonate with me? Well, after a while, I began falling prey to writing more than living and experiencing. I was trying to look at every moment via a reporting lens rather than experiencing the moment as it unfolded. That is not why I was on this trip.

Yes, I wanted to share my journey "back to joy" with friends and readers, but not at the expense of living in the now. Soaking up each moment and/or occurrence without expectation.

For a while, I had a nice balance between being present in each moment with eyes wide open and taking small mental notes as I went along, using them later when time came to sit down at the computer.

Then I started to look at every experience through the lens of observation instead of fully involved, inspired, and uninhibited participation.

When you start trying to manufacture the good times, the good times become elusive. Good times often only come by chance, through kismet, and are distilled for those whose eyes are alert. Once you try to bring a perspective to them, a jaundiced viewpoint that is driven by a desire to record the moments for posterity, you lose the magic.

Now you are looking for the trick behind the marvel, rather than simply reveling in the marvel itself. Sometimes marvelous things should not be questioned, simply enjoyed.

It's funny, right about the time this awareness came, my computer crashed—again!

What is it with technology and me? I swear, it just messes with me on purpose. This was the second time my computer crashed on the journey, the first time being in Indonesia.

Because I was in Spain and it happened on a Saturday afternoon, I was stuck. My flight out to Lisbon was set for Monday at 10 a.m. Thus, at the very least, I would have to do without until the following Tuesday.

I needed an English-speaking Mac repair center.

I finally got things in order on Thursday. Luckily, I was able to retrieve most of my data and have my hard drive upgraded. All in all, it ended well.

The good part, as mentioned above, was the Universe forced me to take a sabbatical.

It wanted me to slow down my reporting and speed up my participating. It wanted me to remember my purpose on this trip: fully experience everything the world had to offer—letting go of the need to feel connected to anything in my day except the beauty the world keeps unfurling before my very lucky, humbled presence!

I had my last dinner in Malaga, Spain, by a gorgeously illuminated cathedral. On the street about twenty-five feet away was this fantastic street performer, a saxophone player, playing for tips. People were sauntering around, eating at cafes, and taking in the wonderful sights of the city at night.

I had an amazing seafood paella, added a few glasses of wine, and then finished it off with some coffee and Grand Marnier. The atmosphere, vibe, weather, and charm of such a grand city had me feeling rather pleasant.

I was reading a book by Rumi, an author who always makes me ponder.

During dinner I had a long conversation with, how shall I put this— Aw, screw it if people don't understand—I talked with God.

If you wish to call it the Universe, conscious, Allah, Brahma or my split-personality, that is fine. For me, I know exactly who was there and have zero doubt as to the person on the other end of the dialogue.

But you see, that is the trick. There is no trick.

He will talk with you anytime if you know how to call on Him. It starts with gratitude.

Your first words need to approximate "Thank You. I love You. I am sorry it has been so long. Can we chat?"

He desperately wants a relationship with you. With all of us!

***

I will reiterate a point I brought up earlier in the book: Almost every prophet from all faiths and walks of life has reiterated we can talk with the Divine Maker at any time during our day. Please, take some time research this truth for yourself.

I did. When I see people respected for thousands of years, across multiple spectrums of culture and upbringings, reiterate the same veracity over and over and over again I figure it is time to take heed.

Once I decided to give it a try, using the techniques taught by these sage folks, I came to find they were right. Thus began the process of learning how to develop my ability to tune into, ask for and thankfully receive messages from this very Divine Voice.

It's there... I swear to you on my heart. He is there! Waiting....

Again, if you are not buying what I am selling it's cool. I just want you to be happy and fulfilled.

***

To sum up the conversation, I would say He told me this:

"Be yourself. Be authentic. Be original. Be fully present. Be aware. Let go of and release all expectations. That is how you truly live in the moment each and every day.

"If you come into any situation, event, or relationship with a preconceived notion, a premeditated desire, you have tainted the flow of it. You must train yourself to forget any notion of outcome; simply allow life to unfold as it does, with only a wide-eyed attitude and an acceptance of what happens.

"It is in the relinquishing of objective that you become the participant, not just the observer.

"Report later, live now!

"Get back to finding your joy. Then give it all away.

"Bring inspiration to every day. Be humble and grateful for the time others share with you; it is in sharing with others you find the meaning of life: truth, love, and relationship.

"Keep giving back. Every time you do, I smile, because you are really giving back to me by understanding compassion. For that is the trait I most adore.

"We, up here, all of us who love you, are behind you 100 percent."

There ya have it. Straight from the Guy upstairs!

This was my message. I needed to hear that, despite my ineptitude, I was on the right path and, for the most part, I was doing the things necessary to make my Dad proud.

I beg you to sit down and ask for yours, if it doesn't come quickly, be patient and wait. Keep asking, keep thanking and keep listening. Once He knows your ears are sincerely attuned you will start hearing His whisper.

***

I will finish this off with a story. The last night I was in Lisbon, we gathered almost everyone in the hostel and took them all to a dance festival supposedly being held in the streets. We did not know what to expect.

As we were walking toward the event, I was in front with a young man from France who was taking a five-day vacation. He was also staying in the same dorm room as I was. Thus, we had already chatted a bit about the past and my trip.

He asked me to distill some wisdom from my whole trip if I could. Without blinking an eye I said the following:

"The best piece of advice I can give you is to drop your expectations. Let go of your need to control how your day goes. After all, none of us has any control whatsoever if you really look at it objectively.

"So, I just wake up each day, say thanks for getting another chance to do something nutty, and then head out of the hostel to go find something new. Some days I come across brilliant, astonishing places, people, and events. Other times, the days are just okay. And every once in a while, I have crappy days.

"But if I keep calm, find some humor in the situation, and realize it is just another bump in the road—I somehow come home at the end of the day mostly happy.

And tomorrow, if I am blessed, I will get the chance to be more, to be better.

"Be present. That's it! Be there, be involved, be focused, and be motivated to have an effect.

"Be the closest thing you can to your true self. The one that is always asking to be set free!

"The world, and by very real proxy, your life, is indeed exactly as you make it."

Back to living for today! A Portuguese day pregnant with possibilities!

I will leave my expectations on my pillow. Let them have their own dreams while I am out allowing life to embroider my days with the serendipitous and unexpected.

I will report my findings ex post facto from here on out.

HUNTING FOR BEAUTY...

One night while out with my friend, Angela, in Lisbon enjoying a particularly festive event she asked, *"What is one of the big lessons you have learned on this trip Stan?"*

Without blinking I replied, "The more I search for beauty, the more she shows up first! It almost becomes automatic; I don't even have to look for her anymore. Often, she just skips right across my path while I am walking down the street.

"She is everywhere. She is in every country, on every beach, and in every city street. She is literally all over the place. All you have to do to get her to start showing up is actively look for her. Open your eyes. Look around where you stand right now and you will see she is right there, in the mix.

"Once she knows you are not only chasing her, but appreciating every single time she turns up—she will start to come looking for you. Like any lover, if she knows she has caught your attention, she will reveal herself even more. Because she is a giving lover, the very best kind."

Angela said, *"Don't you mean 'If you look for beauty, she will let you see her? That is how she shows up'?"*

"Somewhat, but it's more encompassing than that. Not only will she start to show herself, she will start to show up unannounced. She will show up because she knows you care, you want to see her, and you love what she shows you. She will walk your way before you even know she is on the same street. If she knows your eyes are wide open, she will unveil her succulent splendor."

Angela asked, *"Give me an example. Right now if you can please?"*

"Sure, look at this scene right now. We are standing outside of a bar in Lisbon, Portugal, on some random back alley street. We have tasty sangrias in our hands that cost us one euro. People are walking around everywhere, up and down these back alleys, arm in arm, cocktails in hand, laughing and enjoying themselves.

"We have this eclectic mix of people with us tonight. All of them are warm, charming, and genuinely nice. We got to sit in a Portuguese restaurant, enjoy some splendid Portuguese food, participated in spirited conversation with people from all over, and were entertained by male and female fado singers while we ate.

"You tell me, is this all incredible or not? Right now, right here—this very moment you and I sharing. With all these drunken goofballs around us spread out on the sidewalk, chatting away—is this not what the beautiful moments in life while traveling are all about?"

Angela looked at me, wide-eyed, broke out a big smile, and said, *"Dude, high-five. You are the best. Thank you for sharing that. I am definitely going to steal if from you."*

As they say, the highest form of flattery is to pilfer from another.

> When I run after what I think I want,
> my days are a furnace of stress and anxiety;
> if I sit in my own place of patience,
> what I need flows to me, and without pain.
> From this I understand that
> what I want also wants me,
> is looking for me and attracting me.
> There is a great secret here
> for anyone who can grasp it.
>
> ~ Shams Tabrizi

It's the truth, peeps. More than just about every other lesson/moral/truism I have learned on this trip, this is the one that continues to resonate with the highest frequency:

Beauty is everywhere!

She waits, longing to be seen by you.

She waits, desperate to be appreciated by you.

She waits, wishing for nothing more than to be loved by you.

She waits...

And if you show her you love her, she will start showing up on her own.

Every single day!

Sometimes solely for your pleasure, but usually she wants you to share her with those in your company!

She is the best kind of ample opportunity lover.

SLOW-DOWN BOSS...

My new favorite term: slow-down boss.

I am staying on Gili Air island in Indonesia. It's a wonderfully small island that has no cars or motorized vehicles of any kind.

Tammy and I were sitting on the beach, watching the sun go down and chatting with a local waiter serving us dinner.

I asked, "Do you like working here?"

He said, "Yes, very much. Our boss is from Australia. We love him. He wants us to treat the guests well, take care of them, and have fun at the same time. He is a slow-down boss. No need to rush, just get it right. Be polite, be kind, and enjoy your time at work.

"Slow down, focus on each task, and be the best in each moment!"

That, my Western world peeps, is how you build a good team.

Are you a slow-down boss?

Are you simply focusing on the task at hand or are you multi-tasking, thinking you can accomplish it all at once?

When you ponder the idea, multitasking is just another way to distract yourself from giving your absolute best to the moment at hand. It is just multiple distractions, with no task receiving your very best.

Are you enjoying your work, treating people with kindness, and ensuring your customers are taken care of?

Are you having fun? If not, maybe consider decelerating.

Forget this whole busy-busy-busy lifestyle being shoved down your throat.

Take your time. Make one, and only one, person happy at a time.

The others will wait if they see how you took care of the last person.

And if they don't, they weren't your kind of customer anyway.

SHE'S GOT THE WHOLE WORLD IN HER HANDS...

It's 6:00a.m and I am frantically rushing to get a motorcycle taxi for a bus leaving Saigon to the Mekong Delta. I jump into a 7\11 to grab a drink, as I am walking out I see the captivating scene.

In the middle of chaos all around, there is a mother just loving on her new baby in the morning sun. The baby is spread out on her lap, naked as a jaybird.

She is sitting on a plastic chair IN the street. Not off to the side of the road, but about three feet from the side of the road. Again, in the street!

Bikes, cars, vans, motor scooters, trucks and people all over the place, flying by – it's a bustling and busy world, no time to waste.

Everyone has got to be there yesterday. Drive at hyper-speed or get 857,652.73 scooter tire tracks on your back. Seriously, there are a million scooters on the road at 7a.m., all riding so close to one another you can reach over and wipe the smile off their faces if so inclined.

Yes, they smile as they play cat and mouse with disaster daily. I like that about the Vietnamese — Undaunted!

Rush hour. In Saigon, this means high velocity traffic insanity. Every morning commute in this amped up city is a direct challenge to Fate.

Life in the fast lane!

She knows of none of this. She is totally oblivious to the bedlam flying by every second.

An invisible force surrounded them, shielding the sanctity of her devotion and adulation.

She is filled with agape, the love that consumes.

The newborn naked child is life in the smallest of bundles, squirming on her lap. Yet this small bundle also represents a love more gigantic and vast than all the seas on the planet.

In the middle of 2016 she transports me back to the beginning of motherly love.

I am transfixed, mesmerized, and humbled.

Mother and child—I am watching a love unmatched by anything offered up by the Universe in terms of splendor!

I cry on the back of the bike, in the middle of total morning mayhem, at the beauty of life.

We are all the same. We want to feel the same joy of agape. The love that is all-consuming!

For a split second, I feel their love inside my heart.

For just a brief moment, I share in their luminescence.

Is there anything more pure, more authentic, or more astounding than the love between a mother and child?

I haven't found it yet and I have been to many a faraway place.

It truly is to me the tie that bonds us all.

A mother's love is the closest manifestation on this earth of God's love—unyielding, unending, and untainted.

Infinite in its scope.

Singular in its sincerity.

Benevolent beyond comprehension.

Is there any doubts Mother's are God's Gift to Mankind?

Without question, the most riveting moment of my entire trip!

WHAT CAN I SAY ABOUT YOGA?
HOW ABOUT THIS...

When traveling on this type of journey, with changing environments, constant new faces and beds a daily occurrence; you need to find a way to stay centered, grounded. When not in the comfort of familiar surroundings it is quite easy to lose your bearings.

For me, that is where the practice of yoga comes in. I carried a yoga mat with me the whole way and spread it out in every country. Once my feet step onto the mat, I am home. No matter where the soil, I have a way to connect with both the land beneath my feet and myself.

A lot of people journal, some people blog. Others spend a lot of time chatting with the very people at home they needed a break from. Me, I go do yoga.

Why? Well...

When you're lost, yoga leads
When you're exhausted, yoga energizes
When your zest has vanished, yoga reinvigorates
When I was broken, yoga rebuilt me!

If you're wounded, yoga mends
If you're hurt, yoga heals
If you're vanquished, yoga helps conquer again.
If I need answers, yoga has the questions!

When your stomach is in knots, yoga unties them
When there is discord, yoga bestows harmony
When you're sad, yoga comforts
When all around me was dark, yoga illuminated!

If you're overweight, yoga trims
If you're underweight, yoga builds

If you're clumsy, yoga gives grace
If I am toxic, yoga purifies!

When you've got problems, yoga provides solutions
When you're stressed out, yoga brings serenity
When you've forgotten who you are, yoga is the mirror
When I battled demons, yoga offered angels!

If you feel old, yoga regenerates
If you feel ignorant, yoga shares insight
If you crave knowledge, yoga offers wisdom
If I strive for less, yoga gives me more!

When you are alone, yoga is a friend
When you are cold, yoga offers warmth
When you lack self-esteem, yoga inspires belief
When I was afraid, yoga gave me courage!

If your heart is shattered, yoga repairs
If you crave intimacy, yoga embraces
If you feel disrespected, yoga honors
If I forget how beautiful I am, yoga reminds me!

In the end, I find yoga takes and gives.
It takes what you don't need
And gives what you do need

Like the best of relationships, it lets me be ME!

SILENT NIGHT...

What would happen if, for one day, the entire world decided to be quiet?

Think about it for a few seconds. If we could get everyone to be as quiet as possible for an entire day, with the only activities being food previously prepared, served, and eaten in relative silence, what would the world feel like that day?

Nobody works. Nobody! Nobody opens a single store, goes to an office, or even walks the streets. Every single person on the planet stays home for one day. Nary a soul does a home project.

Oh, for fun, let's further agree there shall be absolutely no TV, radio, or instrument turned on, played, or strung. No taxis, no buses, no trains, and no flights—anywhere.

Finally, at night we shall leave all lights off. No illumination except a few candles to provide enough light for the bathroom. All switches off!

So let's recap. No movement. No noise. No light. No cooking. No activity. No talking when possible. You can't leave your home. You stay as silent as possible for twenty-four hours.

You are not even supposed to make love!

Now listen. Can you hear it? Can you block out all the noise and hear the melody of a world where silence is the only noise reverberating throughout the land? Can you hear the sounds of silence?

If you can't properly conjure all this setting portends to offer, then I humbly suggest you go to a special little island in Southeast Asia wherein this very phenomenon occurs—Bali.

Believe it or not, such a holiday does exist, it does unfold exactly as I have said above, and it is one of the most surreal twenty-four hours you will ever experience.

It is aptly titled Nyepi Day! Or, as the pronunciation so perfectly sums up the eventual outcome, nappy day! As in taking a nap. Thus, for all intents and purposes, it's sleep day. That is the one and only activity you are supposed to focus all your energies on. Sleeping!

I know—it sounds brilliant, right? And it is. But it's also bizarre. Especially if you are not from the country and do not have a home. Even more so if you have no idea the whole thing is happening, and to what extent, until about six o'clock the night before!

Let me digress for a moment since I threw in the last comment. I have found Asia to be charmingly frustrating for numerous reasons; one of which is the fact you can talk to ten different people and still not have all the answers you need as to what is going on and/or why.

It's like putting a jigsaw puzzle together. First you find out something is going to happen. You get a little info from the initial person you talk to who tells you such event is going on. Then, as you begin to talk with other folks, the event, and what transpires all around it, is much more involved than you could imagine.

So, with each subsequent individual you talk to regarding said event, you are given more and more information as to what the protocol is, how you are to behave, what activities are or are not occurring, what the premise is, why it is celebrated and so on.

For no single holiday in Asia can be simply explained or comes without several rules. Respecting tradition and cultural heritage is of utmost importance in all Asian lands.

All of it is tied up in religious, cultural, ancestral, political, and societal history. None of which is ever a straight line when it comes to how this particular group of Asians came to weave all these details into a sacrosanct day. Let alone the overwhelmingly sweet characteristic all Asians display—that of humility.

For the most part, I find they are reticent to offer up information unless specifically asked. Out of respect they usually try not to overstep their position. This means it takes developing relationships over time, having numerous conversations with locals, and doing your own research in order to fully grasp how some holidays play out on foreign land.

Now, as this relates back to Nyepi Day, I had no clue as to all of the restrictions and how they affected my next twenty-four hours until the night before. Which not only precluded me from both fully understanding and preparing, but also left me stuck with decisions previously made that were now unalterable.

What made it more exasperating is like every holiday in every country, a lot of businesses started closing down at noon the day before. I didn't even know I would need to go shopping until 5:30 p.m.

Who, when staying in a guesthouse or hostel, would think that the entire staff of the establishment would literally not show up for a day. I am not kidding. "Here you go, sir, customer staying in our place, the keys are over there. We will see you in a day or so."

I made the excellent decision to move the day before from a four-star resort to a smaller guesthouse. *Excellent* being a gross exaggeration of a very bad move!

I should have known when, upon checking into the much cheaper guesthouse, the young Indonesian lad at the desk said, "You want to stay here? Tomorrow? You sure? You know it is Nyepi, right?"

"Well, I think so. Why wouldn't I?"

"Day of rest tomorrow! No business open. Everyone sleep all day."

"Okay. I guess I have no choice."

And I paid for my room. It was about 2 p.m.

An hour later I was chatting with a lady who also was staying at the guesthouse. She asked, "Do you have some books ready for tomorrow?"

"Well, I have one I am about to finish. But I figure I can just hang at the beach, do some yoga, read a bit, and relax."

"Hmmmm, I don't suppose anyone has told you we can't leave the property tomorrow?"

"Huh? You are kidding, right? I thought it was just all businesses closed and basically relax day."

"Nope, nobody is supposed to walk the streets unless it's an emergency."

"Wow! Glad you told me. Guess I need to make sure I have entertaining stuff to do tomorrow."

Oops! Did I mention I had just checked out of a four-star hotel that had three pools, two hot tubs, and was located directly on the beach?

An hour later, about 4:30 p.m. , I was eating a late lunch in the restaurant tied to the guesthouse. The lovely Indonesian woman who ran it asked, "Are you ready with food for tomorrow?"

"What do you mean? Won't the kitchen be open for the guests staying here?"

"No, I am afraid not. Everyone go home. Nobody work. Kitchen closed. No food or drink until next day."

"Sooooooo, I have to feed myself all day?"

"Yes!"

Crap. I had nothing in my room. No hotplate. No refrigerator. Double crap, my room at the four-star hotel had a fridge.

How am I going to feed myself? What kind of food do I need to buy and what can I get knowing I have nothing to cook with, let alone heat water on? After obtaining directions from the accommodating lady running the kitchen, off to the market I went.

It was now 6 p.m. I was in the market. All of us know what it's like to go to the grocery store on Christmas Eve, whether it is day or night. The whole scene is a mess. The store is flooded with people in a state of mind just shy of frenzy, trying to get "X" or "Y" because many of the stores will be closed tomorrow.

As opposed to the hoped-for ambiance of everyone being in good cheer due to the occasion, there exists a vibe closer to desperation because the clock, combined with our perception of how the holiday "must be," is whittling away at everyone's patience.

You know that feeling on that day right?

Walking into the store I was immediately confronted with the same scene, except times ten energy-wise! Amped up, hectic, helter-skelter, and bemusing are descriptions that come to mind.

The frenzy level was through the roof!

It was a funny environment because half the people in the store were locals who knew exactly what was going on, how to prepare, and what they needed to finish off the last details.

The other half were travelers and tourists manifesting varying degrees of bewilderment. Most of us still didn't understand exactly what would happen the next day, much less what to procure based on what our hostel/guesthouse rooms afforded in the way of cooking potential.

I was faced with the reality that all I could buy were fruit, veggies, bread, chips, water, and nuts. Everything else required refrigeration or cooking devices unavailable to me. Even the morning instant coffee would be hit or miss depending how hot the water from the bathroom sink could get.

It is what it is!

After about an hour navigating my way through the hurried crowds, conversations revolving around what exactly was going on the next day, foreign language product descriptions, and food selections, I was on my way back to the guesthouse. I felt like a squirrel in late fall, stocked up with nature's snack bounty.

Earlier in the day I met a young lady from Austria on the beach; her name was Katrina. We agreed to get together around 7:30 for the parade that night. I got back to my room, put a few beers under ice in the sink, showered, and was ready to head out the door.

As I was leaving I stopped quickly to greet another traveler who had checked in that day too. As we exchanged pleasantries and such, I said to her, "Well, at least we seem to have a few cool guests here. That way we can all sit out in the courtyard area tomorrow finding ways to pass the time."

She looked at me with a quizzical expression. "Didn't you know we can't leave our rooms the whole day? We are not allowed to leave our rooms until the next morning."

"Whaaaaaattt? No, I had not heard that yet. But it seems I keep getting another portion of the story as the day goes on. Ah, I love Asia."

This came to haunt us all in a very cruel way later in the story. Stay tuned.

The parade was called the Ngrupuk procession, equal parts fascinating, hilarious, bizarre, festive, unique, and unsettling.

Throughout the day we were able to catch glimpses of some of the float creations as the groups who built them carried them down the main street on the way to the parade starting point. It created a level of excitement in the town and gave us a glimpse of what was to come.

Nyepi opens the New Year of the Balinese lunar-solar Saka calendar, and it comes back every year on the day following the dark moon of the kedasa month. This year it fell on March 9th, which would open the year 1938 of the Saka era. This Saka era dates back to the conquest of Northern India by the Scythian king Kanishka, in 78 AD, and the calendar is still in use in some parts of India.

As near as I could finally ascertain, the holiday is about warding off demons, paying them proper respect for the influence they can wield in this life, then telling them to move on for another year—thus, leaving you and your family to live a life unaffected by the demons roaming the land looking to create havoc in people's lives.

The Ngrupuk procession consists of what I will call the demon walk. The locals spend a few weeks creating elaborate papier-mâché parade floats of scary creatures, some of them standing twenty to thirty feet tall, all erected on bamboo base structures requiring easily sixteen people to carry them.

And let me tell you, these demon creations are way, way out there. Freddy Kruger designed these floats on magic mushrooms! Because he hates kids it seems he wants to create even more nightmares than with just movies.

How do I describe them... Imagine the ugliest human-like characters you can conjure, then:
    A.   Have them be masculine in essence, because all demons seem to be men
    B.   Give them all gruesome faces with downright mean expressions
    C.   Give them really, really, really, long, creepy nails
    D.   Bestow upon them enormous, humongous, gigantic breasts
    E.   Supply them with a set of balls and a huge dong
    F.   Make them outrageously fat
    G.   Adorn them with oversized fangs and Dumbo-like ears
    H.   Design hands and feet triple regular size and astonishingly lifelike
    I.   Do everything possible to ensure every kid in town has multiple nightmares for the next month

Sounds fucked up, right?

And it is to a certain extent. Yet, they have such a playful attitude during the procession, it brings a levity to the event despite the macabre nature of the creations.

As Katrina stated, "I understand different places have different customs, idols, and gods. And it seems as if everyone here takes it all with a grain of salt. But the overt, grotesque depictions of body parts and genitalia certainly suggest an odd sexual undertone exists in this culture."

I had to agree. Therein lies the beauty of travel. You get to see a mind-altering visual spectacle of another society's culture, watch them interact during this sacred event, have your notions of what is normal or acceptable challenged, and you are left with a keen insight into how the people of the land think, behave, and celebrate.

The locals have a really good time with the whole thing, laughing, playing music, wearing costumes, lighting incense, eating snacks, and generally enjoying the festivities. They delight in the outlandish depravity depicted by the characters!

During the procession there is a point where the locals carrying the float have to walk in front of an area of stands filled with many of the town's residents. Then, choreographed with a live band, they must do an elaborate dance for the crowd.

The dance needs to relate to the demon represented on their float and quite often involved a fair number of intricate moves. Remember, there are sixteen guys underneath this float, which must weigh six hundred pounds, and they have to maneuver this twenty- to thirty-foot-tall structure sitting on their shoulders as they complete their demon dance sequence.

I swear they give it their best effort to make the dance routine special. At the end of the day, from where I sat, it was akin to watching a construction site with a lot of heavy-duty equipment being operated by blind people.

About 10 p.m. Katrina and I decided we had seen enough. Plus, as we understood it, we had to be home by midnight (later in the evening, as I was returning from walking her home, I found out the holiday did not truly start till sunrise). We both wanted to lounge under one of the pagodas on the beach and stargaze.

I can't stress this enough: Gazing up at the Southern Hemisphere while languidly lying on the shore of one of the many soul-enriching islands in Southeast Asia is one of my favorite things to do in life.

Which is what Katrina and I did. Because the entire country was already shutting off its lights, the skies were littered with stars—as if God threw bottles of sparkling silver glitter all over His favorite canvas, the vast universe.

While we sat there, sometimes chatting away and other times saying nothing at all, we became aware one of the floats was being carried toward the shore about a hundred feet away. As the men underneath made their way to the water, a group of people surrounded them, singing songs, drinking beers, and cajoling the float bearers onward.

Upon reaching the shore, they placed the float in the water, walking a few feet into the ocean so the back of the float was just barely on the edge of the waterline. They all started cheering when a man lit the float on fire.

Papier-mâché floats tend to burn rather furiously and with great flair. Or should I say great flare?

The entire float burst into a huge mountain of flames, and the locals went crazy with glee. We could see and hear bottles of beer clanging together, people laughing loudly, hugs being exchanged—the air was filled with revelry.

As the flames began to subside from their inferno nature, the locals pushed the float out to sea. It, to me, felt reminiscent of those old burial scenes in movies where they light the corpse on fire and push it out to sea on a raft. When you think about it, a fitting end for the demon in question.

My friend and I could not help but sit transfixed by the incident as it played out before our eyes. We both smiled, eyes lit with fascination and contentment, knowing we had been privileged to partake in such a grand cultural display that evening.

How can you ever forget such a crazy, surprising, authentic, random, and goofy event?

As mentioned previously, after walking my friend back to her guesthouse, I stopped at a bar on the way home, had a beer, found out another rule of protocol, and then went back to my room.

The one saving grace of my room was that it came with a balcony. I popped a beer open, sauntered outside, and was chilling out when the lady staying in the room next to me peeked her head around the divider and said hi.

Next thing I knew, I was having a two-hour discussion with her, mostly centered on consolation as she had essentially been swindled out of her retirement funds due to what I would call an ill-advised real estate purchase in Bali.

I am not going to get into it except to say I came across several people, male and female, who found themselves in the same predicament. They came to a foreign land, fell in love with it, saw their money could go a long way, and decided to purchase property.

Sounds great, right?

Unfortunately, most countries don't let you own land outright as a foreigner. Thus, as an ex-pat looking to buy, you often wind up entering partnerships with locals because they have the ability to purchase property.

And the ownership position always favors the local. For that matter, the contract usually does too. What do you think will be the outcome of a foreigner against a local in the court system of the country the land rests in?

Suffice it to say, the system and situation are very tricky, and way too often ex-pats learn difficult lessons about the dream of living in a faraway land. Be warned, friends, do your homework.

What made this particular person's story peculiar was her steadfast belief that the Department of Homeland Security was behind everything that happened to her. It was 3 a.m. I was pretty much on my way to drunk. I had a crestfallen woman sitting next to me, pouring out her story of anguish while refusing to accept she made some very *suspect* life decisions that had come back to haunt her.

Here is where it finally dawned on me how cruel the travel gods can be in an ironic way.

You see, the next morning there was to be a solar eclipse. Not just a little one, but a full-on eclipse that was to be spectacular! And guess what? According to all the websites on the Internet, the absolutely, positively, unequivocally best place to view this astonishing natural phenomenon was BALI...

It sank in that this brilliant occurrence would be unfolding in three hours, and while I could have a front row VIP seat on the beach, located a mere five hundred feet from my guesthouse, alas, I would get to see no such marvel.

Crap! Double crap! At my old four-star hotel, I could have stood outside my room and, due to the layout of the grounds, had a perfect view of the sunrise/eclipse. The angle available from my current balcony did not catch the sun until about 10 a.m.

Swallowing a tablespoon of chagrin served up by the travel gods, I decided to call it a night.

I awoke the next morning around nine and groggily walked out onto the porch for a stretch, surveying the atmosphere.

Immediately I noticed something was missing. Quickly I deduced it was the sound of the morning rustle. No matter where you are, each place has a cornucopia of sounds that come together to form the medley of the morning. The morning hustle and bustle of a new day's beginning.

There was no noise. There were no cars, buses, voices, machines, or humans causing any sounds to breach the silent divide.

Stillness permeated the air, a quiet so foreign it was temporarily disquieting. In a mental sense, that is. Yet, there was a serene ambiance.

Okay, I thought. *Well, gonna be a long day, pal. Do your best to go with the flow, rest, and accept the way it is.*

I am not sure I can adequately describe what that day and night were like. Strange. Frustrating. Restful. Mindful. Time bending.

There was another element imbuing the vibe of the day. Slumber! Heaviness weighed over your energy. The kind you could not fight off. I ended up taking two separate naps that day. I tried to do some yoga but could muster only a half-hearted effort. I tried to write some but my mind was hazy.

Talk about the power of connected conscious behavior!

By nine that night I was a little stir crazy. After two long naps, plenty of lying around with time for daydreams to freely roam, reading some books, and doing a little writing, I felt restless. When you are traveling, you are so used to being on the go that stopping completely feels limiting.

I began concocting a *Mission Impossible* plan to scale the wall around the guesthouse and explore the town. The only people on the streets were the cops walking up and down the main roads with flashlights.

How cool would it be to wander around when an entire town is shut down?

Alas, I realized it would not be the best of ideas.

So I sat on my balcony and looked up at the sky. The more I looked, the more I started to really tune in. The more I tuned in, the more I was captivated beyond belief.

Remember, the entire country has all the lights turned off, everywhere! All airports were shut down. There were zero planes in the skies for twenty-four hours. Can you imagine how vibrant the sky was that night? How bright, distinctive, and magnified everything was? The total darkness of the land allowed the brilliance of the universe to shine like I had never, ever witnessed before.

I swear to you. The sky was pulsing. A palpable and penetrating pulse! I could both see and feel the physical vibrations of time. I am not kidding. I was not hallucinating or imagining. The skies above literally had a pulse, much the same as a beating heart.

For the record, several other travelers I talked with over the days following Nyepi reached this same conclusion. All of us who tuned in were changed that night!

I wept! How could you not? I was shown something that before I could understand in theory, but not comprehend in reality. Now and forever, I do.

The Universe is a living organism. It has a heartbeat. It is very much alive in the sense of having a collective energy underlying all things!

My heart, your heart, every single heart beating on the planet has attachment to this collective energy, or heart.

When you think about it, it is the everyday noise of our hyper-busy world that distracts us from tuning in to this wonderful force. Noise, when raised to a certain level, functions solely as dissonance. Dissonance creates a diversion.

Noise is the best way to divert your attention away from that soft whisper in your ears, the one telling you the more you tune in, the more you will hear the melody of harmony.

How strong would the pulse be, how many people would start tuning in, if the whole world shut down for one day? I wonder if the reason we don't hear more from the Universe is because we are creating so much noise; whatever it's trying to tell us can't get through the dissonance.

How much more would we hear if we stopped creating so much dissonance?

I wonder if the same can be said in terms of us listening to our own hearts...

Nyepi was without a doubt the most unique holiday experience of my life. I am amazed at the breadth of randomness that transpired during those twenty-four hours. I could not have conjured such a day in my imagination on the best LSD. This was one of those *life is outrageously more creative than art* situations I adored watching unfold. Salvador Dali would be proud of this day!

Honestly, I did not think it was possible for an entire country to shut down. For everyone to buy into the idea, do their best to uphold the rules, and thereby allow a day to exist with no effort whatsoever.

Yet, it is possible.

It really opened my eyes to how much the Universe has to say.

Can you imagine what secrets we could hear if the whole world shut down for a day?

We might actually hear each other's hearts for the first time.

What a crazy thought.

SOUL MATES CROSSING
OVER THE RAINBOW...

I lost one of the dearest, closest, and most treasured of friends while on this trip. A true blue—yes, they do exist—soul mate.

Absolutely crushed me when I heard the news. I cried, by myself, for hours.

She was one of the finest people I have ever known. I didn't have a big sister—I had Lee instead. And her friendship was such a blessing. A gift beyond measure!

I met Lee when I was 20 years old while waiting tables. She was in the midst of a divorce, about to become a single mother of two. She was about fifteen years older than me, yet we immediately hit it off.

As it turned out, she lived around the corner from my home. So after work we would go to her house, have a puff and a cocktail, and shoot the breeze. Seeing as how it was always after work, I would often end up staying over until two in the morning.

One night I came home and my Mom was rather upset upon learning I was spending time with this older woman. Mom's being Mom's, she was worried I might be getting myself ensnared by a 'cougar', as we call them.

The next day I shared this with Lee. She cackled and said, "Oh honey. Tell you what, come over, pick me up around three and we will go have a chat with her. I will get this straightened out in a jiffy." Thus I did.

We walk into my house, I make the introductions and there is some small talk. At which point Lee turns to me and says, "Go get lost for awhile. Isn't it about time you went for a run or something? Us Mom's are going to have a chat."

I left as ordered and kept myself busy for a couple of hours. Upon my return I find Lee and my Mom in the kitchen, glasses of wine in hand, standing over the stove cooking up dinner. They were laughing, sharing recipes and bonding.

My Mom turns to me and exclaims, "you can spend as much time with Lee as you want; she is good in my book." Lee gives me a sly grin and a wink, implying "Problem solved!"

I never asked nor received any info as to what they discussed. From then on it didn't matter if I stayed at Lee's till the next morning, she had my mother's implicit trust. That is how Lee handled stuff - head on.

I will miss her nimble and extremely well read mind. I will miss her out-of-this-world cooking. I will miss the way she looked at me with the most loving of eyes, always seeing me for who and what I was...

And loving me just the same!

I will miss her motherly nature, caring and compassionate demeanor, along with her immense ability to comfort everyone who spent time with her. I will miss her loyalty, through thick and thin. No matter what, I knew she always had my back. I will miss her wicked sense of humor, the way she could point out and analyze the truth, putting that certain Lee spin on life.

She was nobody's fool. Nor would she suffer them for very long. While astoundingly tolerant, you knew when she had enough. And you best listen up.

I will miss her wise, measured, and intelligent counsel.

Whenever I had an ethical problem, a moral dilemma that had me stuck, I would always, and I mean always, call Lee. Her moral compass proved a great and valued resource while navigating stormy seas.

Every time she provided solid advice, the kind that helped you clearly identify the options and relevant merits of each choice therein.

I will miss the way she loved and adored you, Andy, her husband. I can say for sure you made her last twenty-something years the best of her life. Whenever I was around you both, there was a special kind of love, the love that accepts and appreciates. A love without judgment—supporting, forgiving, and reinforcing!

I have told you both before, your marriage was one of the most enjoyable from afar relationships I had the privilege of not only watching up close, but also participating in.

There are good friends, better friends, and then the best of friends. Lee was all three rolled into one. She made me a better man, and more importantly, a better person. I thank God He ensured we met. For only He could be so kind!

I can't say good-bye because I don't believe in them. I always say, "See you on down the road." I said it to her the day I left on this trip. She was the last person I saw before I boarded the bus to the airport in the States.

Now, on those nights when I long to hear her voice, I will have to meet her in the stars. I know she will be there, as she always has been.

I will carry you in my heart forever, Lee Nancy Haley Rubens Turner.

You know what is the saving grace for me? The last words I said to her as we hugged and said good-bye at 5:15 in the morning were...

"I love you, Leepert. So very much!"

"Right back at you, honey," was her response.

Seriously, how many times can you say those are the very words you last uttered to someone before they went to the other side?

Soul mates never really leave you, do they?

Somehow, someway they are always there. Dead or alive, right by your side!

SOME STRUGGLES ARE UNIVERSAL....

When staying in Saigon, I was introduced to a man named Doc Doc by an ex-pat friend living there. Doc Doc was a young man in his mid-thirties, diminutive in stature, but very sweet and sharp as a tack!

Doc Doc ran a little enterprise out of a tiny metal cart, spanning about three feet in length and two feet in width, in the D-1 District right on the street, next to what amounted to an outdoor restaurant.

His business front was selling tobacco products. His real game was selling weed.

Yes, peeps, weed is everywhere in the world. And wherever there is weed, there is a guy facilitating distribution.

And guess what? Not all these people are bad.

Take Doc Doc. I visited with him three times over the course of my trip in Vietnam. Each time I stayed a little longer as my chats with Doc Doc, while very difficult and limiting, were always warmhearted and funny.

Life had developed in both of us a shrewd eye for the games we all must play to survive in this world—games that are a waste of time, rarely bring out the best in men, and keep the world from recognizing what really matters.

Doc Doc had quite the little capitalistic enterprise going. Whenever I sat with him there was a steady stream of customers stopping by to grab some pre-rolled joints or a couple of dime bags. His clientele was a mix of Vietnamese locals and foreigners from all over the world.

I would like to believe he enjoyed my company, as I don't think a lot of foreigners ever sat and chatted with him. Most folks conducted their business rather quickly and moved on, including the locals. It is the nature of the business, and we were, after all, still hanging out in a communist country.

On my second visit with Doc Doc, he invited me to sit down and have a beer with him. We sat on tiny plastic stools, drank a beer, smoked a joint, dealt with his customers, and amicably chatted the night away. Despite his limited and broken English, and my total lack of ability to speak Vietnamese, we were able to carry on fairly decent conversations. Sign language, charades, and facial expressions can go a long way when communicating with people who speak a different language. Along with a lot of patience!

It was during this time he shared with me his plight. He was the oldest son in the family. His father passed away when Doc Doc was a young teenager. He was left with the lead role in a family that included two younger siblings.

His mom was sick and essentially bedridden. She had been so for over ten years. He not only supported the whole family, but also provided for her medical expenses and was the essential caregiver to her. Simultaneously, he had been supporting and/or helping his younger siblings find their way in the world. One of them was in university, the other about to start in the fall.

It is important to understand in Asia many children live at home until their late twenties or early thirties. They spend much more time ensconced in the support network provided by family. So, you get the picture of what this young man was trying to deal with while surviving in a rapidly developing country.

He shared with me how despite all the pressure, he loved his mom and would do what was necessary for as long as it took. "That is what sons do!" he said. A sentiment that struck a deep chord with me!

How funny the many ways my mom's fingerprints are all over this trip, embroidering certain days with moments that remind me so much of the lesson, which was a big theme for her, that life is how you respond to struggle.

Doc Doc described how he had to drop out of school at the age of twelve and start working to put food on the table. How he had limited options because of his size and lack of education and/or connections. How he never had a father to teach him a skill or trade.

Here is an interesting fact. Vietnam's population has a unique demographic:

Fully 65 percent of the country is under the age of thirty-five; 86 percent of the population is under the age of fifty-four.

These are astonishing numbers in terms of much the country is filled with young people giving a go the best they can, without much counsel from elders as they weave through what we all know is an often precarious life.

Family structures are such that many young people have been forced to take on adult roles at very early ages. We are talking about a very young population, with many of the elder role models gone, striving with all their might to attain what we in the west take for granted.

This is all happening with nowhere near the education system in place necessary to give all these young people a fighting chance for decent lives, let alone success.

Thus, as with all societies in this stage of their evolution, people do what they have to in order to survive.

Doc Doc is no different.

I am constantly shown that no matter where we live, we all have the same stories, struggles, and hardships to overcome. The degrees of difficulty or circumstance may be different, but the essential reasons behind the choices people make are always the same no matter where they reside on this revolving merry-go-round we call Mother Earth.

It reminds me of a saying, "How smart you are often depends on where you are currently standing in the world."

What seems to be the smart and easy decision in one country can be infinitely more layered and complex in another. The choices we make are often forged from the circumstances we operate in and the relevant opportunities that are present rather than lofty idealism.

From one spot on the planet, you could say because Doc Doc is doing something illegal, selling a banned substance, he is making a bad choice.

From another spot you could say he is being entrepreneurial, capitalizing on a supply/demand marketplace and doing whatever is necessary to provide for his family.

From yet another spot you could decide weed is a plant; therefore, it is absurd it is illegal, and people should be allowed to do as they wish with their bodies. If he is profiting from it, good for him!

I can tell you from my spot on the planet, sitting right next to him with a beer and joint in hand, happy to share an experience with a man from another culture treating me kindly, I found him to be just another human being doing his best, with the most honest and sincere intentions.

In his mind Mom and siblings came first, and he was going to do whatever it took to ensure they were taken care of. Is it more honorable to take care of an ailing mother for a long period of time or less honorable to sell, well, grass?

After all, weed is indeed just grass.

Is it more ethical to help put your younger siblings through high school and college, thus ensuring they have better opportunities, or less appropriate to facilitate what until approximately fifty years ago was considered medicinal by most cultures for thousands of years? After all, organically grown medicine that heals ought to be considered a good thing, right?

As Doc Doc saw it, he was taking the hand dealt to him and playing it. I can relate to that. How about you?

Studies show most of us form an opinion within seven seconds of meeting a person.

SEVEN SECONDS!

Considering all the valuable time we waste daily doing completely fruitless tasks in an effort to distract ourselves from,
well, ourselves, I find it a shame we can't, at the very least,
give others the opportunity to unfold over a slightly longer
period.

Say, the length of time it takes to smoke a joint with some
diminutive man in a communist land.

Before you or I judge, we might consider giving that stranger
in front of us the benefit of the doubt.

As Doc Doc reminded me, the most pleasant surprises come
from the people you least expect. I found Doc Doc's story of
perseverance and dedication both endearing and admirable.

Nobility and honor come in different forms, take on a plethora
of manifestations that upon first glance could appear otherwise.

Like beauty, it's up to us to find out the heart that lay beneath
a person's choices.

THE SEARCH FOR ENLIGHTENMENT IN BALI...

Ubud, Bali.

I hate to say it, I really do, but I found this place inauthentic in so many ways! Somewhat pretentious!

The book and subsequent movie *Eat, Pray, Love* killed this place, which is a shame, because it is beautiful. The locals are wonderfully kind and superbly accommodating.

Luckily, I was able to see the other side almost every day, because of both my living accommodations and the fact I went out and found it. There is such rich, colorful landscape outside of the town.

We saw giant volcanoes with lovely lakes resting at their base, surrounded by small villages. We went whitewater rafting through the jungle, ensconced in a surreal mix of mountain walls, waterfalls, and rice paddies. We bathed ourselves in holy waters while performing sacred rites in an effort to both respect our hosts and experience the cultural heritage ourselves.

I woke up every day and practiced yoga by myself in front of a spectacular valley of rice paddies as the morning sun crested over the hill. It was replete with a gushing river down below, birds up above, and animals of all kinds offering their particular greetings to a new day—all of which played the song of serenity, the melody setting my movements and thoughts.

I had the pleasure of dining with the owner of the magnificent resort where we stayed. He is a master martial artist and has owned the land on which the resort was built for over thirty-five years. He built a place that is truly unique and exceptionally reverent of nature.

As a side note, one of the most interesting things I remember from our conversation was this:

I asked him, "How many times have you needed to call upon your training in real life, in terms of getting into or out of a fight?"

His answer: "Never!"

Sandy, Alex, and I had the pleasure of seeing my favorite Bali band together at a thriving nightclub. I even had a couple of fantastic massages. And again, overall, the people are especially nice.

So yes, there were parts of Ubud that I loved! Absolutely!

On the flipside, there is this whole bat-shit crazy search for enlightenment. It's so hypocritical, unaware, self-absorbed, fake, and ironic. And the symbol of it all, to me, is the scarf. The lightweight, multicolored Asian scarf that runs about five feet long and is usually about eighteen inches wide.

It seems to be the official announcement that person either A) is on a journey to the path of enlightenment or B) has achieved enlightenment. Here I am, world, protecting and preserving my throat chakra in case the Dalai Lama calls upon me for prayer hour.

Maybe it is akin to the well-known requirement of carrying and wearing a shell as you traverse the road to Santiago.

I am 100 percent being sarcastic.

The place is like a fashion show for overly appearance-conscious yoga enthusiasts, which, if that were what the admitted purpose of everyone there copped to, it would be called!

Everyone walks around resplendent in stylish, upscale, and effortless ensembles. It takes them more time to get ready for the yoga class, along with the post-yoga class "glow" look, than it does to actually take the yoga class.

Flowing shawls, cotton shawls, silk shawls, half-shoulder shawls, knit shawls—you get the point. Cotton vests, cotton pants, fifty bead necklaces and bracelets, brand-new yet purposefully worn-looking journal and pen in hand, off to the coffee shop looking fabulous I go to record my search for enlight-enment in my high-priced, yet stylish yoga clothes.

Instead of laying their souls bare, they are covering them with a much more lightweight and breathable version of, yet all the same defining, armor. Their search still has them focusing on outward appearances as opposed to turning their attention inward.

It's a thousand degrees out—what in the world does anyone need a six-foot-long scarf for? All it becomes is a hot, wet rag around your neck. Heck, wearing a shirt is a pain in the ass.

Here is the real reason it seems fake to me.

When you travel to foreign lands like Bali, especially from fully developed western countries, you can't help but notice how good you have it. How lucky you are. For simply being born where you were born, if anything.

Because many of these people are really poor! You realize poverty does indeed have various levels or degrees. You are shown what it means to work for "nothing" in comparison to the wages commonplace in your culture. These people take hours to do something for you and earn the equivalent of what you pay for a single piece of gum at home. They make in six months what you bring home for three days' work.

Most of them will never, ever leave Ubud. Let alone Bali.

Therefore, it seems more than evident that it is a requirement for travelers to give back. Especially when the predominant portion of people here are willing to work for your money, whatever way possible.

Yes, there are beggars. Not a lot considering the reality of the world they live in. Almost without exception, they are com-prised of old people, kids, handicapped folks, and mothers. That is about it. Every once in a while, I would have a drunk ask me for money, but it was rare. In the USA, I get hit up for money by drugged-out or drunken beggars multiple times a day, every day of the week.

This is where I get super annoyed at all the wannabe enlightenment seekers. Because, quite simply, they forget to take their yoga off the mat!

There is a well-respected healer here who has people from all over come to meet with him. With regards to women, every single one must take their shirt off. No matter what the condition or healing desired. The healer then feels each lady's breasts for a minute or two. After this he takes a stick and pokes it into certain areas of the body, pressing deep and with emphasis. After some painful moments for the female participant, he finishes by spitting on them.

Oh, and of course a blessing.

I mean, what the fuck? Are you serious?

I talked with three women who went to see this guy. Two of them joked he was feeling them up just to get his jollies. Enlightenment? I mean come on, I can go with a lot of stuff, but this guy's routine is ridiculous.

And yet that is how badly people need to look outside themselves for answers when all along each of us knows the path to our healing lies within.

But come on over and I would be glad to spit on you if that is what you need. I am that kind of friend.

***

One day I am walking down the street to find a place for lunch. It is in the middle of town, a ton of people walking around, cars, scooters, street vendors, and such all over the place.

Up ahead, on the left of the sidewalk, I see a young lady sitting on the pavement with a baby in her arms, and she is breastfeeding the child. As always, it is about 1,765 degrees out, the sun blazing down hard on the streets.

As I get closer I can see the emaciated frame on the mother; she is wafer thin. Literally, she has no breasts for the baby to draw milk from.

I reach into my pocket and give her the equivalent of about five bucks in U.S. dollars. Essentially, the price of a Starbucks! Not a big deal, but not cheap by Bali standards either.

This is the third or fourth time I have given away money like this to a mother here. I am no saint; let's make that clear. I am someone who believes in giving. Too many good things happen because of it.

I strongly feel it is an obligation to share some of your good fortune when visiting a country wherein their standard of living is significantly, no, outrageously, lower than your country's.

How can you not realize your good fortune by simply being born in a developed country and feel humbled in the face of such drastic differences in wealth?

How can these feelings then not beseech you to share some of your hard-earned money with the very people who are hosting you in their land?

Over and over again, I saw wealthy people stroll right by poor people without even blinking. After I gave the lady the money, I walked on about twenty-five paces. Then I stopped to turn around and watch what happened as others walked across her path.

One by one, I saw these fabulously and fashionably garbed yogis saunter on by, almost all of them with shopping bags in hand carrying more new outfits, without so much as smiling at the woman. Not one out of fifty.

Worse, not one single yogi gave her a dime! Every yogi who came to Ubud was more focused on the next Ecstatic Dance party at The 'Famous Yoga Place' than they were on the real path to a happier life.

People, if you really and truly wanted to find enlightenment, to see a reflection of your better self, the one you so desperately seemed to be looking for, you just walked right on by your chance.

It is in giving you receive the gift of enlightenment. You see a reflection of your compassion, your empathy, your kindness, and your love.

You are afforded the chance to be the very best humanity has to offer, and in doing so, you understand the concept of and walk in the light of nobility.

No article of clothing will make you feel as good as you do when you hand over five bucks to someone who needs that money way more than you need another silk scarf.

Just seeing the smile that materializes on their face will provide hours of energy to your day! And as sure as I am standing here, I can guarantee you will be blessed sometime very soon after giving that five-dollar coffee away. It always happens.

Enlightenment isn't in Warrior Two pose, it isn't in any healer you dig up, it isn't in your cotton shawl—it is in your heart. It illuminates the most important things, feels most alive when activated by a simple act of love.

Maybe I am being unfair. Maybe I am judging too harshly here. Maybe you are right, I don't know all the people who walked by the mother with child along with all the reasons no one gave her any money. Maybe the next thirty people did give her money.

I don't know, I saw this happen over and over for ten days while there. A big disconnect between the type of people visitors said they wanted to be when coming to Ubud and the type of people they actually tried to be while there.

The expression "Some people can't see the forest but for the trees" kept coming to mind.

In the end, I guess what I am getting at is we all need to do the best we can to remember illumination usually comes on the path to enlightenment, not necessarily at the end of the journey.

Just as we need to stop and smell some roses along the way, we need to sow a few seeds too. You can't bloom like a lotus without stepping in the muck.

If you come to Ubud in the search for your best self, do me a favor—show it! Instead of looking for that "*Eat, Pray, Love*" moment; create a moment that connects you in a visceral way to the ties that bind us all, the human experience.

Give a piece of yourself to someone who needs a little help. Watch as enlightenment's cool and refreshing energy washes over you even in the midst of stifling heat.

Give and you will receive exactly what you are looking for. It is the only real outcome of karma.

Forego buying the new one-third linen, one-third cotton, and one-third blessed by whoever shawl.

You may find wearing your heart on your sleeve is much more comfortable and enlightening than throwing that silk scarf around your throat chakra.

I can assure you it will get you closer to enlightenment than you were two seconds before...

FOUR STUNNING MINUTES...

As per usual during our stay on Koh Chang Island, for that matter in all of Thailand, the roosters awaken Mark and me.

God bless life in the country, even if it begins at 4:45 a.m. every day for the last twenty-plus days.

We are sharing a double bed in our little cabana on the beach. Finally, after staying in a run of places that make a barn look like four-star accommodations, we pony up some more cabbage and rent a sweet spot. Waves caress the shore nary twenty-five feet from our front porch.

Mark is on a budget. I have to, shall we say, twist his arm to increase his daily outlay in the name of a good night's sleep. Something I have not had since our arrival in my "most favorite" of lands.

I can honestly say I never slept more than maybe four hours a night for the first month I was on this trip. My energy level was off the charts. Combine this with the aforementioned roosters, throw in scooters that blaze around the country at all hours of the night/early morning, and deep REM is as elusive as the dreams of my youth.

Like hope—out there somewhere, tangible yet fleeting, part myth, mostly yearning.

No matter what I try, I cannot find that splendid slumber wherein restoration recuses itself for a respite!

On top of this fact, I have come down with the Asian forty-eight-hour flu/stomach virus/dizzy/fever ailment in full swing. Basically, the eventual immunity system assault that happens to everyone within the first six weeks of visiting such exotic places—happens every time I come over to Southeast Asia.

And, I had to go through a three-hour underwater swim test yesterday, part of my endeavor to get certified again as a scuba diver. I almost drowned in a fricking pool, which, if you know me, is like a fish forgetting how to swim.

But, at the end of the day, who cares! I am in Thailand, sleeping on a beach.

As we slowly dust off the morning dew, Mark realizes I am in bed next to him. With a quizzical look on his face, he asks, "How did it go?"

I look at him and grin. "Well, I gave her the best four minutes I had in me."

He immediately laughs out loud to the point it makes him cough for a few seconds.

When he regains his breath, he retorts, "Well, since all men lie about their sexual escapades, usually overstating by about fifty percent, that means you actually lasted about two minutes, huh?"

Now it is my turn to have a hernia-inducing laugh.

"Hey, give a guy some credit. I had the guts to admit it certainly is less than what I would like to consider my capabilities as a lover to be. It *felllltttt* like four minutes."

We are both giggling at this point.

"Although, you may be right. After all, she did indeed, and I quote, say to me when we finished 'Is that it? Are you done?' Which made me feel particularly manly."

Mark starts laughing so hard he rolls off the bed onto the floor. I am on the bed hunched over because my stomach hurts from all the laughing.

Mark puts his hand on the bed, raises his head, and asks, "Wait a minute. You went back to her room, right? Why are you here?"

"Well, she kicked me out about ten minutes after we finished our fleeting moment, as much as it pains me to use that description."

Mark loses what is left of his cookies. He is in absolute hysterics. Tears are cascading down his cheeks.

"Dude, come on. You saw me yesterday. I was dying. My head was on the table the entire time as you and the gang talked and had fun. The pool test for scuba killed me. I took not one but two sleeping pills, smoked a huge J with you, and went to bed.

"She came to our door forty-five minutes later. I was totally passed out. I was drenched in sweat. She wanted me to go skinny-dipping with her. Asked me twice. We were making out on the porch, and my skin was dripping wet with perspiration.

"I told her we could go back to her cabana since it was her last night. By the time we got the lights off, it was kinda on; everything happened faster than I would have liked. It was great. She is sexy as hell.

"However, I had nothing left. Before I knew it I was done. I fell back in bed and she hit me with the 'Are you done?' question. I just started to laugh.

"'Honey, I am crushed. Look at me...' I said to her. I recited all the reasons I had very little to give that were just mentioned to you. I said I was sorry but wished this had happened a night or two sooner, when I was at full sail so to speak.

"So, I suggested we see how I felt in the morning, but meantime, since she had to get up early to leave, why not just pass out. I thought we were good to go with that, but no sooner had I started to slip away I hear her saying, 'Maybe you should go home now.'"

Mark loves every minute of this brutally honest retelling of this ego-damaging evening of mine. Can't say I blame him; it was pretty dang funny.

With a grin spanning ear to ear, he calmly says, "I think it is fair to say you were her bitch last night!"

"FUCKER...." I throw my pillow at him.

He continues through tearing eyes as he tries to stifle his uttermost inner glee, "Think about it. She came to your door for a late-night booty call, seduced you on our porch, dragged you to her cabana, bedded you, albeit not with results one might write 'Penthouse Letters' about, and then promptly kicked you out the door when it was all said and done."

"OMG, you are right! I feel so dirty."

We are both now just piling it on because it is more fun than admitting it's still only 5 a.m.

"On the bright side, you got some action on a random island in Thailand, and you don't ever have to let another man know what actually happened..." Long pause. "Especially seeing as how I will take care of that for you from now on."

"Rat bastard," I retort.

With a more serious tone he then asks me, "Wait a minute. What was it she said when she came to the door last night? Something about feeling stunning; what the heck was that all about?"

"It actually has to do with our very first conversation that I would like to think may redeem me as far as her long-term memory of our encounter and how it went overall. One can only hope something has her thinking fondly of me after last night."

"Well, I hope it was one hell of a conversation, buddy, 'cause in this particular activity, being the fastest is not considered the best."

He once again and for the fifteenth time busts out laughing!

"Rat bastard," I repeat.

MAKE THAT A REVOLUTIONARY FOUR MINUTES...

To be clear: I slept with one woman on this trip.

There was some, shall we say, couch hockey with a few other ladies. With them it was more good-natured fun than anything else. Some light kissing, a little touching and grabbing—people on holiday enjoying the moment!

And there was a negative experience with a lady I found fetching, but that is for another time.

Make no mistake, I met many talented, beautiful, intelligent, fun and warm ladies. Seriously, the world is filled with these wonderful women empowered like never before.

As I have mentioned, about 80 percent of them were under twenty-seven. And a large number had boyfriends either with them or at home. I found there are not a lot of single women travelers over the age of thirty-five, which is somewhat odd considering how many single women there are in that demographic.

Also, there was the whole language barrier thing in many places. To say the least, it makes connecting a challenge.

But I wasn't looking for a bunch of hook-ups this time around the world. I was really and truly hoping to meet someone special. If it wasn't The One, then if something did happen it needed to be with someone with whom a deeper connection had been established.

Deep, intimate connections are not easy to come by on the intimacy front when you only have twenty-four to thirty-six hours to spend with a person. You are staying in shared hostel rooms, you are sightseeing, and everyone is going to a different place the next day.

Not saying it hasn't happened previously, but at this point in my spiritual development, anything less is simply not worth the effort.

Sex without meaning is wholly unfulfilling! Believe it or not, some men truly do feel this way. I know—it is shocking to me too.

Therefore, it ended up being a sweet and refreshing blessing that I did meet such a woman and have the whole relationship flow in the way described above.

She is a very special lady who, no matter what happens in the future, will sweetly linger in my mind and heart when I look back on this trip. And yes, believe it or not, it is the very same girl from the previous story. The girl on the receiving end of the greatest four minutes of her life! (That is a joke by the way.)

Want to know how it all happened?

I was sitting at a table on the beach in Koh Chang. I had just woken up from a brief nap. It was time for Mark and I to have a few frozen rum concoctions, break out the backgammon set, blow each other a bunch of shiiite, and enjoy the always splendid setting sun as gentle waves swept over the shore.

Except at the moment, instead of Mark sitting next to me at the table, there was this beautiful German woman with tears streaming down her face. I had been talking to her for exactly ten minutes. And she was now crying.

Nice work, huh? Smooth operator I be...

Her name is Bebe.

As small droplets gently rolled down her cheeks, I noticed the afternoon sun was hitting her face with that certain golden hue which only comes this time of day. She had crystal blue eyes, a warm smile, and elegant features.

I thought, *Wow! Look at this gorgeous woman sitting in front of me, opening her heart because my story struck a deep personal chord within, and here she is sharing painful emotions— letting her love flow unfettered and unabashed.*

Without filtering my thoughts, as she paused to take a deep breath, I blurted out, "My God, you are absolutely stunning in this moment. Do you realize that?"

She reacted with a bit of shock. "What?"

"I realize my story elicited in you a deep reaction based on what transpired with your uncle, so please do not think I am finished talking about it with you. But right now, in this moment, considering we met ten minutes ago, seeing you just open up like this and looking at your beautiful face, tears streaming down your cheeks and the setting sun shining on your countenance with that certain light—well, I think you... Your whole spirit...is...stunning!"

She smiled at me, paused for a long time, looked down at the table, absorbing what I said and what just occurred, looked back up and said, "I haven't had someone call me stunning and beautiful in a very long time."

More tears softly cascaded from the Pacific Ocean that were her eyes.

"Well, you are—without a doubt. Due to my status as a man, I have the inherent authority to decree it so." I gave her a wink.

Her mood lightened a bit. We took a few sips of our drinks, listened to a song I played on my phone, and watched as the sun took its leisurely stroll to visit the other side of the planet.

After a while I said, "Tell me about your uncle."

The conversation flowed nicely from there until Mark came out and joined us.

For the rest of the evening, my new lady friend accompanied us for dinner and then drinks over at another guesthouse where we had already made some friends. A nice way to get to know each other, if you ask me!

The next day she was going scuba diving. Mark and I went snorkeling on some islands with our new "little sis," Stacie.

That night we all gathered again for dinner, drinks, and revelry.

During a break in the conversation, she turned to me and said, "You know, as I was diving today, I was thinking about what you said to me yesterday. It kept running through my mind all day. You made me really think about who I am."

"I hope my comments have stimulated good thoughts instead of bad."

"Well, both, I guess. But it has more to do with what is going on in my head than anything else. I am still working on it."

Throughout the evening there were times when we managed to slide back into a conversation about the topic. She asked me to define my version of *stunning*. We talked about the conversations we all have in our heads, and how sometimes we let those conversations lead to thought patterns that actually hurt us.

We weaved our own dialogue into the entire fabric of the group's conversations.

As the evening wore down, my lady friend and I sauntered back to the guesthouse along the shore. We were chatting away, gazing at the Southern Hemisphere skies, and dipping our toes in the water. Mostly being silly, carefree, and whimsical.

Later on, as we basked in this incredible setting, ocean waves lapping the shore, a gentle breeze caressing our skin, the sky strewn with stars—the most romantic of settings—I said the following out loud: "It would be nice to kiss a beautiful woman right now."

Crickets.

Nary a sound!

Not even a glance my way.

My words whisked away with the winds. I was the proverbial tree falling in the forest with nobody there to listen. Ground control to Major Tom?

Hmmmm... I thought. Wasn't the reaction I was hoping for. I can hear Harry Carey, my all-time favorite baseball announcer for my beloved Cubbies, now. "A swwwwwing and a MISS!"

The remaining time we spent on the shore was a combination of chitchat and simply soaking up the splendor. Not too long after we both decided to adjourn for the evening.

The next day my Asian flu symptoms started rearing their energy-draining heads. Despite this Bebe and I were able to hang out here and there.

Unfortunately, this happened to be her last day. We had dinner on the beach, hung out with our little sis, and talked away most of the night. That day I had gone through the pool test for my scuba certification. I spent most of the night with my head on the table, hanging on for as long as I could.

I am not going to lie, I thought, *Well, she doesn't seem to feel the way you do, and time is now nigh. May as well say goodbye and hit the sack.* I gave up, bid my adieus, and turned in for the night.

This is when I took the sleeping pills, smoked a joint, and passed out—determined to hunt sleep down like a leopard hunts a gazelle.

Forty-five minutes later, there was a knock at the door. The door opened slightly and Bebe said softly, "Stan?"

I groggily came to life. "Hey, what's up?"

She replied, "I am feeling stunning now!"

You know the rest.

What you don't know is what she shared with me later. You see, it had been awhile since someone had told her how precious, how unique, how special, and how gorgeous she was.

Often, when nobody around us takes the time to remind us, we can forget that each and every one of us is truly beautiful.

It had been so long since someone reminded her, she had for-gotten herself. She had lost sight of her own beauty.

Thus, she needed to spend the next few days rearranging her mind. Parsing through her own negative thoughts so she could start letting the warm light of positivity shine upon her again.

Unwittingly, my words sparked a revolution.

She had to overthrow herself.

To her credit, she immediately started to doing it once she recognized what had been going on for far too long. Also, to her credit again, she decided not to let our moment slip away.

I mean, how can one not feel empowered by seizing the day—and being promptly rewarded for doing so with an entirely for-gettable romantic interlude?

I kid. The outcome of that particular night was truly irrelevant in the grand scheme of who Bebe is to become.

Remember, revolutions don't happen overnight. Neither does change. It takes time for ideas to go from seed to root to blos-som. At the end of the day, one word symbolized the planting of the seed—stunning.

Bebe knocking on my door was more about her than me, or us. It represented the seed sprouting, breaking out of its shell. As much as she did want to be with me in a womanly sense, she wanted to take back the reins of her relationship with her own image, first and foremost.

Turns out, sometimes the funniest experiences can become the seed for something much more special. Especially if watered with kind words and nurtured by loving intentions.

I talked to her with kindness, pointing out only what I saw in her. Who I saw her to be. Then I sat with her and reinforced the message, watered the seed, until I felt the message had at least been absorbed.

Once the message was received, she did all the work. She is the one who rearranged her mental landscape. I was just the guy who took the time and showed the care and concern to sit down, remind someone how truly splendid they are, and then listen.

Luckily, my act of kindness ended up being a blessing in my life too.

I may not have touched her for long, but I like to think I both did it in the right places and in the right way.

The situation brings to mind two expressions:
1.) *"I've learned that people will forget what you said, people will forget what you did, but people will never forget how you made them feel."*   ~Maya Angelou

2.) *Words have power.*

I would like to think more than any of my words, more than any of my actions, Bebe will remember me for the way I made her feel. And that is something I can live with quite well.

That being said, it was my words that formed the basis for our relationship. Particularly one word—stunning!

One word. That's it.

One word. And someone was reborn.

Certainly, the effect that one word can have has a lot to do with the other person's past, with the way they view them-selves, with the internal dialogue they have going on—more often than not we have no idea whatsoever as to what is tran-spiring in their heads.

Yet one single solitary word can set them off in either a posi-tive or negative direction—completely unbeknownst to us.

Think about how many personal revolutions we could start if we all sat down across the table from another person, paused for a second to recognize how special they are, and then let them know it.

Would we not start the revolution to end all revolutions?

Could a few kind words from you change the world? How about just one someone's world?

A few kind words are free and have been known to produce the best return on investment known to man!

224 | STAN CROSSLAND II

UNFINISHED BUSINESS...

I was closing in on the end of my time in Paris. For whatever reason I had been unable to make up my mind as to whether I would go to Amsterdam or head straight to Ecuador for the last segment of my trip.

Due to other detours I had already made, time was now ticking. Basically, I had twenty-two days before my promised return date to retrieve my erstwhile companion, Mr. Miles, from the wonderful peeps taking care of him.

Spending quality time in Ecuador was of utmost importance, as I had been researching the country for years now, thinking it might be the place I wanted to move to next. I needed to know if this dream matched with reality. Would Ecuador still be my goal after this "walkabout," thus causing me to start earnestly planning the move, or would I need to shift my focus elsewhere?

But I was in Europe. Amsterdam was a three-and-a-half-hour train ride away. It was right there. How could I not go considering I might not be back for who knows how long? My dear friends and fantastic hosts, Alex and Carolyn, patiently debated the pros and cons with me over the course of the week.

I was flummoxed!

My decision-making ability was beginning to erode. The demands of travel, carrying around a viral infection through four countries, and the constant daily mental gymnastics your brain does was all taking a toll on my executive decision-making skills.

At ten on Wednesday night, as I was once again mired in the airfare matrix process, my phone lit up with a Facebook message.

I opened it up to see the following from Bebe: "Got a crazy idea. Shall we meet in Amsterdam for the weekend?"

By now, the revolution was in full force, a friendship had bloomed, and identities had been revealed.

Let me share with you how this unfolded through some of our conversations on FB. It is in the unfolding of relationships I find the most joy.

Stan: You are indeed a stunning, warm and fun lady. I wish for you the best. I mean that. Walk with your head high and keep sharing that lovely smile of yours. Safe travels....

Bebe: Hi, good to hear that you are feeling better. Yes, that was only a very short story, but a story. It was a pleasure meeting you. Everything happens for a reason.

Stan: Glad u made it home, lovely lady. Keep Koh Chang in your heart to warm u on the way to work.

Bebe: I will, Stan...and of course I keep you, too. You are a wonderful person, with always a warm smile in your face. Thank you for this lovely time.

My breakthrough was feeling stunning... Seeing my own beauty... You are deeply connected to that feeling.

It just happened... And it was wonderful.

So, I won't ever forget you. I wish you a most wonderful life with all the beauty it has to give. It seems unlikely that we ever meet again, but you never know ... And you never know when it is time for paying back.

Stan: It was indeed my humble pleasure to SEE U again. We are all so very beautiful, each in our own way. Sometimes life makes us forget that. I sincerely hope, from now on, you never do.

And for the record, u kicked me out of your bed. So I expect at least a dinner out on the town when I come to Germany.

Bebe: True, I did. ... I'm sure we could have done better at all.

And for the record, it was me calling you out of your bed ... And I'm glad I did.

Kissing you was just awesome, Stan... It still feels strange, like two parallel universes. I'm physically here, but my mind is in Thailand. Better, still connected to that incredible feeling of living the moment... without fear and worries... being free and being me... with the certain knowledge that everything happens for a reason.

I keep that feeling with me. Anywhere I go. And hopefully it implements my life day by day here in Germany.

Stan: Remember that night we saw the Milky Way, the Southern Cross, Orion's belt and such. I will never forget it. Have fun, lovely lady. Stay stunning

BTW, did you even hear me when I said I wanted to kiss you that night? That was the night you would have had me at full energy. Ha.

Bebe: I know, Stan. But unfortunately I did not trust the flow of life... did not trust this beautiful night... I did not feel stunning... I wish I had. There was all the magic the universe had to offer... And there was you.

To say it with your words... My demon tries to steal my beauty. My self-love!

Stan: Keep being the best you... And tell that demon to take a hike.

Bebe: I did that already—and told him to never come back. Wrong person.

How are you, Stan? Are you happy? Healthy? Lonely? Tired? Do you miss home or people? If you like, tell me.

Stan: Yes, for the most part I am happy. And yes, I get very lonely at times. So many beds sleeping by myself, so many experiences alone. It can be hard. But I came on this trip to find my inner joy, so I must find joy in the loneliness too.

Do I crave the companionship of a partner, someone to love and have love me back—unequivocally!

Do I yearn to be intimate with a woman again? Very much so! It's funny, I have had many female companions on this trip. But none have seen my uniqueness yet! Except, at least I hope you did.

So do I miss some friends? Of course! But most people, even friends, have busy lives and often our only connection is through Facebook.

FB isn't real friendship.

I give and wait. I know my time will come. I believe.

Meantime, I continue to work on myself.

How is all that for an answer?

Bebe: First of all, an honest one. Thank you.

Yes, everybody wants to love…. And being loved—being seen! That is the purpose of life. But first of all you have to love yourself with all your rough edges. I think this is what life is all about...

But when we do not see our own beauty, how can we see the beauty in others?

Stan, I could see your beauty...in the way you treated me.

You looked at me, you listened, you were friendly and funny, you smiled at me. You were present. And of course you were charming, you said nice things to me, but never forced me. You treated me respectfully and politely...

You took me as I am.

Thank you for that. All that turned my inner eyes to see my own beauty again... To feel stunning, let that feeling be part of my personality!

All this happened because I met you. And I could not tell you this if I had not seen and felt your beauty. You are a beautiful and warmhearted man, Stan!

You give more than you get back... at the moment. But what goes around comes around.

You are a lovely and amazing person I was lucky to meet. I hope I could express everything with the right words. As it is not my mother tongue.

Stan: You did great. Thank you for all the kind words. It means a lot.

As I said within the first five minutes of meeting you, you are indeed stunning. You know what I loved? When you started to cry as I described the situation with my mother and how it made you think of your uncle. You just let your heart speak for you through your tears. It was beautiful.

Later on after a minor injury in Bebe's life:

Stan: Stay patient and work on other areas of the body for the time being. You happy otherwise?

Bebe: I try so... Good you remind me. I should feel happy more often because I have many reasons to feel so. I am nearly healthy, I have all material things I wish, friends, a good job. I think sometimes I forget how lucky I am.

But I think sometimes I miss a partner, a proper relationship so I can share all that.

And you, Stan? Are you happy? I wish for that...

Stan: I know EXACTLY how you feel, sweet lady. It is tough, you get to a certain point in your life and the game of dating is, well, somewhat a bore and tiresome.

You just want to be with THAT person. The person who sees and recognizes the beauty within and accepts the, shall I say, weaknesses too.

Bebe: Quite so!

***

Thus, you can understand why it took all of two minutes to decide Amsterdam was now firmly in the "Whiskey a-go-go" phase.

We met in Amsterdam on Thursday afternoon. We enjoyed an amazing weekend sightseeing, bike riding, chilling at cafes, and so much more.

Amsterdam is a brilliant city! Hands down one of the best people-watching cities in the world. Why? 'Cause everyone is active and outdoors. Everyone is riding bikes.

No other city I know of gives you such an opportunity to see all its inhabitants. A constant, yet ever-changing kaleidoscope of humanity on display for your viewing pleasure!

I think it best to let your imagination take over in regards to what might have transpired over the course of the weekend when consenting adults meet in an exciting foreign city, grab a hotel, and let loose.

You aren't interested in the details anyway, right?

However, considering all that is at stake with regards to both my ego and reputation, and knowing everyone at this point has to be curious as to whether or not I redeemed myself, the following are a couple of tidbits on the subject.

The first day we arrived we went out and had a blast. So much so we were back at the hotel by 8:30p.m., with daylight still shining, both feeling quite happy.

And we both had one purpose: "Let's Get It On" as Marvin Gay would say!

When the spirited, high-octane affair ended MUCH LATER, we were lying in bed, and Bebe turned to me and with a sly grin said in her thick German accent, "Well, that was a little longer, no?"

At which point we both broke out in hysterics. Gotta love a girl with a sense of humor.

As you can imagine, when you have a hotel room for a weekend, such activities may happen more than once.

Upon finishing up our second such occurrence, which, while maybe not making time stand still, did make the concept of time irrelevant, Bebe again turned to look at me and uttered, "Well, that was fine, yes?"

Her eyes got wide as she broke into a smile.

"No doubt we are improving," I retorted. "It's all about practice."

On our last day we sat and ate some breakfast before Bebe had to leave. As we reviewed the weekend, Bebe looked at me and stated, "Well, I think we know what the title of this chapter should be for your book."

"What's that?"

Delivered with a mischievous grin she says, "Unfinished business!"

I had to spit my sip of coffee back into the cup for fear of choking from laughter.

We paid for the meal, walked outside, hugged, and then shared a tender kiss.

"I don't believe in saying good-bye," I told her. "Rather, I like to say see you on down the road, my sweet lady..."

"Good bye Stan. Thank you for everything. Stay stunning!"

And with that she turned to walk down the stairs for the train.

The following are our FB messages after the weekend:

Bebe: Thank you for enjoying Amsterdam together... In many ways...

Stan: Glad you made it home safe. Thanks to you too for a really fun weekend. I had a great time with you. Thanks so much for joining me, sweet lady. "Unfinished business" is the best type of business, no? You are such a lovely person. I am very thankful and happy we got to spend time together.

Bebe: Yes, that was a real fun weekend. Very spontaneous! Expect the unexpected. Thank you right back for your company and easy being. That was meant to happen. Enjoy Ecuador. Much love.

***

I have learned to never say never! You just don't know what life will drop in your lap. Too many times I have had to go back on such a declaration.

Both of us, I think, realize our future is not together. Did we ever discuss this? Nope. I think we both just knew.

Guess what? That is fine. I can assure you neither of us will ever forgot the other for as long as we live. Which, when you think about it, confers upon us somewhat of a relationship.

We shared identities. We shared magical moments. We shared our loneliness.

We shared hope. We shared laughter. We shared our frustrations with society and our lives.

We shared frozen coconut drinks, massages on the beach, dancing in the sand, and the Southern Cross. We shared days in Amsterdam—riding bikes around the city, watching people and boats go by as we sat at cafes, giggling uncontrollably after getting baked and generally being goofballs.

We shared the exuberant joy of forgetting, just for a few days, the rest of the world existed.

We saw each other as what we are: stunning and beautiful.

Nothing more, nothing less! We let each other be real, open, and honest. The best way to describe the arc of our relationship is lovely!

Both of us gave the other what we had at the time, and we got what we needed at that time in our lives. It was an unexpected, hilarious, heartfelt, sincere, and rejuvenating connection.

Travelers live out of a backpack. Your whole life stored in one bag as you frolic around the world. Possessions are few and far between, thus you learn to carry little concern for things.

Travelers simultaneously live to fill another virtual backpack along the way. It is the bag that holds all your memories from the journey.

If you are lucky, you come home with a backpack practically empty, meaning you learned to let go of stuff, while your virtual backpack is overflowing with stories, sights, and friends.

Once the current trip is over, this is the backpack you will travel with for the rest for your life.

I am pretty sure Bebe and I will be happy to carry this story around for the rest of our lives, always with a smile on our faces for revolutions, star-filled skies, and second-chance lovers.

Sometimes travel is risky business, other times it can become business as usual, in this instance, unfinished business turned out to be good business for all interested parties...

Who knew revolutionary words could reap so many rewards?

THE QUEST FOR ARTISTIC PERFECTION...

I had the pleasure of meeting a local artist on Gili Air Island. He made jewelry by hand from coconuts, painstakingly etching the design first, then carving the rest with a knife. After the piece was finished in terms of layout and carved design, he completed the job by sanding each creation until it had a smooth surface.

Each piece was at maximum three inches by four inches. His work was very precise; therefore, it required a lot of focus and concentration. He labored over each piece with a steady dedication for the endeavor at hand.

Usually, each work of art took anywhere from five to eight hours to make, evidently requiring a fair amount of patience.

I asked him one night as we sat, sharing some rum and chatting the night away, "How do you keep calm throughout the process, not tire with respect to the amount of detail each piece requires?"

He answered, "You must accept the flow of time. You must find the rhythm of time each carving insists upon. Forgive each work for what it wants from you. In order to tap into the creative spirit, you must forget the concept of time versus effort; just observe the process as opposed to having an agenda. Finally, you surrender to the evolution of your inspiration. Before you know it the piece comes to completion.

"You see, my father taught me the most important philosophy: accept, forgive, feel it, observe, surrender, and then love. That is the key to life."

I thought, *That is terrific!* I said to him, "Can you expand on that philosophy a bit in terms of how you fit into your overall life?"

"Yes, yes. I would be happy to," he replied. "What can you control? Nothing really. Only your choices! Only the way you react. The mind is a tool that needs to be sharpened, tamed, and directed. The first skill is to learn how to accept. Accept what is in front of you. Not necessarily agree with it, but simply recognize it exists—whatever it is."

He continued, "If you first accept it, acknowledge its existence; then you can begin to deal with it.

"Next, forgive it. For being there! Forgive life for what it is asking of you. Forgive yourself if you don't know how to deal with it. If it is something you don't want, forgive the universe for giving it to you. Forgiveness leads to equanimity.

"Once you have equanimity, you can then begin to simply feel it. Experience the feelings that revolve around it. Absorb the truths it is presenting. Feel how your body, heart, and mind are reacting to it. Feel your heart beat in that moment, your gut, your muscles, and your blood flow. Equanimity allows you to feel without attachment."

He asked me, "Okay, are we good so far? Do you understand what I am saying to you?"

"Yeah, I am with you. Please, keep going."

"Now, you are ready to observe. Observe your initial reactions to it. Observe your physical and mental symptoms. What are they telling you? What does your gut's reaction mean? Is your heart sad, happy, or indifferent to it? Do your muscles constrict or release? Is your stomach upset? Does it bring back memories of another time, place, or moment? Why did it trigger that memory?

"If we have accepted it, forgiven it, and felt it—now we have it identified. Observation, with equanimity, affords you the opportunity to clearly see what it is, for what it is.

"Observation gives you perspective. Perspective opens up the ability to rise above it. To see it from afar, from a distance, with a detached demeanor! Detachment severs your need for a particular outcome.

"Most importantly, you then must surrender to it. Surrender to the situation, person, or task. Surrender to the moment.

Surrender to the effort that will be required, surrender to the time commitment, and surrender to the energy you must put forth.

"Surrender to the finish, the outcome, irrelevant of its form, before you start! When we surrender, we are no longer in opposition to what it is we face. We are in communion with it. We are no longer at odds with it. We are immersed in it, infused with it, and aligned with it. Through surrender we cross the bridge of understanding. We end up on the shores of service to it. And in service we then find meaning, purpose, and passion.

"So you see, once we agree to be of service to it, we are then free to do what is necessary. We are agreeable to see it through to the end, irrelevant of the result. Through service we can wholly, completely turn ourselves over to it without fear, without regret, and without animosity. We can fall in love with it.

"Once you truly love something, you always have enough time, patience, and understanding to do whatever is required. Love has always and will always give you enough to do what needs to be done.

"My work is my love, so I can do whatever my lover asks of me, for that is what lovers do—give freely, without attachment, without the need for a particular ending, without wanting anything in return.

"When love is the power you use to move forward, you care not of power in any other form. It is the power of love that guides each work of art to its eventual finish.

"Any manifestation of love is already perfect by its very nature. I never have to worry about how my creations will end, as I already know they are perfect before I begin."

And there, folks, is the process of art and life in a nutshell, delivered by some random artist on some random island making random art out of coconut shells while we sat there drinking rum—leaving me in sincere appreciation of the simplicity in his explanation.

Here is the kicker, and I swear on my mom's grave it is true.

His name is Zen.

Go figure...

(I have taken the liberty of expounding on and modifying some of his explanation. The conversation took some time due to his broken English, and his words were, shall we say, simpler in description. Nonetheless, his earnest desire to share his philosophy was very endearing. And the essential truths therein still remain the same.)

THE THIEF IN THE NIGHT...

Who is this thief you speak of

Who is stealing your dreams?

Who is stealing your peace?

Who is stealing your serenity?

Who is stealing your love?

Who is stealing your kindness?

Who is stealing your will?

And, most importantly, why are you letting him?

After all, thieves can only steal things.

So the question still remains: who is stealing from you?

It is your dream to live, no?

It is your peace to spread, yes?

It is your serenity to hold, no?

It is your love to share, yes?

It is your kindness to give, no?

It is your will to forge, yes?

And, most importantly, why are you allowing this to happen?

After all, a thief can't steal you.

So the question becomes: why are you stealing from you?

What is happening to your dream?

Where did your peace go?

Why has serenity forsaken you?

When did love walk out the door?

How did kindness get misplaced?

Who let will be overtaken?

And, most importantly, isn't it time to gather them all back?

After all, they really weren't taken, were they?

So the question begs: when will you reclaim them?

Your dream starts anew today!

Your peace returns now!

Your serenity unfolds in this moment!

Your love manifests this very second!

Your kindness is given all day!

Your will fortifies here, in the place where you stand!

And, most importantly, nobody takes them again.

After all, they are your blessings to give and receive, right?

So the answers to the questions are in you.

The thief can no longer steal the treasure

When you realize the treasure is YOU!

THE DYNAMIC DUO—SANDY AND ALEX...

These are my girls.

Two of the most brilliant, beautiful, compassionate, and loving friends a person could ask for.

They carried me through my mom's passing.

Ensconced me in their love, held me in their arms so tenderly, and sat with me in my grief.

I don't know why, to be honest. We had only just become friends a few months before.

But some kind of crazy kismet happened.

They saw my heart and I saw theirs, and that is all it took.

For whatever reason, they decided to love me.

And I loved them right back, wholeheartedly!

Fast-forward to today.

We spent two unforgettable weeks together in Bali.

We laughed, we explored, we sat in wonder, we shared stories—we came to see each other even more clearly.

And the vision I have of them is, well, stunning!

They shine like the Southern Cross in the night sky.

I cannot thank you both enough for embracing me, for holding my heart and cherishing my soul.

They have made me a better person and I am grateful for it.

I lost my mom and my big sister in the span of five months.

Two irreplaceable souls!

My heart was wounded.

But, as life would have it, I got two new ladies to help fill the void.

Serendipitous is an inadequate word; nonetheless it will suffice!

Thank you both for loving me in such a tender, caring, and sweet way.

For lifting me up, embracing my brand of beauty, and reminding me that just when you think nobody cares, some people do.

For showing me the joy of finding new friends never loses its luster.

Forever in my heart you will both reside; it's as much your home as it is mine!

THOUGHTS ON BREATH...

Whether you are talking about yoga or life, breath is everything.
How you breathe sets the tone for how you move, behave,
think, and feel.

It is with these thoughts in mind, I humbly offer the following;
whether you are walking down the street or flowing through
your practice on the mat:

Breathe in Expansion, Extension and Elongation
Breathe out Doubt, Disbelief and Disgust

Inhale Resourcefulness, Reinvigoration and Rejuvenation
Exhale Inadequacy, Inability and Isolation

Breathe in Stamina, Strength and Steadiness
Breathe out Fatigue, Fear and Futility

Inhale Engagement, Exaltation and Effervescence
Exhale Tightness, Timidity and Tumult

Breathe in Fortitude, Forbearance and Forgiveness
Breathe out Atrophy, Animosity and Anger

Inhale Resiliency, Regeneration and Reincarnation
Exhale Surrender, Stubbornness and Solemnity

Breathe in Care, Compassion and Courtesy
Breathe out Intolerance, Indifference and Impropriety

Inhale Blessings, Benevolence and Beauty
Exhale Resentment, Regret and Remorse

Breathe in Healing, Harmony and Health
Breathe out Illness, Ineptitude and Incongruences

Inhale Relaxation, Reciprocity and Release
Exhale Blame, Bias and Bitterness

Breathe in Life, Love and Liberty
Breathe out Shame, Sorrow and Stagnation

Inhale Majesty, Magnificence and Marvel
Exhale Disdain, Delusion and Disappointment

Breathe in the Fullness that Embraces your Divinity
Breathe out the Emptiness that Occupies the Void

Inhale the Grace and Generosity of Life
Exhale the Unwanted and Unnecessary

Let Fresh, Cleansing and Purifying Air Fill your Soul and Spirit

HER SPIRIT NOT ONLY SOARS, IT FLOATS TOO....

I am sitting on a bench in Amsterdam, way outside of town on the east side. Out by the larger dock areas where some of the bigger barges, loaded with freight, and sailboats come through the canals.

It is a spectacular spring day in May. The sun is shining, it is a pleasant sixty-five degrees, and people are everywhere. I am on my bike, exploring a new part of the city. Sightseeing, taking pictures here and there, stopping for lunch at an outdoor café—life is good!

Even though I am still only at about 80 percent in terms of my health, I am happy to see improvement each day.

My last day in the city as a matter of fact!

So I decide to purchase a joint.

I ride around for about an hour and end up resting on a bench that overlooks a channel.

I spark up the joint. Life is better!

About halfway through the joint, I start thinking about my dear friend Lee. She is the one I wrote about earlier that went to the amusement park in the sky. I had a few nicknames for her that accrued over the years, of which the most frequently used was "Sleepert."

As I said, thoughts of Sleepert were permeating not only the smoke from the joint, but also the haze that was now my mind.

How much she thoroughly enjoyed living here for four years, how many stories she told me about her time with Andy here, how much she adored the culture and the people.

Without any real awareness I said the following out loud:

"Sleepert, I miss you so much. I finally got to experience the place you so adored. At least now I can talk with Andy about it and remind him of the good times. It certainly is fitting I am toking on a 'fat one' in Amsterdam, thinking fondly of you."

Tears of both remorse and joy start streaming down my face. I look out over the water and start to pan to my left. What do my eyes fix upon but a little sailboat quietly making its way up the channel. There were four people sitting on the deck enjoying the ride.

The boat was about forty feet off the shore, and as it moved closer, I could read the name painted along the rear end.

SLEEPERT.

Impossible! I think. *I am just baked and reading it wrong.*

I scrunch my eyes shut, rub them with my hands, wipe away the tears, and try to assure myself that while I am indeed high, I am not in hallucination territory.

Again I open my eyes, sharpen my gaze, read the name on the side of the boat AND NOW the back of the boat.

SLEEPERT.

With some date annotated underneath.

I sit there. Dumbfounded... Awestruck... Astonished...

My heart heats up with a familiar warmth, the kind you feel when by a fire or in the company of a treasured friend.

I know then and there Lee is in the right place. She is okay. And she loves me as much as I love her.

What a GIFT.

I assure you, on my father's grave, this actually happened.

You tell me: What are the odds of a sailboat from another country being named the same nickname I have for my dear friend who happened to live in Amsterdam for a short period in her life, and said boat happens to sail by me at the one ten-minute juncture in my life wherein I am not only visiting Amsterdam, but sitting along this one channel, at this one moment in time, smoking a joint and thinking of my recently deceased friend with same name?

The more I know, the less I understand.

Frankly, my need to understand has diminished too. There is enough science and religion out there explaining and answering so many questions already.

At this point in my life, it's mysteries that get me excited!

THE STANDARDS...

If you are going to Europe at some point or another it only seems evident London, Paris and Amsterdam need to be on the agenda right?

I mean, that would be equivalent of introducing your son/daughter to the 100 greatest rock and roll songs of all time but neglecting to play "Stairway to Heaven" by Led Zeppelin, "Sympathy for the Devil" by the Rolling Stones and "Riders on the Storm" by the Doors.

What music aficionado would allow such a reckless omission?

There are classics, and then there are 'The Standards' by which all else must be compared.

Thus, despite having already visited one of the three many moons ago, I felt it imperative I finally be able to discuss the merits of each when amongst the worldly folks out there.

London was first on the list. As you would expect, London did not disappoint.

For my money, this is THE most cosmopolitan city in the world. London stands above all others, wearing chic, historical and charming as if they are old coats with worn out sleeves that still fit just right while looking damn good whether the occasion is a cocktail party, dinner with friends or a night out on the town.

Come on man, on every corner there is something to catch your eye. Character hangs out here more often than anywhere else because it's the old neighborhood to him; familiar, amicable and yet inspiring no matter how many times he goes home.

And you can always find a spot of tea or a pint depending your mood.

Some places copy others, consciously or unconsciously. Some places are up-and-comers, others staid and over the hill. London is both timeless and right on time, every time, in every era!

History languidly strolls the streets, shyly lurks in alleyways, stands stalwart in the middle of the road larger than life, and stealthily sneaks up on you when least expected. If you can't find beauty, awe and warmth here than you simply are not paying attention and/or trying whatsoever.

Basically, you are immune to beauty. Or when style and substance make an agreement this is where they support each other like 'brotha's'.

One historic building after another, one dazzling museum after the next, one cool and different neighborhood following the other, with an endless parade of peculiar, sometimes odd, yet uniquely endearing people!

The neighborhoods are of such variety from Sloan Square's high-end shopping, to the impressive Financial District, to Hyde Park mix of charm and regal, to the rough and tough brick row houses of Kensington and Chelsea each block has it's own story unfold if you take the time to go for a walk through it.

Foodies come here to drool in public while reading menu's posted in the window from the street. Or, they come just to get that traditional bangers and mash, always satisfying. If it is food from your native land you crave, it most assuredly can be found somewhere at any time of the day or night.

Architecturally, the mix of classic and modern in London is second to none. The buildings here don't simply stand on the streets as much as they command them. History is on every corner, whether it be in the form of exceptional brickwork or masonry, sculptures and statutes, gold and black trimmed neo-gothic street lamps, grand staircase entrances to homes, Victorian style homes lining the avenues, new structures with fantastic sight lines and engineering twists or even the simple street corner bar with requisite historic carved wooden sign.

My favorite place in all of London is Hyde Park. Much as Central Park is such a perfect representation and visual icon of all that is the Big Apple, in the same way so does Hyde Park gloriously display all that makes mesmerizing London unique and special.

It is enormous. I happened to arrive in London during a particularly beautiful spring week, the sun shining every single day I was there. Which meant Hyde Park was in full bloom, bursting with people soaking up much needed sunlight and warm weather. I walked this expansive park several times for hours, reveling in the diversity of terrain, activities, and tranquil nooks.

It is surrounded by such a diverse array of neighborhoods and filled with this eclectic mix of characters you can't help but be simultaneously inspired and spellbound. Add in the fact that London has the most international demographical make-up of any city I have visited and the resulting concoction is this amazing mix of personalities, cultures, trends and history leaving you wanting another pint.

A huge shout out to my friends Kevin and Ruvenna, teacher pals of mine from our days in Korea, who took an hour and a half train ride into the city to act as guides for an afternoon. We went to the Beefeator Gin Museum and Factory, toured Westminster Abbey, The Palace, Big Ben, hit Trafalgar Square and then sat down for some Shepard's pie. They even picked up the entire bill.

Good peeps are a treasure when you are traveling alone.

Along similar lines, so is a sweet stay at a four star hotel, which is what I treated myself to for three days while doing my best to recuperate. I walked into the room on a Friday night, threw my bag on the bed, went to the bathroom and immediately noticed a....

Giant BATHTUB! I have never been so happy in my entire life to see this oval shaped porcelain container of mirth.

It took .00000002456 seconds to decide my Friday night would not be spent exploring whatever juicy surprises London had to offer on this particular night; instead, I would lay ensconced in a bubbly pool of warm, soothing water until I had to call room service for help getting into bed!

One last note about London, I arrived having carried some type of viral infection in my chest that, despite my best efforts, I carried around three countries for about three weeks. I could not shake it and I was starting to lose energy. After a difficult day of searching for the facility that would see a foreigner and a not-so-bad hour waiting, I was able to see a doctor.

She examined my condition, promptly told me I would have been in the hospital in another two days had I not come in, then prescribed medication for my ailments. I thanked her profusely, walked out to the front desk and inquired, "What do I owe you?"

"Nothing sir. Your care is free as part of the N.H.S."

"Wait, what? Seriously, I don't mind paying. I don't live here. It is the least I can do."

"Not required here Mr. Crossland. We believe health care should be available to all. Have a nice stay in London."

"Well I will be damned!" Props to you London! I wish my own country would pull their heads out of their ass on this topic.

Next up, the city of amore, Paris.

***

Paris is like a cat. Regale, finicky, aloof, fetching, moody, pretty, slightly vain and glorious all at once, at all times.

If any of these comments don't sit well with you, well, so be it. I call it like I see it.

Thankfully, my buddy Alex, who I meet in Thailand, was gracious enough to invite me to stay at his flat with his long-time girlfriend, Caroline. What an absolute joy it was to be able to build a wonderful friendship with these "heart of gold" people. I slept on the floor in their one-bedroom apartment, a wood floor to be exact.

Could not have cared less. I adore visiting with my friends in their homes, such a joy to have those half hour conversations before they head off to work, even deeper ones over copious bottles of wine before/during/after dinner (it is Paris after all), have their counsel when it comes to making plans, and know you will come home to a friendly face with eager ears at the end of your day.

They looked out for me in every way possible with a loving touch.

Paris is two different cities in one. There is Paris during the day, then Paris at night.

Both present a totally separate vibe, behavioral pattern and look. As you would imagine, it is the nighttime side of this multi-layered lover that truly shows her magnificence.

Her ubiquitous street side cafes beckon you to sit and have an espresso or vino, depending the mojo you have flowing. Intimate and dimly lit settings seen thru tinted windows, with small tables covered in fabric table clothes, candles and wine bottles. All the tables are squeezed up against one another to maximize space and, I would hope, encourage interchange with the person your leg is rubbing up against out of necessity.

It's not easy to be charming and accessible, while pompous and pretentious at the same time, yet once again Paris obliges in only the way she can. Waiters, store clerk's, civil servants and residents are at once polite and patronizing, willing to please and off-putting. A conundrum.

Then again, if you had so many strangers walking around your city everyday, all day for the past 300 years you might be a little over it too.

Evidently, the city has many a gorgeous historic edifice. You want old school cathedrals, covered. You want pristine, stately palaces, check. You want massive spiked peaks reaching for the skies atop rectangular behemoths made in stone, done. You want imposing cultural institutes with massive columns supporting the entrances, her pleasure.

What makes Paris architecture so Paris is the ornate, detailed facade of the buildings on every street! As much as they are known for their fashion, it would then make sense they extend that same sensibility to how they decorate the erections that house them.

Artistic carvings etched in marble, granite and limestone. Welcoming balconies perched on the sides of carefully crafted multi-story domiciles that allow the owners to participate in the visual spectacle that is Paris from all places. Elaborate, arched entryways leading to giant, foreboding wood doors. The words "Liberate, Egalite and Fraternite" chiseled into both walls made of every substance and the collective minds of all who roam.

Strolling the streets along the rivers, appreciating the bridges spanning them with carved out arches for boats to sail under, "locks of love" on fences everywhere you look, lovers attached at the hip with arms intertwined and heads tilted to rest on each other; even when alone Paris acts through ambiance the role of the lover you wish was by your side.

Her artists, poets, musicians, booksellers and buskers add the true "love is the source of all inspiration" touch to this fair lady of a city.

My absolute favorite memory from Paris is when my friend Celine met me for dinner and thereafter we rented bikes for the rest of the evening. We started at 9p.m. and rode around the entire city until 1:30a.m. We saw everything possible.

They way they light the city at night is certainly something to behold; a magical sight to soak up while on wheels with a balmy breeze cooling the skin. God bless Celine, but she has only one gear, full speed ahead. It was quite the challenge keeping up with her considering her need for speed.

At one point I had to gently remind her I was a tourist and wouldn't mind a tad slower pace so I could take in the beauty with proper appreciation, snag pictures and have a more leisurely experience. Thankfully, she was kind enough to cool her jets just enough for me to accomplish all the above.

We ended up under the Eiffel Tower, as one should, right about the time the normally static lights lining the tower go off for five minutes on a dazzling display for the whole city to see. Such a cool visual display on such a worldwide iconic piece of construction!

Out of nowhere, as we were standing there taking pictures, another couple struck up a conversation with us. They were soon to be married, visiting Paris together for an art show she was the main exhibitor for. The gentleman was a Christian Pastor. Very nice, down-to-earth and easygoing people.

At one point the Pastor takes my hand, looks me in the eye and says, "Do you believe in God?"

I look him square back in the eye and say, "Unequivocally!"

"Good. I don't like to scare people if it is not their cup-of-tea, to use a local metaphor. The Spirit of the Lord tells me you are a good man. He is happy with you; proud of the way you are trying to live. He asked me to share that and tell you to keep up the good fight."

Celine was standing right next to me, stupefied. Can't begin to tell all of you, my readers, how much this comment from a total stranger meant to me. You can't buy that kind of reinforcement and you definitely can't conjure it up on your own.

Thanks Paris. It was real and now I can say with a wistful yearning and squinted eyes "Ahhhhh Pariii..." the next time someone inquires, "Have you been to Paris?"

Time to hit Amsterdam.

✳✳✳

Amsterdam is the enchanter of the three standards if you ask me.

It has the international residential flavor and historical 'oomph' of London, along with the 'articulate adornment of architecture' philosophy and aristocratic atmosphere Paris brings to the table. Just add quaint bridges stretched over tranquil canals everywhere, semi-legal weed, lots of beer, great food, all locals in the city on bikes and floating abodes on water to the mix for the most unique and 'Man, that goes down easy' city cocktails in Western Europe.

Small enough to feel comfy, large enough to allow plenty of wandering, with parks that are so inviting you have a hard time leaving them to go ride your bike some more — Amsterdam is just the right size.

You know that pair of jeans we all have that are perfectly worn in, fit great and still looks terrific when you wear them out on a Friday night?

That's Amsterdam.

Fits everybody perfect, with nonchalance and flair at the same time!

How can you not love a city where 90 percent of the inhabitants ride bikes everywhere, everyday? Morning, noon, night, and late night — this is how you get around. It is fantastic.

It gives the city a quiet hush. The bustle is still there, but without so much of the noise that accompanies bustle! Plus, and this is my absolute favorite factor about Amsterdam, because everyone is on bikes or on foot you get to people watch the entire town.

Park yourself down at a coffee shop or restaurant on a bridge and watch as this ever-changing, always intriguing world walks or rides on by.

Best people watching city I have been to thus far.

I rented a bike for seven days and rode it around for at least six hours every single day. A plethora to see, do and absorb. Soooo much fun. Especially during rush hour!

Yes, they do have rush hour. It's just with bikes instead. And they most definitely have rules of protocol. You better catch on quick or they will politely, but sternly let you know what's up.

Keep your head on a swivel cause bikes come at you from all directions, there are specific lanes to be in based on the speed you pedal, cars are still at play along with a lot of pedestrians, and you better know which way you are going cause they expect you to make decisions and move quick.

Study some history on the Dutch and you will find they have been travelers forever and a day. It is in their blood. The whole dang city is a port. Therefore it stands to reason they would be naturals at hosting travelers too. Exceptionally accommodating.

Food is plentiful and delicious, always served with a smile. Beer gardens abound and weed/coffee shops are sprinkled here and there. Whenever you bring legalized weed to the equation in any city it always has an indelible effect on the "check this character out" factor.

Even if you do not partake I strongly suggest hanging out in one of the shops for a couple hours. A whole different and pleasurable vibe exists when you walk through those smoke-filled yet welcoming doors.

I mentioned the parks above and think it worth a follow up. They have three main parks in the city and a smattering of smaller ones throughout. The main parks are quite expansive with canopy tree lined bikepaths/walkways, quaint gas lamps lining keeping them all well illuminated, weeping willows cascading over small ponds with fountains, terrific sculptures scattered everywhere, open fields for sports/relaxing on a blanket and the safest of ambiances.

Women walk these parks alone, late at night, with a comfort level not usually seen. To me this conveys volumes about the way they are as stewards of civility and decency.

Nobody does the shudder concept better than these peeps. You know, the kind you install on the windows of the outside of your home so that should inclement weather come through you can close them up to protect the windows from shattering due to flying debris.

This city has taken shudders to a higher form than simply function. They are as imperative to the artistic nuance and visual spectacle of Amsterdam as the canals. Vibrant colorful mosaics which convey an inherently whimsical yet avantgarde streak runs through the veins of her streets and people.

One other aspect of Amsterdam I find endearing is the variety and number of buskers, artists and musicians the city attracts. Talented, clever, witty and visually stimulating shows put on by people from all walks of life who love their craft; and what a splendid craft it is to perform and captivate a street audience form scratch.

Live art on the streets is such a welcome gift to these eyes, always reminds me the soul of the world is alive and vibrant.

I spent a significant portion of my time here alone. While I had several conversations with interesting people as I always do during my stay at a super cool hostel and enjoyed the company of my friend Bebe the first weekend, I was still nursing the remnants of the aforementioned viral infection. All told, it took six weeks to run its course through my body.

Thus, beyond the shear exhaustion of having traveled quite a bit of ground over the previous five months, the infection slowly drained whatever was left of my spirit. Amsterdam became the city of tranquility for me. I slept in the grass in parks, chilled at coffee shops, relaxed by numerous bridges, languidly ate meals while reading books and generally went inward with my thoughts.

Don't get me wrong - I had a remarkable experience! I adore this city. It was the perfect setting for me to recover and reboot for the last leg of my journey. Sometimes the infinite silence of people watching leaves a louder impression on your soul than 100 conversations.

Also, again I was lucky enough to have a friend, the beautiful and vibrant Karen C., take me out for a meal and some sightseeing. A friendly face warms the heart so very much when on the road to nowhere in particular.

If you really and truly want to watch a city unfold before your very eyes every day, and in doing so gain a comprehensive understanding of it's people and traditions, park your ass on a chair by a bridge over a canal for awhile, then take a bike ride around Amsterdam, and then park your ass again.

Rinse and repeat repeatedly throughout the day until you leave.

Amsterdam, like Paris, is charming company — quirky, kitschy and without guile. She is the eccentric and captivating girl you could never really get out of your mind, even when hanging out with the stunner.

She leaves that wistful, reoccurring thought "Wonder what would have happened if we…"

VALLEY OF VOLCANOES...

Speechless! That's right — No words... Describe this place? Ha!

Fat chance I could remotely approach the subject.

I am in Cotapaxi Valley, Ecuador. Surrounded by eight enormous volcanoes. All of them reach elevations over 10,000 feet.

Literally, they form a circle around the entire valley.

Breathtakingly gorgeous scenery!

From where we sit, in this giant hammock built for a dozen people, the volcanoes tower over the valley as if guardians of a sacred place.

Yep, a hammock built for twelve—good stuff. Surprisingly, despite the semi-dicey balancing act required, not too many get hurt entering and exiting. Yet, it does happen.

It's a complex equation of travel fatigue, weed intake, and alcohol absorption rates in high altitude. Motor coordination skills, much like inhibitions, tend to falter when such forces comingle.

How in the world does God come up with these places?

Prairie fields spread out before us as the sun rises, some of it utilized for farmland, other parts seemingly left for us to simply gaze upon with thanks, watching wild horses, goats and cows grazing until bellies are full.

Llamas roam the land. Who doesn't love llamas?

At night, while sitting close enough to the fire to stay warm, we gaze upon the Southern Hemisphere skies and view a kaleidoscope of constellations.

So many vivid stars in one sky, I get dizzy several times trying to focus on them all.

A sheer jaw-dropping, word-defying display of majesty!

Behind me sits Pasochoa, its peak topping off at 4,220 meters. We hiked it yesterday.

Brilliant!

When you get to the top, the cold and warm air meet, causing a dense fog to envelop the crater of the volcano. So, on one side you have a clear vista for miles. Turn around, and you can't see your outstretched hand in front of your face.

Nothing.

You know you are standing on the precipice of an abyss, but you can't tell how many feet away the ledge is.

To the left is Puntas, topping off at 4,452 meters.

Flowing clockwise, next up is Antisana, with an elevation of 5,758 meters.

Next comes Sincholagua, with a maximum height of 4,898 meters.

Then we get to Mama Bear, directly at high noon as clock position goes from where we sit, the astounding Mount Cotopaxi volcano. This beauty is actually two meters higher than Mt. Kilimanjaro. She stands an incredible 5,897 meters.

To her right sits Ruminahui, with a total elevation of 4,712 meters.

Then there sits S. Iliniza, with a peak reaching 5,248 meters.

Her sister N. Iliniza stands just a kilometer away, reaching to the skies some 5,128 meters.

Last, but certainly not least, is Corazon. She is directly to our right and asserts herself a healthy 4,788 meters into the sky.

Sitting for hours we watch as each volcano plays a game of visual hide and seek due to the ever-moving fog cover, sometimes offering only a glimpse of one corner, others a breathtaking full view of reflective snow covered caps, then slipping back into oblivion for another who knows how many minutes.

We are not just surrounded by these incredible displays of Mother Earth's indomitable will; we are ensconced in her illustriousness!

As the volcanoes stand watch over this gorgeous valley, they simultaneously impose their resolve upon our psyche and wrap us in a strange sense of safety. Which, let's be real, is tenuous at best. These are still considered active volcanoes.

Such is the nature of nature, no? This incredible ability to inspire wonder, veneration, gravitas, comfort, fear and worship at the same time!

I am staying at a very nutty hostel. They have built hobbit dwellings on the property. Humble round abodes carefully inserted into carved out crannies of earth, replete with round doors and grassy knolls over the roof. Eagerly I await Gandolf's arrival.

There are two large bunkhouses that host about 12-14 guests in each, built in that woodsy cabin style we all associate with mountain living. Wood beams, wood floors, wood bannisters and the musty scent of a wood-burning fireplace. Mix that scent in with the wet clothes being hung to dry by everyone and you have a yummy, pungent log humidor. All of which is ok because of the setting you are in.

The main building houses the kitchen, a big clay kiln, dining area, communal bathroom area and living room with large hearth. Done again in the whole log cabin hideaway look, this is where all the guests gather throughout the day.

Individual hammocks are there for the relaxing and when it gets chilly towards dusk, you can throw on one of the "come one, come all" poncho's to snuggle in while watching the sun slowly make it's way towards brightening another part of the world's day.

Wild flowers grow all over the hostel grounds, a rainbow of colors spread across the grass. Artsy plant displays are everywhere filling up old cowboy boots, pots, pans, wheel barrels and such.

Seriously, I am in a shire for crying out loud.

One of the best features of this little "Lord of the Rings" world is they have no internet access unless there is an emergency or you really, really need it. On top of that, you are in the middle of nowhere. You can't walk to a store. There are no restaurants nearby. No phones and no T.V.

This means you actually need to fill your time by either reading, writing, adventuring or talking. Sequestered with your bunk mates for two or three days, no electronic distractions, going on epic hikes around waterfalls, through streams and up the sides of mountains gives you ample time for getting to know your fellow wanderer.

These are the places that really afford you the chance to unplug. Disconnect. Take a break from all the noise. Allow you to reconnect with the rhythm of nature and the good nature in a fellow man. To see clearly how cool it is to sit in wonder, without a care at all. Free.

You can buy me a book with a hundred pictures in it. Heck, I took over a hundred while here. You can make me an HD IMAX movie of this magnificent volcanic valley. Geez, I already have six videos from a sweet recorder. Neither will ever, ever come close to sitting on this hammock, made for a dozen, looking out over this ridiculous spectacle with a cup of coffee in my hand.

An experience like this can't be properly recorded on any medium. It can only be adequately appreciated up close, in person.

Come on peeps, I beseech you, get up off the couch and get here. Do you want to see a movie about a valley of volcanoes with a shire or actually visit one?

A hammock built for twelve of your friends awaits, and so does a better, more enriched life...

FATHER TIME SENDS A MESSAGE...

Sometimes you have to realize how old you are.

Case in point:

While staying in the Valley of Volcanoes, I sign up for the horseback riding experience. As it is sold, we are going to ride horses all around the valley.

And this is exactly what we do.

Let me state that I have ridden a horse one and only one time before this day. It was one of those tours where all you do is trot behind a group of horses as the leader takes you sight-seeing.

It happened when I was twelve.

This is not such an experience. These horses are able to run free under our direction.

For the sake of brevity, I am going to skip a bunch of the story to get to the end.

I am assigned a horse that, for whatever reason, will not allow any other horses to be in the lead. Throughout the entire ride whenever another rider tries to take the lead, my horse immediately shifts into a higher gear. If further challenged, he then goes from a merry trot to a canter.

Three thoughts: 1) I have never been on a horse when it is in canter mode. 2) Horses are miniature locomotives. 3) Now I get horse riding!

Holy shiiiiittteee! Being on a horse moving that fast is soooo exhilarating. I mean, just a blast. It's enthralling! A one-of-a-kind, pulse-quickening, spine-tingling adrenaline rush!

Fucking Wow!

This is terrific! I am hauling ass on a horse through an out-standingly marvelous valley with rivers, open fields, and scin-tillating scenery, all of it unfolding before my eyes while I hang on for dear life.

Let's reiterate, I don't know how to ride a horse at canter. My left foot keeps popping out of the damn stirrup, which has me bouncing about on top of the saddle desperately trying to grab hold of the saddle handle in an effort to not become the next Christopher Reeve. This must have happened at least six times. It was a fine line between extreme elation and anxiety.

This brings me to the end of our "Stan is not, despite his best hopes, ever going to be a rhinestone cowboy" tale.

We are at the last stretch of field before the ending point. One of the guys on the ride with me had been laughing the whole time regarding my horse's penchant for being the lead dog, as it were.

He thought it would be funny to push my horse one last time. This despite my specifically having told him I had had enough and wanted to simply trot on in the rest of the day—my ass was killing me.

Instead of adhering to my request, he comes alongside my horse and yells, "Hiyyyyyyaaaaa..."

Immediately, my horse takes off. Within seconds we are at a canter. I am already legs akimbo, hanging on for dear life.

I try everything possible to control the horse. Just when I think there is a chance it might work, the guy next to me kicks in with another loud "Hiyaaaaa..."

Son...of...a...bitch...

My horse pops the clutch and hits another gear entirely. Sim-ply put, it takes off like a rocket. Within the blink of an eye, we are at FULL GALLOP!

I imagine at this point, from afar, I resemble the human ver-sion of that toy where a ball is attached to a paddle with a strand of rubber, the goal being to bounce the ball off the paddle repeatedly and as quickly as possible while never allowing the ball to miss the paddle when the string snaps it back.

Out-of-control cowboy on board a runaway horse I be.

At least 756 memories fly across the movie screen of my mind as I do my best to stay atop this freight train of a horse.

All of a sudden, to my horrifying chagrin, my saddle starts to slide to the right and down the horse's side. Literally, one moment I am riding vertically, the next I am riding horizontally. I am now riding the horse sideways, at a 90-degree angle—still attached to the stirrups.

This is not good comes the understatement of my lifetime galloping across the mental movie screen. Next thought is *This may not end well.*

We gallop onward, with Stan unintentionally practicing for the circus, for another 50 feet before...

I miraculously release my left foot from the stirrup and Boom!

My body crashes hard to the Ecuadorian terra firma. Low back, right side. Crushing blow.

I let out a scream.

The only problem is my right foot is still attached to the stirrup. Which means I am still attached to the saddle. Which means I am now being dragged through the valley by a horse with no name, not on a horse with no name, at a full gallop.

There ought to be a song....

Rather than describe the scene, I ask you to rent the movie *Seabiscuit* and watch the part where Toby Maguire's character gets dragged through the barnyard behind the horse while still attached. 'Cause that's exactly what is happening to me, down to the exact image running through my mind as it all transpires.

Stan is a human pinball attached to a horse ricocheting off the ground, bouncing against small rocks and boulders, crashing through sage bushes, careening off little dirt mounds and dragging every limb along for the ride.

"Hello prickly bush, nice to meet you..."

"Go pound sand up your ass" is now crystal clear as far as old time euphemisms go.

This goes on for about fifty feet before somehow, by the grace of God, my right foot wriggles free and I come to a screeching halt, encumbered in bushes and tumbleweed.

First thought, *If I am not dead, just kill me now 'cause I know this is going to hurt really bad in about ninety seconds!*

Second thought, *I am alive. Sweet Jesus, You are da bomb! Remind me to never ride a horse again.*

Third thought, *Do my legs still work?*

Fourth thought, *and I thought the Turkish massage was a bad idea...*

Suffice it to say; I felt the aftereffects for a month.

Despite the crash landing, the horse-riding adventure was unreal. Right up there in the top five things I have ever done. Riding a horse at full gallop is a heart-pumping rush. Doing it in the middle of this astoundingly grandiose valley was surely the icing on the cake.

Riding a horse sideways, while super cool, upon rewind of the tape, is not an experience I suggest for most. Neither is falling off a horse and/or being dragged by a horse.

You can thank me later for providing this valuable life lesson.

Which leads to...

God hammers home the first case in point:

I was certified to paraglide in Korea. Paraglide meaning the kind where you jump off the side of a mountain with a guidable parachute, then fly like a bird in the sky. Absolutely the coolest thing I have ever done. Ever!

Fast-forward ten years later. I am in Ecuador and dying to do it again.

Because it has been so long since I last flew, the owner of the adventure company wants me to go out with him for a test run on the side of a smaller mountain. Which is not a problem because I suffer from CRS, can't remember shiiiite. He wants to see if I can handle the parachute, work the various strings, adjust to the wind, and steer properly. I am interested in finding out myself.

We get out to the site. Incredible views of mountain peaks surround me on all sides. Fresh mountain air in the lungs is so invigorating. Except, it is extremely windy. We wait a bit for it to die down some.

Finally, he thinks the wind is manageable. I get my parachute up, turn around, start running downhill, and wooooooooosssh-hhhh—up I go into the air.

Understand, the purpose of the exercise is for me to stay close to the ground, land again, keep running downhill, take off for a few feet, land again, and repeat. All the while keeping my forward progress in somewhat of a straight line, showing I can work with the winds to control the chute.

Well, before I can process what is going on, a forceful breeze blows, and the parachute picks me up about twelve feet off the ground into the air. I immediately pull my arms down to try and control the chute.

The parachute reacts like clockwork to my command; except the wind is so strong it hurls me back to the ground.

Wham!

I smash to the earth right on the spot where my low back is already in serious pain from falling off the horse four days earlier.

I let out a loud groan. The strong winds keep hold of my chute and start pulling me uphill, backwards while on my back.

On a stone-filled rock quarry of a mountainside!

I am simultaneously trying to absorb the now searing pain shooting up my right side while doing my best to get the chute to drop to the ground.

No such luck.

As I bang off the terrain, already dragged for about fifty feet, I roll around to my front side thinking if I can get my feet under me I can stop the pillaring.

Nope.

Now I am being dragged face first, uphill at about fifteen miles an hour.

The parachute drags me for a total of 150 feet. I mean drags me kicking and screaming up the mountain, smashing into small stones and crevices in the terrain like a wrecking ball. I am turning every which way but loose, trying to get control of the chute.

Finally, the chute falls to the ground and I stop, ten feet short of the minivan that drove us up here.

My instructor comes running up to me. He excitedly asks, "*Estas bien*?" Or, "Are you okay?"

Dazed, confused, and feeling like a villain dragged through town behind a horse in an old western cowboy movie, I gather my scrambled brain and stand up.

He starts laughing.

It is maybe important to relate a few funny facts.

First, while obtaining my certification in Korea, I was taught by a female instructor who spoke minimal English. She was terrific! But think about it—I was learning how to jump off the side of a mountain and fly, and the person in charge of teaching me how to NOT DIE couldn't communicate 80 percent of the lessons I needed to learn in my language.

Nonetheless, we managed to make it work over the six weeks of training and had a ton of fun. My last two flights were for forty-five minutes.

Now I am here in Ecuador, essentially having to get certified again because of the amount of time elapsed since my last flight, and I am yet again working with an instructor who can barely speak my language.

This adds a whole layer of mental effort to the already overloaded nature of learning how to handle all the strings associated with a parachute in strong winds.

Second, I am dead tired. So, not only is my low back already killing me, I have no strength left. Battling a strong wind with a parachute seems more than I may be able to handle.

He asks if I want to go again.

"Sure! Let's go." *Never let them see you sweat.* Or in this case, cry on the inside.

We set me up for another go. I start to run downhill. The parachute unfurls in all her glory.

I get pulled to the right; adjust the chute. Then pulled to the left. I adjust the chute again.

All right, straight ahead we go.

Once again a forceful gust of wind grabs the chute, lifting me about ten feet off the ground.

The instructor yells, "Pull down!"

I overreact, AGAIN, pulling down hard on the chute strings.

Wham! And I mean WHAM! Crashing to the ground smack dab on my sore back, for a second time.

I let out an agonizing scream. Before I can process the pain here I go up the side of the mountain again. Skipping off the surface like a stone over water, I am lifted up two to three feet at a time and planted hard against the turf at least a dozen times.

Again, the whole time I am twisting, turning and fighting with all my might to get control of the chute. It's akin to wrestling a bull with a rope around its neck.

I resemble a dozen empty beer cans tied to the back of a "Just Married" limo leaving the wedding party at full speed because it's a shotgun wedding and the baby is coming.

I had so many bruises the next day...

Despite having the instructor move the car further up the mountain, I end up coming to an abrupt halt no less than five feet away from the back hatch. Minimum 170 feet from where I was first summarily dumped.

You catching this, at the ripe age of forty-eight, I have just been dragged over three hundred feet uphill against my will, testing what actually happens when an immovable object, Mother Earth, and an unstoppable force, me, collide.

My unscientific determination is the immovable object wins.

Once again the instructor comes running up to me. "Ay yi yi, you okay, gringo?"

I lie there, still, mentally surveying the shape of my body.

The little men who run around managing the facility that is my brain report in on the damage. The foreman finally states, "Sir, we have sustained serious damage but the ship remains functional."

Still not believing the report from the man in charge, I reply, "Yeah, I think so."

The instructor looks me up and down, pauses for a second, and states flatly, *"Amigo, usted es dura!"*

Loosely translated, "Amigo, you are one tough hombre!"

My high school football coach would be proud. My chiropractor, massage therapist, and Reiki master are all going to make a boatload of money off me over the next six months.

To my credit, or demise, depending on how you view it, I muster the fortitude to practice for another hour and a half. It takes a lot of effort to run with an open chute downhill while the wind drives you backward.

We finally call it a day. I am done. Utterly spent.

He clears me to fly. The next day I get to live my favorite dream again.

***

For the next four days straight, it rained and was extremely overcast, thus negating any flights.

Each day I stayed in at night, got up early, checked the weather, checked in with my instructor, ate breakfast, chatted with other travelers, and worked on my computer—then preceded to take five-hour naps.

Every day. For five days straight. I slept through the whole afternoon.

On the fourth day it occurred to me this was my body saying, "You are done, my friend. It's over. Maybe down the road you will fly again, maybe not. But at this moment in your life, you simply don't have it."

The unstoppable force that is I had to look in the mirror and acquiesce to the one undeniable force that gets us all sooner or later—Father Time.

There have been few times in my life, and I mean few, where I have to say, "Dude, you need to be smart and recognize you are no longer invincible. It's about time you acknowledged some adventures can no longer be embraced if you want to give the Indonesian taxi palm reader's prophecy of having kids a chance, and live to raise them."

That afternoon I went to the instructor and asked for some of my money back. We worked out a deal, which was good for each side, shook hands, and said good-bye.

As I was walking out the door he repeated, "Hey, *gringo, usted es dura! Adios, amigo.*"

I may not have flown again, but at least I have some random paragliding instructor in Ecuador walking around thinking that while some Americans can be a pain in the ass, others can take a beating and still come up with a smile on their face.

Never lose sight of the fact that while you may be too old for some endeavors, while you may not accomplish what you set out to do because age has finally caught up with you, you can still walk away with your head held high because you did not quit before life made you.

And you were intelligent enough to know when the beating was a message.

Then again, if the weather had not intervened, I might very well have given it the old college try the next day when I could barely stand up, let alone walk.

Once again the travel gods had my best interest at heart.

I may or may not ever fly again. I hope I will never become the unstoppable object testing the immovable force again.

I will, however, laugh out loud every time I recall what it felt like.

Besides, how many people can say they have ridden a horse with no name sideways at full gallop?

My dream of running away to join the circus is now complete. I will let you judge whether my role was that of daredevil or clown.

THE WINNING TICKET...

We are all so audaciously, ludicrously, and benevolently lucky!

Every single friend I have is blessed beyond measure. Each one of us has already won the greatest lottery in existence. All of us, myself included, got the most prized ticket out there, the one with the biggest payoff.

And I, for one, am going to try my hardest to remember that when I bitch about, well, anything or everything.

For sure, I have gotten down on my knees to atone for the numerous times I have lost this perspective.

Maybe after this story you will too.

It has taken me a full week to process what happened. To be honest, I am not sure I am going to do the subject justice, but I will give it my best.

It is my last night in Saigon. I am fortunate in that my friends Stacie, Jimmie, Wes, and Allie have agreed to come out for a good-bye dinner. As I have said before, when traveling you form bonds with people fast, and the friendships can become profound even quicker.

We go to a lovely Vietnamese restaurant with an outdoor garden on the third floor. We have a nice meal, with lively conversation, delicious food, and tasty drinks. Overall, it is a fun dinner.

One of the cool portions of our conversation has to do with Allie and Wes debating the merits of starting a side business venture in Vietnam. Everyone throws in their two cents regarding the opportunities of their proposed endeavor, how to go about building it, and the way to structure the company.

Later, my friends do indeed launch their enterprise. I would like to think the encouragement I give them had a tiny bit of influence when it came to going after their dream.

Starting a business is daunting. I have done it many times. I respect people who put themselves out there and step off the ledge into the entrepreneurial abyss.

Back to the story.

Jimmie runs two hostels in Saigon. After dinner he tells us there is a pub-crawl organized at one of his hostels, and he wants to ensure it goes off without a hitch. Thus, we decided to accompany him for a drink.

We get there. Twenty-somethings all over the place, having a good time. All the guys are attired in women's dresses, apparently the theme was to find a girl traveler, ask to borrow some clothes and then off in drag they go for a night of revelry in Saigon.

Actually, it's apparently a great relationship builder as Stacie informs me over half the guys end up hooking up with the girl they borrowed the dress from. Ha, go figure. Something Freudian there for sure.

Jimmie gathers the troops, gets the ball rolling with shots for everyone and away we go to the first bar. The group is taken the long way around District 1 to the first pub so they can soak up the crazy atmosphere and sensory assault that happens only at night for the first time.

We take a shortcut through alleys.

So, basically the five of us are ahead of the group, with a few stragglers who hitched to our tails on the shortcut. Jimmie and Stacie are talking with those stragglers. Wes, Allie, and I are chatting away as we simultaneously absorb the pandemonium ourselves. We get to the first gin joint and stand out front.

Now again, I have shared that Saigon is bedlam, sensory overload. People everywhere, scooters everywhere, street vendors everywhere—organized chaos everywhere! All are eating, drinking, selling and partying.

Saigon is just plain nuts.

As we are standing there waiting for the rest of the group to catch up, I turn to my left and...

I see him.

I am utterly SHOCKED!

A little boy, maybe eight to ten years old. A young man in his late twenties is carrying him.

The boy, well, he is the most deformed child I have ever seen. Period!

Nothing on TV, in movies or magazines has ever compared to what I am seeing right in front of me. My first thought, *This is not happening right now, this is not possible!*

His head is literally the size of, say, five human heads. I am not kidding. It is the largest cranium I have ever witnessed. And the most malformed!

You know how aliens are always depicted with giant heads? Well, this young boy has the same skull. It is oval in form, eighteen inches in diameter. His entire head is about two and a half feet tall.

Are you kidding me?

It gets worse.

The boy's legs are the size of twigs. Pencil thin. They are strewn across the arms of the man carrying him, askew or akimbo as it were. Bent in a frightening and wholly unnatural way! There is no way this young boy can walk or stand on his own.

His body is wafer thin, almost emaciated. *Malnourished* is a generous description. His arms are in the same condition. Essentially useless appendages!

Please know, I am trying to describe the appearance to relate to you how shocking it was. How crushing. How befuddling. How utterly incomprehensible!

Flabbergasted, I have to look away.

Then I look up to the heavens. In my mind I say, *There but for the grace of God go I.*

Immediately, I start digging into my pocket. I pull my money out and grab a small bill.

A voice inside my head says loudly, "More!"

I grab a larger bill. The voice inside my head says, "More!"

I am so befuddled I drop some of my money on the street. Ever the vigilant one, Wes quickly picks it up and hands it back to me.

I fumble through the money to find the largest bill I have. I find it, turn around, and simultaneously see Allie digging through her purse for cash too. *I knew I liked this girl,* I think.

Allie gives the man holding the boy money, and I give him mine.

The man looks at the money, sees it is a fairly sizable sum from two foreigners, and starts profusely thanking us. He grabs my hand and shakes it vigorously, repeating, "Thank you, thank you, thank you."

He begins to cry tears of thanks and gratitude.

I look at him, then the boy; our eyes catch one another's, and I say, "May God bless you both." Then I turn away. I am ashamed to say I simply cannot handle what reality is asking of me in that moment.

Looking at the boy is so outrageously heartbreaking I cannot absorb it anymore.

A plethora of thoughts are streaming through my mind:

How is this boy not in a hospital?

How is he not being given care twenty-four/seven?

How in the world are the parents handling this?

How is it possible he is still alive?

How does the entire community not care for this child?

Where is government help?

I look at Allie and see a tears gently rolling down her cheeks. She is beyond consolation. She is on the verge of losing it completely.

I can see in her eyes we are thinking the same thing: *How can life be so cruel? How can we be so fortunate?*

Wes is stone silent. Literally, frozen in place by disbelief.

After about a minute of silence I say, "What the fuck did we just see? Did that really happen? I can't deal with what we just saw."

Allie says, "That may be the saddest thing I have ever witnessed. The worst part is we don't even know if that is his child. The parents could very well rent the child out for others to use as a begging device. I know it sounds horrible, but that's how it is here—you never really know what is real." She finishes with "I wanna cry!"

I say, "I can't imagine his parents would subject him to something like that, but you may be right. Nonetheless, at least we know we tried to do the right thing."

Again, all around us is complete chaos. The streets are packed with people, drinks and food being consumed at every turn, laughter and music ringing through the air. The atmosphere is electric.

And I would say this man and boy are invisible to 99.9% of them.

We realize we need to let it go for the moment or it will destroy the rest of the evening. We do not bring it up again.

But it keeps coming up in my mind over the next week. Every few hours it haunts my thoughts. I oscillate between being happy I did something, then admonishing myself for not doing more.

For not grabbing the child's hand, along with the young man's, and praying over him. For not giving them every penny I had in my pocket.

For not grabbing them both and going begging with them, cajoling other foreigners to pony up some party money.

Imagine the effect I could have had on their take that night if I had just stopped my fun, for one night, to help a fellow human being in dire distress.

Come on, people, this is me we are talking about. The guy who can talk with a wall and have a pleasant conversation!

Yesterday, as I meditated about it I heard a voice in my head say, "It's okay, Stan, you helped. You gave. You answered My call. You listened when I said more. Yes, you could have done more. Make no mistake, I am proud of you for both helping and realizing next time you should do more. This was a good lesson. Make sure you put it to use the next time one of My children comes across your path."

Forgiveness from above provokes an immeasurable level of humility. Of course, I cried! I wept tears of sadness and joy.

I did what I did and it's done—no use beating myself up over it. Learn from your shortcomings and do better next time.

Lucky? Damn straight we are lucky. Beyond our wildest dreams, more than any of us have a right to be.

We are healthy. We are all—for lack of a better term, even though I don't like using it—normal.

We have five fingers, five toes, legs and arms that work. We have skulls as they are meant to be, with brains in them that function.

We have awareness. We have intuition. We have compassion. We have the ability to affect and effect change.

We have potential. Ability. Courage. Empathy. Forgiveness.

We have every tool we need to be the best we can be.

We have been given everything. Before we ever even got here. With no credit to be taken by us whatsoever! Just dumb luck/chance/fortune.

As I can attest, these gifts are not given to all.

We have the whole world in our hands, yet we spend an absurd amount of time looking in other places for it.

Winning lottery tickets, you, me, all of us—we already won the lottery! Stop buying the ones peddled at the store and give the money to someone or some organization that needs it.

I promise you this, if you do, you will indeed be blessed in some other way. It might not necessarily come back to you in the same form, meaning money, but a blessing will be bestowed upon you.

Look, my life has repeatedly reinforced the long-held premise "the more you give, the more you get." It is impossible to out give God, Karma, the Universe, or whatever you want to call the dynamic.

As I said, victory has already been bestowed upon you. At worst, consider it payback. Or pay it forward, as in a down payment for the possible next life!

You can remember that you already won the cosmic lottery and therefore be thankful for such a gracious gift.

You can wake up tomorrow, smile from ear to ear, and go out into the day a messenger of thanks, compassion, and hope.

Answer me this: are you a benevolent winner or a stingy one?

Are you taking things for granted or giving things with thanks?

Lastly, what are you doing with your winning ticket?

FAST FRIENDS...

So many of my friends are knee deep in the family life, career sphere or whatever, fighting the good fight and staying focused. Many asked me to post as much as I could of my adventure on Facade Book so they could in a small way live vicariously through me until their time comes.

A task I took to heart. Here's hoping the plan worked.

In that vein, I travel for two main reasons. First, the exotic places to be seen. Second, the wonderful, eccentric, unique, 'suck life dry' people you are blessed to cross paths with.

Life on the road bonds you in furiously fast and profoundly unforeseen ways!

You have seen the pictures and read some stories, now meet some of the peeps.

To Jessica... It's as if our hearts immediately recognized one another, again. You are pure joy, unfettered & carefree. The light inside you beams thru those beautiful eyes, shining love on all you come across.

Thanks so very much for our fascinating talks & all the vibrancy you bring to a simple discussion. I wish you & Medhi happiness & the healthiest of babies.

To Joseph... You my friend are a sweet prince young man. To be a part of your coming of age, to watch you before our eyes realize you are indeed beautiful, no matter anyone else's opinion, was an absolute pleasure.

I am very confident your new life will be filled with love & adventure, all those things you thought you had missed. Trust me, you are arriving at your destiny right on time.

And if you ever forget, just grab a hat & go for a walk, recall the things we all said to you & about you. Know you are loved & supported all the way across the world.

To Eckhart... You had me when I asked how long you have been travelling & you said "Well, I rode that motorcycle behind you here from Germany." At which point I was like "Sit down, I have to hear about this crazy man's adventure."

The indomitable spirit in you is beyond inspiring. You person-ify the "I can do anything I set my mind to" philosophy & your nonchalance about it all leaves me shaking my head, saying "What an incredible young man."

I hope your marriage to the gorgeous Iranian lass is long & fruitful.

Also remember, your family doesn't necessarily need to see the real you to still love you completely. Continue being you, but let their expectations be theirs.

To C. Reed... Or as we call him, "King Reed!" Your generosity, graciousness & hospitality truly humbled Mark and myself.

We had such a blast with you on both our day about town and with the infamous liars dice gang. All of your friends made us feel at home immediately, evidenced by how much crap they gave us from the start. That is when you know people like you, so we took every zinger as a compliment.

Truly, a gentle man & a gentleman!

To Viggio and Martin... Our boyz in the hood! Hanging with the two of you crazy characters was like walking back in time for us. You are both excellent young men, hilarious, kind & astute. Both of you had us in stitches all day, every day.

Your zest for life, ability to mix with any crowd & willingness to truly listen to others will serve you well as life continues. Zip lining, Korean feasts, random temple hopping at night, parkour with Mark – whatever it was you made us smile just by being so terrifically nutty. Our little brothers in the Shakara Gang!

To Kevin... Our German friend with a huge heart & the willing-ness, in action, to back it up. We were humbled to be a part of your special B-Day party as uninvited guests, what a feast.

And let's face it, when a man comes over to your table, plops down a bottle of rum and says: "Enjoy, all guests at my party need to feel at home. Drink up gents, have fun, thank you for being here." Well, how can you not immediately develop a fondness for that person? Our talks were special; I will not forget them, or you.

To Jim M from Chi-town... You can literally be the funniest person on the planet at times. And you have such a soft heart. I am grateful we were introduced through our girls Sandy and Alex.

To Stacie... You are such a gem. A stylish, elegant and sparkling sapphire! Your smile lights up the room & your laugh breathes fresh much needed oxygen into the air. Thanks for your breezy attitude and welcoming heart. What a treat we got to meet in different countries and develop such a special bond. You know I got ya' covered girl.

The little sistah' we never had & the kind of yogi mama we all love, you brighten the life of all in your path.

To Alex and Cedric... Our French comrades! You were a humorous shot in the arm. Thanks for jumping in with both feet and simply looking to share your charms with the rest of the gang.

Alex, you and Carolyn are fantastic people. I had such a splendid time staying at your flat in Paris. Honestly, and I mean this, the highlight of that city was getting to know you both. All the long talks in your home were what I most cherish about travel.

Cedric, you need to get on stage. No doubt, you can entertain a group. Thanks so much for rallying to meet me for lunch in Paris.

Yusuf, Yuyu and Rapeeporn... Our Thai/Turkish family by adoption and affection, many heartfelt thanks for your generous spirit, loving care and genuine extension of welcome to all who visit your fine home. This is the second time I have come to Thailand and had a local family adopt me as if one of their own. A very, very special feeling indeed!

Koh Chang really means Yusef and Yuyu's beach house to us. Nam, you are more than something special, you are a treasure. Beautiful, sweet, precocious and smart! I hope you dream big and go far. The world can be yours if you put your mind to it.

My boy David... I knew I liked you the minute you said, right after you learned I am from Chicago, "Man, I really hope your Cubs win it this year so you can experience the joy we did in Boston!" Thanks for the warm conversations, joints on the beach and staying in touch.

Jessica, Frederick, Disa, Franc and Dante... My adopted Swedish family on Phu Quoc. Just lovely people w amazing kids. They were conversational, eloquent and involved. Such a pleasure to see wonderful parents doing a great job of raising outstanding kids. Many blessings to you and thank you for your gracious company!

Allie and Wes... A big shout out for being such gracious hosts while staying at your home in Saigon. Your generosity of spirit was endearing. You carved out time from busy lives to entertain us at every turn. Heck, Allie made us some fantastic soup from scratch. Does it get any better?

Noura and Matt... Matt, anytime only one other guy joins me 200 yards out in the water to get hammered by giant waves in the name of body surfing you have my respect. Such a pleasure spending time with you and your lovely lady. Between Ubud tour guide day and our goodbye party we became brothers, a bond I will cherish.

To Tude and his band... Best band in all of Indonesia. You are mellifluous, soulful, rockin' and one hell of a guitar player. I loved hearing you every time. My fondest memories in Sanur are from you.

To David C. and Charles D.... David, we meet for three hours while watching a huge storm roll over the Gili Air island and had one of the most intriguing, insightful discussions of my whole trip. Thanks for being real.

Charles, we spent many an afternoon and evening watching waves crash over the shore, drinking rum elixirs and discussing all the things men should discuss once the pretense and power struggle is dropped. Thanks for being a sweet straight shooter.

To Emily and Angela... The two of you took me back in time to a space occupied by two other girls from my youth, and it brought such an enormous smile to my face. You are intelligent, charming, beautiful and funny as hell. Thanks for making me laugh so hard my stomach hurt.

To Kenny... My man in Lisbon. We walked and talked and walked and talked until our feet hurt. Thanks for being the sounding board I needed after many months on the road with the youngsters, sharing your personal story, years of dedication as a fireman and zest for finding those special places that still make us feel alive.

To Catarina and Penha... I asked if I could pet your dog in Lisbon because I was so homesick for mine and you said, "Sure!" Next thing I know we are drinking pitchers of Sangria along the river for five hours with your friends. You are so bright and bubbly, thanks for sharing your city with me.

To Hammer and Ruvina, along with Karen C... When people take the time to meet you, break bread and show you their fair city for a day it is indeed a special gift. Thanks for your friendships, how to get around tips and warm welcomes. This weary sailor was glad to find some ports in the storm.

To Jeannie and Marc-Andre... My sweet and pleasant roomies in Lisbon, eager companions on our excursion outside the city, and opinion changing millennial friends. Your company was delightful. I thoroughly enjoyed our talks about what makes your generation tick and the fact you took some of my perspectives to heart. You give me much hope for the future.

To Sue from Wales... Nothing like a 14,000-meter mountain hike the day I get off the plane from my last sea-level spot to whip us both into shape huh? Notwithstanding the fact it took us 2.5 hours to cover the first 12,000 meters and another 2.5 to cover the last 2,000 meters, I say we did well. Your companionship in Ecuador was a refreshing and welcome bond, making my experience there more special.

Last but certainly not least, my boy Markus. To my brother in travel, thanks for being, well, undeniably you! It all started with an email asking, "Wanna meet in Thailand in January?"

You are one-of-a-kind. When together, we have this crazy kismet energy that draws all kinds of random people to us, each new character leaving another memorable encounter. We laughed more than most people do in a year and we have such terrific discussions.

I adore you because you make the word frugal seem extravagant, crack fantastic perfectly timed dry one-liners at the absolutely appropriate and inappropriate moment, literally take ten minutes to tie your shoes (seriously???), are exceptionally endearing due to your rather large but well hidden heart and always have my back.

No matter where you are, all you have to do is call and I am there.

Peeps, I could go on. There were many others who touched my heart in the deepest of ways, made me laugh till I hurt, showed me kindness and compassion and lifted my spirits exactly when I needed it the most.

I am a blessed man indeed for all the folks who touched my soul. Thank you so much!

NON SEQUITUR THOUGHTS, UNSCIENTIFIC OBSERVATIONS, AND SHORTIES...

→ If I ever write a book—hey, wait a minute, this *is* my book! Ha, what do ya know—I would declare you are not a traveler until you check out for at least six months. Anything less, it's just a vacation.

What's the difference? A tourist goes away to forget their lives for a bit, a traveler goes away to find an entirely new one.

Heck, it takes six weeks to unplug. Another six weeks to deprogram. So, it's not until about month three that you begin to take the reins. You ride a high for a while and then the inward journey really starts to kick in.

We all have one to go on; it's partly why we left.

The best soul surfing comes when you have let go of your homeland, dropped off a bunch of your past along the road, and still have a few months in front of you to craft, absorb, and embrace the new you.

→ As a backpacker you have to take it as it comes, take it with a grain of salt, take it on the chin, take it easy, take only as you need, take things as they are, and take it or leave it—but always, you must take it in stride so you can take it all in.

→ In doing so, you learn to give what you have, give up your assumptions, give in to the unknown, give without expecta-tion, give and take, give your past a break, and, therefore, give your future a fresh start. If you are taking the time to fig-ure yourself out, you get the bonus of forgiveness.

→ Travelers make up the best of what every country in the world has to offer, people-wise. Whether from Iran, Kenya, Austria, or even America, travelers, because of their inherent thirst to see the world and be open-minded, are the most accommodating people from all the cultures they come from.

So they are much easier to get along with; you form much quicker friendships and are constantly surprised at all the stereotypes broken down because of the quality of people you come across.

It's rare you confront travelers who are straight-out assholes.

→ By the same token, the assholes you do come in contact with are more often than not travelers who are being stubborn about what they are accustomed to back home, with no respect for the culture, customs, or traditions and the simple fact that what they are used to, service- or product-wise, is not available. Some people just can't go with the flow.

Exceptionally rare is the local who is a dick!

→ Throughout Southeast Asia you will hear a saying uttered by the people of each country to Western travelers over and over again:

"Same same, but different!"

It means whether you are trying to purchase a product, service, or experience, it will be similar to what you are familiar with, yet slightly different. So don't worry, all is fine. Now buy my stuff!

As every single Western traveler will attest, quite vehemently, "Same same but fucking different" is really the case.

No, it is not anywhere near what we are accustomed to, so stop trying to tell me so because I have already learned to say, *Fuck it, it's Asia. It is what it is!*

→ When I got off the plane in Bangkok after having been gone for twenty-six years, I took a deep breath—pulled in as much of the air as I could. As I was exhaling, the following thought occurred:

"Ah, I am home again."

This place has a certain charm I have found nowhere else. The gentle people, pleasing climate, gracious Buddhist traditions, exceptional countryside, serene temples and delicious food synergistically create an ambiance that pacifies my weary soul.

I am forever blessed for having been given the chance to explore and befriend such a truly unique country, occupied by the warmest of souls.

→ Nobody does "chillaxin'" on a hammock better than the Vietnamese. They take it to a level artistic in form, pitching hammocks wherever possible. Zen masters of the afternoon nap.

→ Some of the most brilliant, random, hilarious, insightful, and memorable exchanges come with taxi cab drivers the world over. If you take the time to interact with them, and you get one who speaks fair English, it can be a blast.

→ There are givers and there are takers. It's easy to spot each kind when you are traveling. If you can't discern between them, you are in the "taker" category. Kind like sitting at a poker table and wondering who the sucker is—it's you!

→ There is an inverse relationship between how much a place to stay costs and the friendliness of the guests. Experience has shown over and over again the more money you spend, the less friendly the folks seem to be.

→ Necessity is the mother of invention. People with the least amount can do amazing things once they put their minds to it. Ingenuity is alive and well. Just when you think you have seen it all, yet another person from the deepest depths of poverty creates a marvelous machine that leaves you giddy at what people can do.

→ Nothing makes you feel more stupid when traveling than the fact you only speak one language. No matter how many degrees or accomplishments you have, multiple language-speaking people are cooler than you.

→ The more you give, the more is given to you. Start sharing. Not because you want something, but because someone else needs something. If you give with a pure heart, just sit back and watch the benevolence that comes to your life...

→ Selfless prayer arises from the presence of God, in the heart, and is answered before it is uttered. When you pray for your fellowman, your foe or friend, without guile, the prayer is already answered. After all—where do you think the prayer came from?

→ Food for thought: Are you in love with your thoughts? I ask because you sure seem quite attached to them.

→ Ecuadorian bus trips are the most entertaining of any land I know. Locals jump on the buses, ride along for twenty minutes or so, and try to earn some money. The ways in which they do so are a delight: from singing, to magic, to storytelling, to food treats and mini vaudevillian skits. Never a dull moment and several performances per ride.

→ Home is wherever love is. Thank God for guesthouse and hostel owners along with all the families who decided they want to welcome weary travelers from all over the world as a business endeavor. Nothing is more appreciated than a warm, friendly haven in the midst of foreign lands. *Fortunate* best describes what it is like to have total strangers treat me as family.

→ You never, ever know who is watching. Beyond the Guy in the sky, I mean. As I am walking the streets of Saigon a young lady approaches me selling random goods spread out on the small serving tray affixed to a strap slung around her shoulder. Gum, breath mints, and such. She is very shy and quiet.

I buy a few packs of gum and something tells me to dig a little deeper than normal. I hand her the equivalent of ten dollars. Big money to give to a beggar here! Her eyes light up; she breaks into a huge grin and bows several times before skipping away.

As I begin to walk away, with a smile on my face, a police officer directing traffic stops what he is doing and walks directly over to me before I get to the other side of the intersection.

Again, he just abdicates his job directing traffic, letting everyone do as they please. This decision could result in catastrophe based on the way people drive here.

"Thank you," he states and puts his hand out.

"Sure. For what?" I extend my hand.

"She is deaf. No parents. Lives on the streets in alley behind you. I watch over her every day. Most foreigners give her nothing. You are a good man."

With that he turns, blows his whistle loudly and goes back to restoring order to the traffic bedlam.

→ You never know who is waiting. Waiting for you to be the civil traveler. It's Terry's last day on Gili Air Island. She is about to go back to reality and take on an important new career role helping foster children back in the States. The job will require a heavy workload, fraught with emotionally challenging and heart-wrenching cases. Thus, her desire is to be frivolous and carefree all day.

Also, she wants to try mushrooms for one and only one time. So we go to the restaurant serving up mushroom smoothies. I mean, what can happen? The island can be walked around in its entirety in less than forty-five minutes.

And I haven't done 'shrooms in forever.

As we await our order, we see a few locals across the bar having a few afternoon beers. We say hello in the local dialect. They respond in kind. In the end, we chat back and forth with them before our drinks arrive, we down them, and are on our merry way.

Epic day of fun in the sun, outrageous amount of laughing! Fast-forward eight hours. It is now 11 p.m. and we are at another restaurant/bar a couple spots up the beach. A local man approaches us as we listen to the band and sway in the island breeze.

"Hi! I am Moe. I wanted to thank you for greeting us today earlier at the bar."

We are surprised by his excellent English.

"Many foreigners don't even show us the courtesy of being civil while visiting our beautiful island home. My friends and I were thankful you did not hesitate to engage in conversation."

With that he proceeded to buy us beers for the next two hours while we peppered him with questions about life on the island, their culture, and how friendships can start from a simple hello. He was gut-busting hilarious. He implored us numerous times to come stay with his family on another island.

We demurred but thanked him profusely for his generosity of spirit. Being nice to strangers can lead to such wonderful moments.

→ Some of the most memorable moments on my journey, ones I will cherish forever, occurred when I did nothing but sit at a table with strangers, multiple cappuccinos/espressos or beers strewn about, and waste the hours away talking about nonsense.

I had conversations that were hysterical or absurd, conversations that blew my mind, conversations that touched my heart, and conversations that actually changed me.

It never ceases to amaze me as to how much of an impression one person can leave on you even if you only talked for 20 minutes while waiting for a bus in 1,000-degree heat.

→ Have you ever seen a whirling dervish? Outstanding! I got to watch one for the first time ever in Istanbul. Dressed all in white, with a blouse-like top, boots and a cylindrical hat atop his head, he spun and twirled his way round and round for, I swear, two hours straight.

For two hours he never lost his composure, never tripped or stumbled, never became robotic or stilted in movement. Light as a feather, he spun with such effortless grace and ease, as if controlled by an unseen puppet master from above.

His devotion to the craft left me in awe. What a truly fetching spectacle!

→ Singapore Airport is the resort spa of airports. I could stay in the airport terminal for days, lead a yoga retreat and be happy.

→ Not wearing shoes for essentially three months, I have determined the following: shoes suck! How we got roped into thinking the opposite is beyond my comprehension.

→ Breaking bread with another is the single best way known to man to turn an awkward 'hello' into a giant bear hug 'good-bye'.

→ So look, we all read the dire "don't drink the water" warnings regarding less developed countries right? We are made to believe you will die or suffer some other horrible fate. I watch foreigners go to extremes in an effort to only consume bottled water.

Which all makes me laugh. Why you ask? Well, as I sit with foreigners drinking their bottled water I also happen to notice they order one alcoholic cocktail after another filled with ice.

And it strikes me odd it never occurs to them that the ice is indeed made from the local water supply. No, I am sorry to inform you that in Asia, India, Mexico, Cuba or any other less-developed country the ice is not filtered.

Trust me on this, it is not happening. They are not taking 2,842 bottles of water and freezing it in little trays everyday so you can enjoy your favorite elixir chilled. Next time you go out for the night and have five or six rum and cokes with ice know you just drank the equivalent of two glasses of local water.

On a good note, I haven't seen one friend die yet, thus I think you will survive too.

→ I have found when you're at the breaking point due to frustrating travel issues making the day brutal, strangers making your experiences getting somewhere extra difficult and irritating, language barriers forcing your brain one time too many to play charades and comprehend the incomprehensible, train schedules looking like hieroglyphics and all else which transpires on those certain days where the travel gods seem to be having a grand time watching you take a beating ...

It is right after all these fucking hassles the most brilliant parts of your trip unfold.
Stick with it peeps, there are rainbows at the end of long, hard roads waiting for you.

→ Some of the best, brightest and most beautiful art in the world does not require you to enter a building, nor pay an admission fee. Yes, there are fantastic sculptures in every city around the world, but for my money, the free stuff on the walls quite often blows you away.

That's right, graffiti is one of the most intriguing art forms on the planet if you ask me. Open your eyes and start looking around; you will be surprised to see how many dazzling, promising young talents work with spray paint.

→ Special thanks to Ana and Ewelina... The awesome ladies who took such excellent care of me while staying in Lisbon at the fantastic Good Morning Hostel, winner of the best hostel award and most awesome breakfast! Second place went to The Student Hotel in Amsterdam simply because the design and atmosphere is way cool. As mentioned, Yuyu's Golden Beach on Koh Chang wins most friendly guesthouse.

→ In order to enter the fullness of any relationship, to experience the total spectrum of what a nourishing relationship has to offer—you must be able to render yourself completely vulnerable!

If you are unable to be sincerely vulnerable in a relationship, you are missing out on the true depth, the most valuable treasures found therein.

The key is learning how to offer up your heart, put yourself in that position of vulnerability without selling your soul. Without giving away your identity. Without losing who and what you are.

You can do both.

You can love freely and without expectation, without knowing how the ending will turn out, even get hurt, and still be a whole person. Still able to absorb whatever happens, knowing your heart was genuine, you gave it over without fear, and it was the other person's choice not to cherish it.

It's still your heart. You didn't give it away forever. Nor did you give away all of it.

Really, you only gave away a portion. The rest of it still resides in you.

Each time you give your heart freely, you gather strength and courage. You become more full.

It is in embracing your vulnerability you find power. Every time you give in to being vulnerable, and survive, you access more internal fortitude. The power to be you without worry, care, or concern!

When you can give your heart to another and have no worries as to how they treat or handle it, you are finally unencumbered by the seemingly arbitrary pain this world can inflict. You are free in a way few will ever comprehend.

I hope to get there soon enough. Maybe you can join me there, it would be lovely to visit this esteemed and much sought after paradigm together.

WHY DO YOU STILL DO IT?

1) Accessibility
2) Availability
3) Affordability....

No other generation in the history of the world has ever seen the above three factors collide the way they do right now—to our benefit!

Again, let me be clear, no other humans throughout the entire span of humanity have had the ability to do and experience what we can today!

How astoundingly cool is that?

Explain further if you would please, Stan.

Sure! At no time ever has society had access to all the countries in the world the way we do at this time. Out of all the countries in the world, there are maybe ten you can't enter. Or, you don't want to enter. That's it. Otherwise, if you follow the proper procedures and you come from a relatively respected country, you can go virtually anywhere.

Think Cuba two months ago for Americans. Think Russia in 1980. Realize how many Eastern European countries we are then discussing. Think China in 1950. Think about how much of the Middle East has been off-limits for so many years.

Go back in time. Invariably one large country and another large one, ruling over many lands between them, were at war, or multiple countries were at war. For crying out loud, my former President said Iran is the axis of evil, and yet I can still visit there if I really want to.

Next, the possibility of going to far-off, remote, desolate, enchanting, rural, jungle, island, or mountain locales is right there for the taking. All you have to do is go online and start researching the who/what/where/when/how part.

And guess what? Most of the time someone already has it all mapped out for you.

You can now get there by using your feet and a backpack, mule, horse and carriage, tuk-tuk, rickshaw, bicycle, motorcycle, car, moped/scooter, van, truck, bus, plane, train, helicopter, snow-plow, snowmobile, snowshoe, parachute, parasail, paraglide, snorkel, fishing boat, hydrofoil, sailboat, and on and on...

There is no shortage of people and companies who can safely transport you to just about every spot on the planet. Some-how, someway someone can help you find your little version of paradise.

Never, ever before has traveling been so affordable on such a grand scale. Air travel has made flying to the opposite ends of the earth as reasonable as buying a large screen high-defini-tion TV.

Right now, this very minute, I can buy an around-the-world ticket that takes me 360 degrees around the planet over the course of a year for about $6,000.

Outstanding! Un-flipping-believable!

You can fly from New York to Bangkok for the cost of a new couch. Both require you to sit on your ass for a while, but only one gives you memories that last a lifetime.

If you are lucky enough to be from a developed country, you can live for a full year abroad in some countries, with an upgrade in lifestyle, if you saved three to four months' wages at home.

There is a bonus reason to add to the mix of why. Perhaps the most important feature of them all! Not only are all these places accessible, available, and affordable, but...

We can get there in forty-eight hours or less, almost without fail. Most of the time we can get there within twenty-four hours. Amazing! Let's be real, time is our most precious com-modity, right? Well, now more than ever, time is on our side when it comes to traveling to faraway lands.

There is an expression: Time flies, but you are the pilot.

Never before could we cover so much ground with so little time lost to the very endeavor of getting there. Add to that the subsequent time left over to explore what each place has to offer, and the time value of travel has never been higher.

Like no era in the past, time is now the wind beneath your adventurous wings! Not the impediment that takes the wind out of your sails.

These four reasons, taken together, present to me a carpe diem situation I choose not to lose out on whilst lucky enough to be on this planet. Part of any opportunity is having the inherent ability to recognize you have one in front of you.

Now look, as if the above reasons aren't enough, we have the obvious ones. Hopefully, they have come across strongly enough in the book via my stories and thoughts, but I will reiterate them now—the people and the places!

Come on, you can't fully fathom how fascinating, unique, beautiful, kind, compassionate, and loving people of the world can be. I have said it before and I will say it again, 90 percent of the world is comprised of good people. I know this because I have experienced it firsthand.

What's more, this brilliant planet is overflowing with wondrous spectacles that leave you standing in awe. They are everywhere. They are spellbinding, mesmerizing, and captivating. They can leave you speechless, breathless, and clueless!

How can I not seek out more of these people and places? How can I not search with wonder for wonder? Once I have found it, how can I not go curiously in search of it again?

Wandering for wonder is significantly more intoxicating than surfing for shows on the tube, or as I call it, bubble gum for the eyes.

Lastly, there are a few more reasons that make travel so appealing versus other lifestyle choices. Before I list them let me assure you, my choice to be a traveler has come with its own price. Every decision we make has a cost versus benefit scale.

I have paid the price of not having what most people label as stability—stability in career, family life, friendships, home, community, and the bonds created therein.

Being ensconced in a strong, loving, and supportive community is to participate in a very special life. The ties that bind by staying in one place can be profoundly enriching. This is an aspect my choice will most probably never allow to exist for me in the sense most people understand.

I have learned that "out of sight, out of mind" unfortunately carries weight. The number of people who truly keep in touch over my years as a traveler is significantly less than what some of my friends seem to enjoy, having stayed in one place for a long time.

Yet those relationships that do last with us travelers tend to occupy such cherished places in the recesses of our minds because we went through something few others will ever understand. They have a special glow, warming the heart during the lonely moments.

We conquered a certain part of the world, for Christ's sake! At least in our minds! If you can't be a legend in your own mind, where can you be one, right?

In no way am I saying either life choice is better than the other. I am saying for travelers, the open road is often the only place we feel alive.

This leads to the less tangible reasons I like to travel. It comes down to two factors: the challenge and the moments.

Let's be clear. There are those who go on vacations and those who go on journeys. Some travel to forget their life for two weeks to a month; others travel to live a different life for six months to a year, or more!

Traveling challenges you every day. Usually many times throughout a day. Sometimes all day and night! Often many,

many days in a row! Consistently forcing you to accept, adapt, absorb, abide, acknowledge, and acquiesce.

It strips you down, leaving you naked and exposed. There is no fallback. It's all on you.

Traveling tests your patience, your preconceived notions, your perception, and your personality. It requires you suspend what you consider to be the way things should get done for the way things are done here, where I am today, according to their custom.

It humbles you in ways you had no idea you needed to be humbled.

You must extend yourself beyond your comfort zone on a daily, if not hourly basis.

You have no choice but to expand your notion of what is "acceptable" as lifestyle choices.

You are forced to not just change, but go through a meta-morphosis. And rarely is it the kind that leaves you less than what and who you were before!

The other reason I keep traveling is for those moments— those singular, dynamic, magical, joyous, maddening, inspir-ing, frustrating, rejuvenating, sparkling, befuddling, spellbinding, life-affirming, and heart-connecting moments!

Stupendous sunsets, star-filled constellations, soul-soothing beaches, captivating cities, bewitching cultures, transfixing structures, culinary delights, mesmerizing markets, historical monuments, sweet treats, nutty buskers, flavorful street merchants, transportation tribulations, and every other goofy, crazy, inexplicable if you weren't there predicament— they all coalesce into a kaleidoscope of experiences that enrich in ways nothing else can deliver.

Mix in the exotic, random, unique, colorful, beautiful, kind, compassionate, refreshing, alluring, sweet, helpful, consider-ate, guileless, and loving people who participate in most of the above-mentioned moments with you—and what you have left is a bank account filled with a currency worth more than anything you can measure on a scale.

A currency that can't be traded, borrowed, stolen, sold, or given away. It stays in your account forever! It fuels the heart and sparks the imagination long after the purchase date. It never goes stale or spoils. Actually, this currency seems to not only increase in value, but has richness, a wealth of its own, inherent in the retelling, whose value is priceless.

You could spend your money on coffee every day for a year at Starbucks. You could take those same funds and, at the end of the year, buy a ticket to some far-off land. I can tell you for sure:

You will not remember one single sip of coffee!

You will remember almost every moment of your trip!

Carpe diem, we always hear. Seize the day!

Right now, to me, it is seize the times. Seize the opportunity. Seize the adventure. Seize the world.

> Don't be satisfied with stories,
> how things have gone with others;
> unfold your own myth.
> ~Rumi

It is my sincere hope I see you out on the road less traveled, sooner rather than later. First round is on me!

WHEN YOUR DUST SETTLES...

> There are only two mistakes one can make along the road to truth;
> Not going all the way and not starting.
> ~Buddha

Riddle me this... Why do so many of the platitudes about life have words such as road, journey, path, street, and travel? Think about how many metaphors, analogies, and such talk of "finding your way."

Recall the number of posters, images, and pictures we see every day that show a solitary person walking down some distant, ethereal path toward a greener pasture where harmony infuses the air and whisks away all your cares.

Why is the individual in the scene alone 98.7654321 percent of the time?

Is it because, at the end of the day, the journey to that magical, wondrous, and mystical place called happiness requires a solitary trip down a path on long-lost land no one else seems to know about, but you can find if you just go traipsing about with intent and purpose. An adventure tour we all know lies within whatever street, avenue, path, or boardwalk you physically stumble upon at this moment.

Or is it because when all is finished in your life, when the dust finally settles, you will walk the final path alone?

They tell me if you have done it right, the living part that is, you will skip down the road to the light at the end of the last tunnel, luminescent in contentment and satisfaction of a job well done!

Then again, fairy tales, while mostly for kids, are science fiction, aren't they?

Dear readers, meet Lee. Lee, meet the people kind enough to grace us with their time and attention.

On the opposite page is a picture of the last physical vestige of this adored confidante. Yep, those are indeed her ashes. The spot where this picture was taken is where her dust settled!

Today is the last time I will ever spend with her in a tangible way. From here on out, all our memories get stuffed into the backpack my mind carries of those who touched me with such sweetness. Now we walk down an imaginary path with no illusions to distract us from clearly seeing one another.

Yes, I talk to her often. And yes, she is right there, adding her two cents where she sees fit.

Now she has had the opportunity to see the entire video of my life, every second of every day, so there is truly nothing left to hide. I see her more clearly than ever, and vice versa.

No doubt, our conversations are more one-sided. That being said, her answers are distinctively her and unmistakably present in both delivery and content.

I am at a place called Glass Beach in Northern California. I drove two and a half hours north to spend this one last moment with her alone, just the two of us.

Lee was an adventure seeker like me. Neither lost nor found, somewhere in the middle, I guess. Curious. Thirsty for knowledge! Straddling that fine line between searching for the innocence she lost along the way and accepting what she found to be her truth in the midst of such a loss.

I am comforted to know God called her home from the lost and found bin that is this life.

Over the past few years, I have regretfully attended funerals where the person whose life being celebrated was not afforded the luxury of being surrounded by a plethora of loved ones. For various reasons, the funerals, more specifically the burials, were scantly attended. Yet, the people being lowered into the ground, or spread thereupon, had lived full lives. They had influenced, touched, graced, and loved many. They left their mark.

In the end, to the earth they returned on an invisible chariot with seating for one.

The last road is to destination unknown, a path whose scenery nobody brings pictures, stories, or trinkets back home to share with family and friends.

Each time I felt a certain sadness that these people who I loved were sent off with such a lack of fanfare. We all hope to leave behind a positive and lasting effect, right?

You can have a large family and still die alone. You can have a life rich with friends and outlive them all. You can give thirty years to a company, and they won't have any idea who you are six months after you walk out the door.

When you think about it, we spend more time alone with our thoughts than with anything or anyone else.

Recently I have read several articles about elderly people who were interviewed about what they would have done differently in their lives. Looking back, what were their biggest regrets?

Almost to a person the answers revolved around the same issue. Nobody talked about that bad job, that horrible marriage, that terrible city they lived in. Nor did they bemoan money lost, lovers lost, or loss of hope at certain times.

Always the answer had to do with the opportunity they did not take, the move they did not make, or the person they did not go after.

Always it was about the chance they walked away from, the risk they were too afraid to take, or the bet they should have made on themselves.

Always, always, always it was about what they did not do versus what they did do!

One of the suggestions I received long ago from a mentor I took to heart, and still follow to this day, is to head over to a local graveyard when I am confronted with a big life decision.

While this may sound macabre to some, think about it.

When you are sauntering around a field of gravestones, reading over the inscriptions that try to describe the person in one or two sentences, absorbing the ancestral history of the area, realizing how many lives have come before you and how many more will come after—well, you can't help but strip away the stuff that doesn't matter and get to the heart of what is important.

I find the experience humbling and inspiring, deflating and uplifting. Invariably, I end up understanding one truth more than any other—it's my life, I have a limited amount of time, and I better not waste it.

Every time I walk away crystal clear as to what I should do next.

Since my return home I have spent the last few months with Lee's husband, Andy. It's been a tough transition for him, but it looks as if he has come out on the other side of the ordeal standing tall.

This makes me happy. As I am sure it does Lee.

One of the conversations Andy and I have had repeatedly is the importance of two imperative creeds to live by:

Life is about movement. And, life is for the living.

Moving on and moving forward!

Moving up.

Moving away from the negative and toward the positive.

Moving closer to the version of you that best suits you.

Moving to your truth, your joy, and your serenity.

Moving forward into the great unknown that is the next day.

Action begets more action. Cause creates effect.

Participation precludes seclusion.

The moment you stop moving is the moment you start dying.

Life is letting go; death is holding on.

Life is living with your fears.

Living with your shame.

Living with your inadequacies.

Living with your disappointments.

Living with your choices and living with your actions.

Life is in the unfolding.

Life is for embracing the challenge, for reaching higher.

Life is leaving no room for "if I had only…"

> Is it a mystery to live; or a mystery to die?
> ~Bob Dylan

Considering we will never know the answer to the second part of the question, I am inclined to look for all the mystery contained in the first.

More than any lesson, truth, reality, takeaway, memory, or experience on this trip, I came home with something even more valuable.

Something I desperately needed to find again.

Something I thought may have been lost forever.

Something life had come close to, but not close enough, beating out of me.

That something was the love for the mystery.

I remembered what it was like to be a kid full of dreams, not yet exposed to the toxic realities of our day.

To think about the unlimited possibilities of each day as opposed to the setbacks of my past before my feet hit the floor.

A few side benefits came about too!

First, my belief in the goodness of others was restored. I was reminded that what I saw in others was simply a reflection of me. And if I was to forgive myself, I needed to forgive them too. As I stated earlier, "I am in you and you are in me; together we are everywhere!"

Kindness is everywhere. It outnumbers evil by the millions.

Second, my excitement for people, sights, sounds, adventures, and even heartbreaks had been rekindled. In so many ways I was reborn on this trip.

The world is filled with such nutty, crazy, cool, astonishing, brilliant, staggering, stupefying, enchanting, befuddling, charming, and bizarre places and people, it boggles the mind!

Throw in your kismet, chance encounters, *it's a small frickin' world* meetings, *WTF just happened* encounters, *did that really just happen* situations, *he/she may be the nicest person on the planet* Samaritans, *this driver is going to kill us* moments, soul mate sightings, and *that dish was out of this world fantastic* experiences, and you simply cannot replicate them in any other way than to hit the road, Jack!

Having no idea where you are in your life, I can only hope this book, at the most minimum level, made you smile a few times. Maybe even caused you to start a whole new journey of your own. The one that takes you off the beaten path, down a desolate road to a place only you can find—the depths of your heart!

Or maybe, just maybe, you might consider putting everything on hold and getting out there. Step off the merry-go-round and get on the roller coaster! Save up, plan carefully, buy that one-way ticket, and see for yourself what can happen when you step off the ledge into the unknown that is travel.

Seriously, what do you have to lose?

Will 365 cups of coffee ever taste as good as some outrageously delicious Vietnamese soup on the side of the road in Saigon?

Will a new high-definition TV give you more viewing pleasure than watching the sunset over the Blue Mosque in Turkey?

Will your kids grow, learn more, and become more enlightened if you enroll them in gymnastics class or take them to live in Bali for a year, especially considering it will cost you less to live there for one year than it does to live at home for three months?

Nothing, and I mean nothing, would make me happier than to hear from you readers this book promulgated change. In whatever form, however your life needed to transform, it would be the greatest gift ever if you told me I helped you down the road to a better you.

Sometimes you have to put your ordinary life on hold, hit the pause button, and walk away from the routine—the day-to-day patterns that become so comfortable, so familiar, we forget they can lull us into complacency.

We can settle. Settle for a life not touched by divine lunacy.

For my money, travel is the ticket to rejuvenation.

Reinvention.

Reincarnation.

Revitalization.

Reckoning.

Renewal.

Travel, when done for extended periods, say, at least six months straight, challenges you.

It brings out your primal instincts again.

It forces you to come to terms with you.

It reminds you life isn't over until you say it is.

It shows you how blessed your life has been.

It teaches you exactly what you need to learn.

It brings out the best in you.

It makes you stand up and scream...

"I am still alive,

And I want more!"

If you are lucky enough to have a long life, and some young kid comes up to ask what you regret, what would you like the answer to be?

When your dust settles will they say he/she got busy living or got busy dying?

Will you be satisfied or will you ask your children to spread your ashes in all the places you decided not to visit?

Can you stand here today and say with absolute veracity you went after it?

You may be incomplete. You may not have done everything right. You may leave a bunch of loose ends. You are no doubt imperfect. But from here on out, you can decide to achieve perfection the only way possible: be perfect in your effort to suck life dry.

As goals go, we can all live with that, no?

From the depths of my heart, thank you again for coming along on this walkabout! The pleasure of your companionship has been all mine.

REUNITED...

The erstwhile Mr. Miles...

The reason I came home...

Stan's best friend...

The Bob Marley of dogs...

The dog Old Souls seek for counsel...

The dog that would have made me rich if I had a nickel for every person who came up to me and said, "Man, your dog is something special!"

To which I reply, "I know, it's crazy! I don't understand either..."

The reason I found myself, after having been separated from him for four and a half months, crying like a baby in the back of a bus from Quito to Banos, Ecuador, while driving through incredible mountain scenery, as they showed some random dog movie, with Spanish subtitles, before the movie even got to the tear-jerker moment.

Which, of course, had many a local on the bus wondering, "WTF is up with the gringo in the back?"

I am forever indebted to my buddy Andy, who went above and beyond by caring for my dog while I was away on my adventure. Andy turned to me this afternoon and said, "Your dog is so fricking cool. Never met a dog like him in my life. I am not exaggerating when I say he literally saved me after Lee passed away. He just intuitively understands stuff most humans are clueless about."

A huge, immense, and heartfelt thank you for watching over the "dog that abides," my good friend!

People spend time with this dog and tell me they are changed. How does that happen in five minutes with a non-speaking fur shedding machine?

You could offer me a million dollars for a trade and I would say, "Nah, keep it."

Try me. I won't even blink.

I am humbled he chose me as companion and friend.

God's gift to Stan!

BOTTOM LINE...

"Come on Stan... Give us the most important lesson you learned. It's a bottom line world and we need a moral to end the tale. Something to walk away from your 'walkabout' with."

Seriously? After all the golden nuggets I have laid out heretofore ye wanteth more?

Honestly, the epiphanies I encountered were so copious, were such a veritable cornucopia of personal wisdom; my attempts at adequately describing them all would be woefully inadequate...

Therein lay the point of my entire book – you need to go out and reach for your own paradigms. Your own verities!

Because I love my peeps, I will leave you with two lessons I am diligently trying to remember every hour of every day since my return:

The seed of ALL happiness is gratitude!

And, I am exceptionally beautiful!

Guess what, so are EACH and EVERY one of YOU.

We need to step letting the world tell us differently.

Much love to you dear reader...

For information regarding Stan's
current adventures along with
other great travel materials
check out

www.justunplugandgo.com

or

www.howtravelchangedme.com